COMPILATION

OF THE

INTERNAL REVENUE LAWS

OF

THE UNITED STATES

IN FORCE

AFTER THE ACT OF JUNE 6, 1872;

WITH

AN APPENDIX

EMBRACING THE

ACT OF DECEMBER 24, 1872, AND OTHER INTERNAL REVENUE ACTS PASSED AT THE LAST SESSION OF THE FORTY-SECOND CONGRESS, ENDED MARCH 4, 1873.

PREPARED UNDER DIRECTION OF THE SECRETARY OF THE TREASURY, PURSUANT TO SECTION 45, ACT OF JUNE 6, 1872.

WASHINGTON:
GOVERNMENT PRINTING OFFICE.
1873.

PREFACE.

This Compilation has been prepared in pursuance of section 45 of the act of June 6, 1872, which is as follows:

SEC. 45. That the Secretary of the Treasury is hereby authorized and directed carefully to revise and prepare for publication the internal-revenue laws in force after the passage of this act, with amendments incorporated in their proper places, conveniently arranged for reference, and with a proper index; and that the same be printed as soon as practicable by the Congressional Printer. That ten thousand copies be printed, five thousand for the use of the House of Representatives, two thousand for the use of the Senate, and three thousand for the use of the Commissioner of Internal Revenue.

The Compilation embraces, as required by section 45, the internal-revenue laws in force *after the passage of the act of June* 6, 1872, with amendments incorporated in their proper places, conveniently arranged for reference, and with a proper index.

The last session of the Forty-second Congress ended while this work was passing through the press. The internal revenue acts passed at that session are embraced in an Appendix hereto. Principal among them is the act of December 24, 1872, which provides in effect for the abolition of the offices of assessor and assistant assessor, and that after those offices shall cease to exist in any district, all returns and reports required by law to be made to such assessor or assistant assessor shall be made to the collector or his deputies in said district; also that all duties imposed by law on assessors and assistant assessors shall, after the offices of assessor and assistant assessor shall cease to exist in any district, be transferred to and imposed upon the collector of internal revenue of said district, to be performed by himself or his deputies, excepting that all assessments required by law are to be made by the Commissioner of Internal Revenue, and that all special taxes, including the tax on stills or worms for distilling, accruing after April 30, 1873, be paid by stamps denoting the tax.

Besides the many sections of the laws as printed in this Compilation which are affected by the above specified general provisions of the act of December 24, 1872, that act expressly amends the following sections, viz: Section 110 of the act of June 30, 1864, as previously amended; sections 5, 19, 28, 59, and 103 of the act of July 20, 1868, as amended, and repeals section 43 of the act of June 6, 1872.

Of the changes made by the other acts passed at the last session, attention is specially called to the following: Section 18 of the act of June 6, 1872, (p. 103,) is amended so as to provide for "thirds" as taxable fractional parts of a barrel of fermented liquor; and section 55 of the act of July 20, 1868, as amended, (p. 81,) is further amended.

Attention is also called to the act approved March 3, 1873, to amend the act of July 18, 1866, entitled "An act to prevent smuggling, and for other purposes."

It should be noted that the provisions relating to the franking privilege of internal revenue officers (see pages 1 and 15) have been repealed, from and after July 1, 1873, by "an act to abolish the franking privilege," approved January 31, 1873.

In consequence of the number of acts relating to internal revenue, some portions or all of which are now in force, it has not been found practicable to take any particular act as the basis of this Compilation. The plan adopted has been to bring together, as far as possible, from all the acts, the sections relating to the same subjects under their appropriate titles. This necessarily produces an appearance of incongruity as regards the enumeration of the sections, but there will be found on the margin, at the commencement of each section, the date of the act from which it is taken, which, in connection with the full table of sections, giving the page of every section printed, will, it is believed, render easy the labor of reference.

While pursuing the plan of grouping all the sections relating to the same subjects under their appropriate titles, it has been found practicable to preserve the sequence of the sections of the act of July 20, 1868, (the principal act now remaining relating to distilled spirits, tobacco, snuff and cigars,) and they are all either printed in full in their original order, or accounted for.

Amendments to the various sections are shown in the following manner: Words inserted are printed in italics, and words omitted are indicated by asterisks, with references in the margin to the amending sections wherever practicable. In a few instances the omissions are because of superseding provisions in various acts too numerous to be noted. Where a section is printed wholly in italics it indicates that the words so printed have been substituted for those of the original section, while preserving at the same time the original number and date. Several sections of the act of June 30, 1864, have been thus amended by the act of July 13, 1866, and by other acts. Where the amended portion of a section has been subsequently amended, the words thereby inserted have been indicated by small capitals.

The work of revision has been found to be a task of no little difficulty and delicacy. Repeals by implication have necessarily been treated with much care and deliberation. Some parts of the law have, by repeated changes, as well by express amendment as by superseding provisions, been left in a condition requiring considerable explanation, which is given in foot-notes when not sufficiently indicated in the margin, and by other means. For a specimen section of this kind see section 59, act July 20, 1868, page 48.

The text has been carefully compared with the Statutes at Large, and has been made to conform thereto, including the punctuation.

A Schedule of all Articles and Occupations Subject to Tax under the Internal Revenue Laws at present in force, a List of Acts relating to Internal Revenue, enacted since July 4, 1861, a Table of Subjects, and a Table showing the Arrangement of the several Sections, precede the laws. The Index will be found at the end.

The Compilation has been prepared under the direction of the Secretary of the Treasury, by Messrs. William H. Armstrong and Charles W. Eldridge, of the Internal Revenue Office.

SCHEDULE

OF

ARTICLES AND OCCUPATIONS SUBJECT TO TAX

UNDER THE

INTERNAL REVENUE LAWS OF THE UNITED STATES

NOW IN FORCE.

SPECIAL TAXES.

	Rate of tax.
Rectifiers	$200 00
Retail liquor-dealers	25 00
Wholesale liquor-dealers	100 00
Retail dealers in malt liquors	20 00
Wholesale dealers in malt liquors	50 00
Manufacturers of stills	50 00
and for stills or worms, manufactured, each	20·00
Manufacturers of cigars	10 00
Dealers in leaf-tobacco	25 00
Retail dealers in leaf-tobacco	500 00
and for annual sales over $1,000; for every $1.00 over $1,000.	50
Dealers in manufactured tobacco	5 00
Manufacturers of tobacco	10 00
Peddlers of tobacco, when traveling with more than two horses, mules, or other animals, 1st class	50 00
Peddlers of tobacco, when traveling with two horses, mules, or other animals, 2d class	25 00
Peddlers of tobacco, when traveling with one horse, mule, or other animal, 3d class	15 00
Peddlers of tobacco, when traveling on foot, or by public conveyance, 4th class	10 00
Brewers, annual manufacture less than 500 barrels	50 00
annual manufacture 500 barrels or more	100 00

DISTILLED SPIRITS, &C.

Distilled spirits, per gallon	70
Brandy made from grapes, per gallon	70
Wines, liquors, or compounds known or denominated as wine, and made in imitation of sparkling wine or champagne, but not made from grapes grown in the United States, and liquors, not made from grapes, currants, rhubarb, or berries grown in the United States, but produced by being rectified or mixed with distilled spirits or by the infusion of any matter in spirits, to be sold as wine, or as a substitute for wine, in bottles containing not more than one pint, per bottle or package	10
Same, in bottles, containing more than one pint, and not more than one quart, per bottle or package	20
And at the same rate for any larger quantity of such merchandise, however put up, or whatever may be the package.	
Stamps for distilled spirits intended for export, for expense, &c., of, each	25
Stamps, distillery warehouse, each	10
Stamps for rectified spirits, each	10
Stamps, wholesale liquor-dealer's, each	10

TOBACCO AND SNUFF.

	Rate of tax.
Tobacco, chewing and smoking, fine-cut, cavendish, plug, or twist, cut or granulated, of every description; tobacco twisted by hand or reduced into a condition to be consumed, or in any manner other than the ordinary mode of drying and curing, prepared for sale or consumption, even if prepared without the use of any machine or instrument, and without being pressed or sweetened; and all fine-cut shorts, and refuse scraps, clippings, cuttings, and sweepings of tobacco, domestic or imported, per pound	$0 20
Stamps for tobacco, snuff, and cigars, intended for export, for expense, &c., of, each	10
Snuff, of all descriptions, domestic or imported, and snuff-flour, sold or removed for use, per pound	32

CIGARS.

Cigars and cheroots, of all descriptions, domestic or imported, per thousand	5 00
Cigarettes, domestic or imported, weighing not over three pounds per thousand, per thousand	1 50
Cigarettes, domestic or imported, weighing over three pounds per thousand, per thousand	5 00

FERMENTED LIQUORS.

Fermented liquors, per barrel, containing not more than 31 gallons	1 00
And at a proportionate rate for halves, thirds, quarters, sixths, and eighths of barrels.	
More than one barrel of 31 gallons, and not more than 63 gallons, in one package	2 00

BANKS AND BANKERS.

Deposits in banks, or with persons, &c., engaged in the business of banking, per month	$\frac{1}{24}$ of 1 per c.
Deposits in savings-banks, &c., having no capital stock, &c., per month. (See exemptions post, p. 110)	$\frac{1}{24}$ of 1 per c.
Capital of banks, &c., and capital employed by any person in the business of banking beyond average amount invested in United States bonds, per month	$\frac{1}{24}$ of 1 per c.
Circulation (see post, p. 109) issued by any bank, &c., or person, per month,	$\frac{1}{12}$ of 1 per c.
Circulation exceeding 90 per cent. of capital in addition, per month	$\frac{1}{6}$ of 1 per c.
Banks, &c., on amount of notes of any person, State bank, or State banking association, used for circulation and paid out	10 per cent.
Banks, bankers, or associations, on amount of notes of any town, city, or municipal corporation, paid out by them	10 per cent.

STAMP TAXES UNDER SCHEDULE B.

Bank checks, drafts, or orders, at sight or on demand	$0 02

STAMP TAXES UNDER SCHEDULE C.

Medicines or preparations. For and upon every packet, box, bottle, pot, phial, or other enclosure, containing any pills, powders, tinctures, troches, lozenges, sirups, cordials, bitters, anodynes, tonics, plasters, liniments, salves, ointments, pastes, drops, waters, essences, spirits, oils, or other medicinal preparations or compositions whatsoever, sold, offered or exposed for sale, or removed for consumption or sale, or sent out, removed, or delivered, by any person or persons whatever, subject to the conditions specified in Schedule C, and also the conditions and exemptions in section 13, act July 13, 1866, where such packet, box, &c., with its contents, does not exceed, at retail price or value, the sum of twenty-five cents	1
Exceeding twenty-five and not exceeding fifty cents	2
Exceeding fifty and not exceeding seventy-five cents	3
Exceeding seventy-five cents and not exceeding one dollar	4
Exceeding one dollar, for every additional fifty cents, or fractional part thereof in excess of one dollar	2

	Rate of tax.
Perfumery and cosmetics. For and upon every packet, box, bottle, pot, phial, or other enclosure, containing any essence, extract, toilet-water, cosmetic, hair-oil, pomade, hair-dressing, hair-restorative, hair-dye, tooth-wash, dentifrice, tooth-paste, aromatic cachous, or any similar articles, by whatsoever name the same heretofore have been, now are, or may hereafter be called, known or distinguished, used or applied, or to be used or applied as perfumes or applications to the hair, mouth, or skin, sold, offered or exposed for sale, or removed for consumption or sale, or sent out, removed, or delivered, the same rates per package, &c., as for medicines and preparations.	
Friction-matches. For and upon every parcel or package of 100 or less.......	$0 01
More than 100 and not more than 200..	2
For every additional 100 or fractional part thereof..............................	1
Wax-tapers, double the rates for friction-matches.	
Cigar-lights, made in part of wood, wax, glass, paper, or other materials, in parcels or packages, containing twenty-five lights or less in each parcel or package...	1
When in parcels or packages containing more than twenty-five and not more than fifty lights..	2
For every additional twenty-five lights, or fractional part of that number, one cent additional.	
Playing-cards. For and upon every pack not exceeding fifty-two cards in number, irrespective of price or value..	5

A LIST

OF

ACTS OF CONGRESS RELATING TO INTERNAL REVENUE

ENACTED SINCE JULY 4, 1861,*

NOT INCLUDING APPROPRIATION ACTS OR PRIVATE ACTS.

An act to provide increased revenue from imports, to pay interest on the public debt, and for other purposes, approved August 5, 1861. (12 Stat., p. 292.)

An act to provide internal revenue to support the Government and to pay interest on the public debt, approved July 1, 1862. (12 Stat., p. 432.)

An act increasing temporarily the duties on imports, and for other purposes, approved July 14, 1862. (12 Stat., pp. 543, 560.)

An act to impose an additional duty on sugars produced in the United States, approved July 16, 1862. (12 Stat., p. 588.)

Joint resolution to amend section 77 of "An act to provide internal revenue to support the Government and to pay interest on the public debt," and for other purposes. Approved July 17, 1862. (12 Stat., p. 627.)

An act to amend an act entitled "An act to provide internal revenue to support the Government and to pay interest on the public debt," approved July 1, 1862. Approved December 25, 1862. (12 Stat., p. 632.)

An act to amend an act entitled "An act to provide internal revenue to support the Government and [to] pay interest on the public debt," approved July 1, 1862, and for other purposes. Approved March 3, 1863. (12 Stat., p. 713.)

An act to prevent and punish frauds upon the revenue, to provide for the more certain and speedy collections of claims in favor of the United States, and for other purposes, approved March 3, 1863. (12 Stat., p. 737.)

Joint resolution to provide for the printing annually of the report of the Commissioner of Internal Revenue, approved January 13, 1864. (13 Stat., p. 400.)

An act to increase the internal revenue, and for other purposes, approved March 7, 1864. (13 Stat., p. 14.)

An act to provide internal revenue to support the Government, to pay interest on the public debt, and for other purposes, approved June 30, 1864. (13 Stat., p. 223.)

Joint resolution imposing a special income duty [for the year ending December 31 next preceding October 1, 1864,] approved July 4, 1864. (13 Stat. p. 417.)

An act to amend an act entitled "An act to provide internal revenue to support the Government, to pay interest on the public debt, and for

---

* On this date Congress convened in its first (extraordinary) session after the commencement of the War of the Rebellion, at which session was commenced the legislation which has since produced the present system of internal taxation.

other purposes," approved June 30, 1864. Approved December 22, 1864. (13 Stat., p. 420.)

An act to amend an act entitled "An act to provide internal revenue to support the Government, to pay interest on the public debt, and for other purposes," approved June 30, 1864. Approved March 3, 1865. (13 Stat., p. 469.)

An act authorizing the Secretary of the Treasury to appoint assistant assessors of internal revenue, approved January 15, 1866. (14 Stat., p. 2.)

An act to declare the meaning of certain parts of the internal revenue act, approved June 30, 1864, and for other purposes. Approved March 10, 1866. (14 Stat., p. 4.)

An act to reduce internal taxation and to amend an act entitled "An act to provide internal revenue to support the Government, to pay interest on the public debt, and for other purposes," approved June 30, 1864, and acts amendatory thereof. Approved July 13, 1866. (14 Stat., p. 98.)

An act to authorize the refunding of certain taxes, approved July 27, 1866. (14 Stat., p. 301.)

An act amendatory of section thirteen of an act entitled "An act to amend an act entitled 'An act to provide internal revenue to support the Government, to pay interest on the public debt, and for other purposes,' approved June 30, 1864," approved March 3, 1865. Approved July 27, 1866. (14 Stat., p. 301.)

Joint resolution to prevent the further enforcement of the joint resolution (No. 77) approved July 4, 1864, against officers and soldiers of the United States, who have been honorably discharged, so as to relieve them from the further payment of the special 5 per cent. income tax imposed thereby, approved July 28, 1866. (14 Stat., p. 371.)

Joint resolution to amend existing laws relating to internal revenue, approved February 5, 1867. (14 Stat., p. 565.)

A resolution to provide, in certain cases, for the removal of alcohol from bonded warehouses free from internal tax, approved February 18, 1867. (14 Stat., p. 565.)

An act to amend existing laws relating to internal revenue, and for other purposes, approved March 2, 1867. (14 Stat., p. 471.)

An act to exempt wrapping-paper, made from wood or cornstalks, from internal tax, and for other purposes, approved March 26, 1867. (15 Stat., p. 6.)

An act to prevent frauds in the collection of the tax on distilled spirits, approved January 11, 1868. (15 Stat., p. 34.)

An act to provide for the exemption of cotton from internal tax, approved February 3, 1868. (15 Stat., p. 34.)

Joint resolution to provide for a commission to examine and report on meters for distilled spirits, approved February 3, 1868. (15 Stat., p. 246.)

An act to exempt certain manufactures from internal tax, and for other purposes, approved March 31, 1868. (15 Stat., p. 58.)

An act for the relief of certain exporters of rum, approved June 25, 1868. (15 Stat., p. 78.)

Joint resolution to correct an act entitled "An act for the relief of certain exporters of rum." Approved July 6, 1868. (15 Stat., p. 256.)

An act imposing taxes on distilled spirits and tobacco, and for other purposes, approved July 20, 1868. (15 Stat., p. 125.)

An act to correct an error in the enrollment of the "Act imposing taxes on distilled spirits and tobacco, and for other purposes." Approved July 27, 1868. (15 Stat., p. 238.)

An act to amend an act entitled "An act imposing taxes on distilled spirits and tobacco, and for other purposes," approved July twentieth, eighteen hundred and sixty-eight. Approved December 22, 1868. (15 Stat., p. 266.)

An act to allow deputy collectors of internal revenue, acting as collectors, the pay of collectors, and for other purposes, approved March 1, 1869. (15 Stat., p. 282.)

An act to amend an act entitled "An act to exempt certain manufacturers from internal tax, and for other purposes," approved March thirty-first, eighteen hundred and sixty-eight. Approved March 3, 1869. (15 Stat., p. 336.)

An act to amend an act entitled "An act imposing taxes on distilled spirits and tobacco, and for other purposes," approved July twentieth, eighteen hundred and sixty-eight. Approved April 10, 1869. (16 Stat., p. 41.)

Joint resolution in relation to female clerks in the Internal Revenue Bureau, approved June 29, 1870. (16 Stat., p. 382.)

An act to define the intent of an act entitled "An act to allow deputy collectors of internal revenue, acting as collectors, the pay of collector[s], and for other purposes," approved March one, eighteen hundred and sixty-nine. Approved July 1, 1870. (16 Stat., p. 179.)

A resolution to determine the construction of an act to provide internal revenue to support the Government, [to pay interest on the public debt,] and for other purposes, approved June thirtieth, eighteen hundred and sixty-four. Approved July 13, 1870. (16 Stat., p. 387.)

An act to reduce internal taxes, and for other purposes, approved July 14, 1870. (16 Stat., p. 256.)

An act to amend existing laws relating to internal revenue, approved July 14, 1870. (16 Stat., p. 274.)

An act to amend section four of the act of March thirty-one, eighteen hundred and sixty-eight, approved July 14, 1870. (16 Stat., p. 277.)

Joint resolution to construe the act of March thirty-one, eighteen hundred and sixty-eight, approved July 14, 1870. (16 Stat., p. 338.)

An act relating to internal taxes, approved March 3, 1871. (16 Stat., p. 475.)

Joint resolution to amend section four, act of July twenty, eighteen hundred and sixty-eight, approved March 3, 1871. (16 Stat., p. 601.)

An act to repeal the paragraphs of Schedule C of the internal revenue acts imposing taxes on canned meats, fish, and certain other articles, approved March 5, 1872. (17 Stat., p. 36.)

An act to provide for the abatement or repayment of taxes on distilled spirits in bond, destroyed by casualty, approved May 27, 1872. (17 Stat., p. 162.)

An act to reduce duties on imports, and to reduce internal taxes, and for other purposes, approved June 6, 1872. (17 Stat., p. 230.—Internal revenue portion commences on p. 238.)

An act for the reduction of officers and expenses of the internal revenue, approved December 24, 1872. (See Appendix.)

An act to remit the excise taxes upon alcohol used by universities and colleges for scientific purposes, approved February 21, 1873.

An act to amend an act entitled "An act to reduce duties on imports and to reduce internal taxes, and for other purposes," approved June sixth, eighteen hundred and seventy-two, and for other purposes. Approved March 3, 1873. Section 5 of this act amends section 55 of the act of July 20, 1868, as amended by the act of June 6, 1872.

An act to amend an act entitled "An act to prevent smuggling, and for other purposes," approved July eighteenth, eighteen hundred and sixty-six. Approved March 3, 1873.

An act relating to the fractional parts of a barrel containing fermented liquors, approved March 3, 1873.

An act to place at the disposal of the Commissioner of Internal Revenue certain copies of the new compilation of internal revenue laws. Approved March 3, 1873.

TABLE OF SUBJECTS.

TABLE

SHOWING

THE PAGES ON WHICH WILL BE FOUND THE SEVERAL SECTIONS EMBRACED IN THIS COMPILATION.

NOTE.—Sections which do not appear in this table either do not relate to internal revenue, or have been repealed or superseded by subsequent legislation, or they are of an amendatory nature, and are incorporated with the amended sections. Sections which simply repealed other sections, or which have expired by limitation, are also omitted.

Act	Section	Page.
Act June 30, 1864, Section	161	116
	162	117
	163	118
	164	118
	165	120
	166	120
	167	120
	168	120
	169	122
	170	122
	171	41
	172	45
	173	138
	174	130
	179	124
	180	133
	181	131
	182	129
Act March 3, 1865, Section	3	33
	4	6
	6	111
	14	111
	15	7
	16	138
	17	133
Act March 10, 1866, Section	3	21
Act July 13, 1866, Section	6	42
	11	28
	13	122
	14	134
	15	134
	16	134
	17	135
	19	39
	28	121
	29	75
	38	78
	41	7
	44	84
	59	17
	60	16
	62	135
	63	125
	64	1
	67	127
	68	129
	70	139
Joint Resolution, February 5, 1867		56
Act March 2, 1867, Section	3	126
	4	32
	5	136
	6	3
	7	125
	14	75
	19	15
Act March 2, 1867, Section	26	18
	28	136
	30	136
	31	14
	32	100
	34	139
Act March 2, 1867, (appropriations) Section	1	9
Act March 26, 1867, Section	2	111
Act March 31, 1868, Section	2	140
	3	42
	5	79
	7	126
Act July 20, 1868, Section	1	54
	2	54
	3	55
	4	55
	5	56
	6	56
	7	57
	8	58
	9	59
	10	60
	11	60
	12	61
	14	61
	15	62
	16	62
	17	63
	18	63
	19	64
	20	66
	21	66
	22	67
	23	68
	24	69
	25	69
	26	71
	27	71
	28	71
	29	72
	30	72
	31	73
	32	73
	33	74
	34	74
	35	74
	36	74
	37	75
	38	76
	39	76
	40	76
	41	77
	42	77
	43	77
	44	78

INTERNAL REVENUE LAWS.

ORGANIZATION OF OFFICE OF INTERNAL REVENUE.

SECTION 1. *Be it enacted by the Senate and House of Representatives of the United States of America in Congress assembled*, That, for the purpose of superintending the collection of internal duties, stamp duties, licenses, or taxes, imposed by this act, or which may hereafter be imposed, and of assessing the same, the Commissioner of Internal Revenue, whose annual salary shall be *six* thousand dollars, shall be charged, under the direction of the Secretary of the Treasury, with preparing all the instructions, regulations, directions, forms, blanks, stamps, and licenses, and distributing the same, or any part thereof, and all other matters pertaining to the assessment and collection of the duties, stamp duties, licenses, and taxes which may be necessary to carry this act into effect, and with the general superintendence of his office, as aforesaid, and shall have authority, and hereby is authorized and required, to provide cotton marks, hydrometers, and proper and sufficient adhesive stamps, and stamps or dies for expressing and denoting the several stamp duties, or the amount thereof in the case of percentage duties, imposed by this act, and to alter and renew or replace such stamps, from time to time, as occasion shall require. He may also contract for or procure the printing of requisite forms, decisions, regulations, and advertisements; but the printing of such forms, decisions, and regulations shall be done at the public printing-office, unless the Public Printer shall be unable to perform the work. *And the privilege of franking all letters and documents pertaining to the duties of his office, and of receiving free of postage all such letters and documents, is hereby extended to said Commissioner.

June 30, 1864.

Commissioner of Internal Revenue.

Salary. July 13, 1866, § 64.

Duties and powers.

July 13, 1866, § 64.

Commissioner may frank letters pertaining to the duties of the office.

SEC. 3. *And be it further enacted*, That the Deputy Commissioner of Internal Revenue, whose annual salary shall be *three thousand* five hundred dollars, shall be charged with such duties in the Bureau of Internal Revenue as may be prescribed by the Secretary of the Treasury, or as may be required by law, and shall act as Commissioner of Internal Revenue in the absence of that officer, and exercise the privilege of franking all letters and documents pertaining to the office of Internal Revenue.

June 30, 1864.

Deputy Commissioner. July 13, 1866, § 64.

Salary.

Duties and powers.

SEC. 64. *And be it further enacted*, That the office of the Commissioner of Internal Revenue be reorganized so as to include—

July 13, 1866.

Organization of the office of Internal Revenue.

One Commissioner of Internal Revenue, with a salary of six thousand dollars; and

One Deputy Commissioner, with a salary of three thousand five hundred dollars;

Officers, clerks, employés, and their salaries.

Which offices are already created, and the duties thereof defined by law; and to authorize, under the direction of the Secretary of the Treasury, the employment of the following additional officers and clerks, and with the salaries hereinafter specified, namely:

Two Deputy Commissioners, each with a salary of three thousand dollars;

June 22, 1870, § 3.

* * * * * *

Seven heads of divisions, each with a salary of two thousand five hundred dollars;

May 8, 1872, § 1.

Thirty-four clerks of class four; *forty-eight* clerks of class three; *fifty-two* clerks of class two; and *twenty-eight* clerks of class one;

Seventy-five copyists;

Seven messengers, three assistant messengers, and fifteen laborers.

OFFICERS OF INTERNAL REVENUE.—APPOINTMENT, COMPENSATION, ETC.

July 1, 1862.

Collection districts.

Assessor and collector appointed for each district.

Limitation of the number of districts.

Additional districts in California.

SEC. 2. *And be it further enacted*, That, for the purpose of assessing, levying, and collecting the duties or taxes hereinafter prescribed by this act, the President of the United States be, and he is hereby, authorized to divide, respectively, the States and Territories of the United States and the District of Columbia into convenient collection districts, and to nominate, and, by and with the advice and consent of the Senate, to appoint an assessor and a collector for each such district, who shall be residents within the same: *Provided*, That any of said States and Territories and the District of Columbia may, if the President shall deem it proper, be erected into and included in one district: *Provided*, That the number of districts in any State shall not exceed the number of representatives to which such State shall be entitled in the present Congress; except in such States as are entitled to an increased representation in the thirty-eighth Congress, in which States the number of districts shall not exceed the number of representatives to which any such State may be so entitled: *And provided further*, That in the State of California the President may establish a number of districts, not exceeding the number of Senators and Representatives to which said State is entitled in the present Congress.

June 30, 1864.

Collection districts and appointments of assessors and collectors.

Districts may be altered.

SEC. 7. *And be it further enacted*, That the second section of an act entitled "An act to provide internal revenue to support the Government and to pay interest on the public debt," approved July one, eighteen hundred and sixty-two, shall remain and continue in full force; and the President is hereby authorized to alter the respective collection districts provided for in said section as the public interests may require.

June 6, 1872.

[1]SEC. 43. That prior to the first day of January, eighteen hundred and seventy-three, it shall be the duty of the President, and he is hereby authorized and directed, to reduce the internal-revenue districts in the United States to not

[1] This section is expressly repealed by "An act for the reduction of officers and expenses of the Internal Revenue. See Appendix.

exceeding eighty in number, and for that purpose he may unite two or more districts, or States, or Territories, into one district, and he shall designate from among the existing revenue officers one collector and one assessor for each new district, or at his discretion he may, by and with the advice and consent of the Senate, nominate and appoint new officers for such new district; and the collector and assessor so designated or appointed shall give bond according to law, and the Secretary of the Treasury is hereby authorized and required, prior to the first day of January, eighteen hundred and seventy-three, to reduce the number of internal-revenue assistant assessors, inspectors, gaugers, storekeepers, and the clerks and employés in the internal revenue bureau to as small a number as is consistent with the performance of the reduced duties of the service, and that he report to Congress at its next session the reduction made under this act, and such further changes in the organization of the internal-revenue service as will promote its efficiency and economy.

June 30, 1864.

Assessors to divide their districts into assessment districts.

SEC. 8. *And be it further enacted*, That each assessor shall divide his district into a convenient number of assessment districts, which may be changed as often as may be deemed necessary, subject to such regulations and limitations as may be imposed by the Commissioner of Internal Revenue, within each of which the *Secretary of the Treasury*, whenever there shall be a vacancy, shall appoint *one *or more* assistant assessors, who shall be a resident of *such assessment district;* and in case of a vacancy occurring in the office of assessor by reason of death or any other cause, the assistant assessor of the assessment district in which the assessor resided at the time of the vacancy occurring shall act as assessor until an appointment filling the vacancy shall be made. * * * * *

Jan. 15, 1866, § 1.

March 3, 1865, § 1. Appointment of assistant assessors.

In case of vacancy in the office of assessor.

July 13, 1866, § 9.

March 2, 1867.

Commissioner may designate assistant assessors for special duty.

SEC. 6. *And be it further enacted*, That it shall be lawful for the Commissioner of Internal Revenue, whenever he shall deem it expedient, to designate one or more of the assistant assessors in any collection district to make assessments in any part of such collection district for all such taxes as may be due upon any specified objects of taxation, and in such case it shall be the duty of the other assistant assessors of such collection district to report to the assistant assessor thus specially designated all matters which may come to their knowledge relative to any assessments to be made by him: *Provided*, That whenever two or more districts or parts of districts are embraced within one county it may be lawful for such assistant assessor or assessors to make assessment anywhere within such county upon such specified objects of taxation as he may be by said Commissioner required: *Provided, further*, That such assessment shall be returned to the assessor of the district in which such taxes are payable.

When two districts in same county.

July 14, 1870.

Assistant assessors specially assigned, to be discharged in certain cases.

SEC. 19. *And be it further enacted*, That as soon as practicable after the passage of this act the number of assistant assessors employed shall be permanently reduced by the discharge of all officers of that class who are assigned specially to the assessment of any taxes which shall have been abolished

Assistant assessors to be further reduced in proportion to the reduction of taxes.

by law; and the Commissioner of Internal Revenue shall be required further to reduce the number of assistant assessors in proportion to any reduction of the service of assessment which has been made, or may hereafter be made, by the repeal of any portion of the internal taxes.

June 30, 1864.

July 13, 1866, § 9. Compensation of assessors. Salary. Commissions.

SEC. 22. *And be it further enacted, That there shall be allowed and paid to the several assessors a salary of fifteen hundred dollars per annum, payable quarterly; and, in addition thereto, where the receipts of the collection district shall exceed the sum of one hundred thousand dollars, and shall not exceed the sum of four hundred thousand dollars annually, one-half of one per centum upon the excess of receipts over one hundred thousand dollars. Where the receipts of a collection district shall exceed four hundred thousand dollars, and shall not exceed six hundred thousand, one fifth of one per centum upon the excess of receipts over four hundred thousand dollars. Where the receipts shall exceed six hundred thousand dollars, one tenth of one per centum upon such excess; but the salary of no assessor shall in any case exceed the sum of four thousand dollars.*[1] *And the several assessors shall be allowed and paid the sums actually and necessarily expended, with the approval of the Commissioner of Internal Revenue, for office-rent; but no account of such rent shall be allowed or paid until it shall have been verified in such manner as the Commissioner shall require, and shall have been audited and approved by the proper officers of the Treasury Department. And the several assessors shall be paid, after the account thereof shall have been rendered to and approved by the proper officers of the Treasury, their necessary and reasonable charges for clerk-hire; but no such account shall be approved unless it shall state the name or names of the clerk or clerks employed, and the precise periods of time for which they were respectively employed, and the rate of compensation agreed upon, and shall be accompanied by an affidavit of the assessor stating that such service was actually required by the necessities of his office, and was actually rendered, and also by the affidavit of each clerk, stating that he has rendered the service charged in such account on his behalf, the compensation agreed upon, and that he has not paid, deposited or assigned, or contracted to pay, deposit, or assign any part of such compensation to the use of any other person, or in any way, directly or indirectly, paid or given, or contracted to pay or give, any reward or compensation for his office or employment, or the emoluments thereof; and the chief clerk of any such assessor is hereby authorized to administer, in the absence of the assessor, such oaths or affirmations as are required by this act. And there shall be allowed and paid to each assistant assessor* FIVE *dollars for every day actually employed in collecting lists and making valuations, the number of days necessary for that purpose to be certified by the assessor, and three dollars for every hundred persons assessed contained in the tax-list, as completed and delivered by him to the assessor*; and the said assessors and assistant assessors, respectively, shall be paid,*

Not to exceed $4,000.

Office-rent.

Clerk-hire.

Chief clerk may administer oaths in the absence of assessor.

Mch. 2, 1867, § 9.

Compensation of assistant assessors.

Mar. 2, 1867, § 9. July 20, 1868, § 59.

[1] See June 30, 1864, section 24 as amended; also July 20, 1868, section 28.

after the account thereof shall have been rendered to and approved by the proper officers of the Treasury, their necessary and reasonable charges for stationery and blank-books used in the discharge of their duties, and for postage actually paid on letters and documents received and sent, and relating exclusively to official business, and for money actually paid for publishing notices required by this act: Provided, *That no such account shall be approved unless it shall state the date and the particular item of every such expenditure, and shall be verified by the oath or affirmation of such assessor or assistant assessor; and the compensation herein specified shall be in full for all expenses not otherwise particularly authorized:* Provided further, *That the Commissioner of Internal Revenue may, under such regulations as may be established by the Secretary of the Treasury, after due public notice, receive bids and make contracts for supplying stationery, blank-books, and blanks to the assessors, assistant assessors, and collectors in the several collection districts:* Provided further, *That the Secretary of the Treasury shall be, and he is hereby, authorized to fix such additional rates of compensation to be made to assessors and assistant assessors in cases where a collection district embraces more than a single congressional district, and to assessors and assistant assessors, revenue agents, and inspectors in Louisiana, Georgia, South Carolina, Alabama, Florida, Texas, Arkansas, North Carolina, Mississippi, Tennessee, California, Nevada, and Oregon, and the Territories, as may appear to him to be just and equitable, in consequence of the greater cost of living and traveling in those States and Territories, and as may, in his judgment, be necessary to secure the services of competent officers; but the compensation thus allowed shall not exceed the rate of five thousand dollars per annum. Collectors of internal revenue acting as disbursing officers shall be allowed all bills of assistant assessors heretofore paid by them in pursuance of the directions of the Commissioner of Internal Revenue, notwithstanding the assistant assessor did not certify to hours therein, or that two dollars per diem was deducted from his salary or compensation before computation of the tax thereon.*

Stationery, blank-books, postage, and publication.

Accounts to be verified by oath.

Commissioner may contract for stationery, &c.

Secretary may allow additional compensation in certain cases.

Limit of compensation.

Collectors shall be allowed bills of assistant assessors heretofore paid, notwithstanding certain informalities.

SEC. 24. *And be it further enacted,* That assistant assessors shall make out their accounts for pay and charges allowed by law monthly, specifying each item and including the date of each day of service, and shall transmit the same, verified by oath or affirmation, to the assessor of the district, who shall thereupon examine the same, and, if it appears just and in accordance with law, he shall indorse his approval thereon, but otherwise shall return the same with objections. Any such account, so approved, may be presented by the assistant assessor to the collector of the district for payment, who shall thereupon pay the same, and, when receipted by the assistant assessor, be allowed therefor upon presentation to the Commissioner of Internal Revenue. Where any account, so transmitted to the assessor, shall be objected to, in whole or in part, the assistant assessor may appeal to the Commissioner of Internal Revenue, whose decision on the

June 30, 1864.

Assistant assessors to make out accounts.

Account to be approved by assessor.

And paid by collectors.

Assistant assessor may appeal to Commissioner.

Amount negligently approved by assessor to be deducted from his pay.

case shall be final. And should it appear, at any time, that any assessor has knowingly or negligently approved any account, as aforesaid, allowing any assistant assessor a sum larger than was due according to law, it shall be the duty of the Commissioner of Internal Revenue, upon proper proof thereof, to deduct the sum so allowed from any pay which may be due to such assessor; or the Commissioner as aforesaid may direct a suit to be brought in any court of competent jurisdiction against the assessor or assistant assessor in default, for the recovery of the amount knowingly or negligently allowed, as hereinbefore mentioned: Provided,

July 13, 1866, §9. Mch. 2, 1867, § 9.

Taxes received on cotton and distilled spirits shipped in bond to be divided in calculating commissions.

That in calculating the commissions of assessors and collectors of internal revenue in districts whence cotton or distilled spirits OR OTHER ARTICLES *are shipped in bond to be sold in another district, one-half the amount of tax received on the quantity of cotton or spirits or other articles so shipped shall be added to the amount on which the commissions of such assessors and collectors are calculated, and a corresponding amount shall be deducted from the amount on which the commissions of the assessors and collectors of the districts to which such cotton or spirits* OR OTHER ARTICLES *are shipped are calculated.*

Mch. 2, 1867, § 9.

June 30, 1864.

Collectors to give bonds.

SEC. 9. *And be it further enacted*, That before any collector shall enter upon the duties of his office, he shall execute a bond for such amount as shall be prescribed by the Commissioner of Internal Revenue, under the direction of the Secretary of the Treasury, with not less than five sureties, to be approved by the Solicitor of the Treasury, conditioned that said collector shall faithfully perform the duties of his office according to law, and shall justly and faithfully account for and pay over to the United States, in compliance with the order or regulations of the Secretary of the Treasury, all public moneys which may come into his hands or possession; which bond shall be filed in the office of the First Comptroller of the Treasury. And such collector shall, from time to time, renew, strengthen, and increase his official bond, as the Secretary of the Treasury may direct, with such further conditions as the said Commissioner shall prescribe.

Conditions thereof.

Bond may be renewed and increased.

March 3, 1865.

SEC. 4. *And be it further enacted*, That so much money as may be necessary for the payment of the lawful expenses, incident to carrying into effect the various acts relative to the assessment and collection of the internal revenues after the thirtieth day of June, eighteen hundred and sixty-five, until the first day of July, eighteen hundred and sixty-six, and not otherwise provided for, be, and the same is hereby, appropriated from any money in the Treasury not otherwise appropriated. And it shall be the duty of such of the collectors of internal revenue as the Secretary of the Treasury may direct to act as disbursing agents to pay the aforesaid expenses, without increased compensation therefor, and to give good and sufficient bonds and sureties for the faithful performance of their duties as such disbursing agents, in such sum and form as shall be prescribed by the First Comptroller of the Treasury and approved by the Secretary.

Collectors to act as disbursing agents.

March 3, 1865.

July 13, 1866, § 20

One collector to be designated to have charge of exportations, where there is more than one in any port.

SEC. 15. *And be it further enacted, That in any port of the United States in which there is more than one collector of internal revenue, the Secretary of the Treasury may designate one of said collectors to have charge of all matters relating to the exportation of articles subject to tax under the laws to provide internal revenue; and at such ports as the Secretary of the Treasury may deem it necessary, there shall be an officer appointed by him to superintend all matters of exportation and drawback, under the direction of the collector, whose compensation therefor shall be prescribed by the Secretary of the Treasury, but shall not exceed, in any case, an annual rate of two thousand dollars, excepting at New York, where the compensation shall be an annual rate of three thousand dollars. And all the books, papers, and documents in the bureau of drawback in the respective ports, relating to the drawback of taxes paid under the internal revenue laws, shall be delivered to said collector of internal revenue; and any collector of internal revenue, or superintendent of exports and drawbacks, shall have authority to administer such oaths and certify to such papers as may be necessary under any rules and regulations that may be prescribed under the authority herein conferred.*

Officer to be designated by Secretary to superintend.

Compensation.

Papers in bureau of drawback to be delivered to collector.

Authority to administer oaths, &c.

July 13, 1866.

SEC. 41. * * * * * * * *

And at any port where there shall be no superintendent of exports, all the duties and services required of superintendents of exports and drawback shall devolve upon and be performed by the collector of internal revenue designated to have charge of exportations.

Collector to perform the duties of superintendent of exports.

June 30, 1864.

SEC. 10. *And be it further enacted*, That each collector shall be authorized to appoint, by an instrument of writing under his hand, as many deputies as he may think proper, to be by him compensated for their services, and also to revoke any such appointment, giving such notice thereof as the Commissioner of Internal Revenue shall prescribe; and may require bonds or other securities, and accept the same, from such deputy; and each such deputy shall have the like authority, in every respect, to collect the duties and taxes levied or assessed within the portion of the district assigned to him which is by this act vested in the collector himself; but each collector shall, in every respect, be responsible both to the United States and to individuals, as the case may be, for all moneys collected, and for every act done by any of of his deputies while acting as such, and for every omission of duty.

Deputy collectors.

Bonds may be required.

Duties and powers.

Collector responsible for acts of deputies.

June 30, 1864.

SEC. 25. *And be it further enacted*, That there shall be allowed to collectors, in full compensation for their services and that of their deputies, a salary of fifteen hundred dollars per annum, to be paid quarterly, and in addition thereto, a commission of three per centum upon the first hundred thousand dollars, and a commission of one per centum upon all sums above one hundred thousand dollars and not exceeding four hundred thousand dollars, and a commission of one-half of one per centum on all sums above four hundred thousand dollars, *and not exceeding one million of dollars, and one-eighth of one per centum on all sums above one million of dollars;* such commissions to be computed upon the amounts by them respectively collected and paid over and accounted

Compensation of collectors.

Salary.

Commissions.

March 15, 1865, § 1.

for under the instructions of the Treasury Department.[1] And there shall be further paid, after the account thereof has been rendered to and approved by the proper officers of the Treasury, to each collector his necessary and reasonable charges for *advertising*, stationery, and blank-books used in the performance of his official duties, and for postage actually paid on letters and documents received or sent, and exclusively relating to official business; but no such account shall be approved unless it shall state the date and the particular items of every such expenditure, and shall be verified by oath or affirmation of the collector*: *Provided*, That the Secretary of the Treasury be authorized to make such further allowances, from time to time, as may be reasonable in cases in which, from the territorial extent of the district, or from the amount of internal duties collected, or from other circumstances, it may seem just to make such allowances.

Stationery, blank books, and postage. March 3, 1865, § 1.

March 3, 1865, § 1. Secretary may make further allowance in certain cases.

May 8, 1872.

SEC. 1. * * * * *

Total net compensation of collectors not to exceed $4,500.

And hereafter the total net compensation of collectors of internal revenue shall in no case exceed four thousand five hundred dollars per annum. (*Extract from an act making appropriations for the legislative, executive, and judicial expenses of the Government for the year ending June thirtieth, eighteen hundred and seventy-three, and for other purposes, approved May* 8, 1872. 17 *Stat., ch.* 140, *p.* 68.)

June 30, 1864. Collector may devolve his duties upon a deputy in case of sickness &c.

SEC. 39. *And be it further enacted*, That in case of the sickness or temporary disability of a collector to discharge such of his duties as cannot under existing laws be discharged by a deputy, they may be devolved by him upon one of his deputies; and for the official acts and defaults of such deputy the collector and his sureties shall be held responsible to the United States.

June 30, 1864. Mar. 2, 1867, § 9. Oldest deputy collector to act in case of vacancy.

SEC. 40. *And be it further enacted, That in case of a vacancy occurring in the office of collector by reason of death, or any other cause*, the deputies of such collector shall continue to act until his successor is appointed; and the deputy of such collector longest in service at the time immediately preceding shall, until a successor shall be appointed, discharge all the duties of said collector; and for the official acts and defaults of such deputy a remedy shall be had on the official bond of the collector, as in other cases; and of two or more deputy collectors, appointed on the same day, the one residing nearest the residence of the collector at the time of his death, resignation, or removal, shall discharge the said duties until the appointment of a successor: *Provided, That in case it shall appear to the Secretary of the Treasury that the interest of the Government shall so require, he may, by his order, direct said duties to be performed by such other one of the said deputies as he may in such order designate.* And any bond or security taken from a deputy by such collector, pursuant to this act, shall be available to his legal representatives and sureties to indemnify them for loss or damage accruing from any act of the deputy so continuing or succeeding to the duties of such collector.

Mar. 3, 1865, § 1. Secretary may designate the deputy in certain cases. Bond of deputy available to legal representatives and sureties.

[1] See June 30, 1864, sec. 24; also see July 20, 1868, sec. 28.

Mar. 1, 1869, § 1.

Deputy collector acting as collector during vacancy entitled to receive same pay and compensation as provided by law for the collector.

Be it enacted by the Senate and House of Representatives of the United States of America in Congress assembled, That any deputy collector of internal revenue who has performed, or may hereafter perform, under authority or requirement of law, the duties of collector of internal revenue in consequence of any vacancy in the office of such collector, shall be entitled to and receive so much of the same pay and compensation as is provided by law for such collector; but no such payment shall in any case be made when the collector has received or is entitled to receive compensation for services rendered during the same period of time.

July 1, 1870.

Defining the true intent and meaning of the foregoing act.

Be it enacted by the Senate and House of Representatives of the United States of America in Congress assembled, That the true intent and meaning of an act approved March one, eighteen hundred and sixty-nine, entitled "An act to allow deputy collectors of internal revenue acting as collectors the pay of collectors, and for other purposes," is as follows, to wit: That any deputy collector of internal revenue who has performed, or may hereafter perform, under authority of law, the duties of collector of internal revenue, in consequence of any vacancy in the office of said collector, shall be entitled to, and shall receive, the salary and commissions allowed by law to such collector, or the allowance in lieu of said salary and commissions allowed by the Secretary of the Treasury to such collector, and that the Secretary of the Treasury is authorized to make to the said deputy collector such allowance in lieu of salary and commissions as he would by law be authorized to make to said collector. And said deputy collector shall not be debarred from receiving said salary and commissions, or allowances in lieu thereof, by reason of the holding of another Federal office by said collector during the time for which said deputy collector acts as collector: *Provided*, That all payments to said deputy collector shall be upon duly-audited vouchers.

July 20, 1868.

Assessors or collectors not to discharge the duties of other assessors or collectors.

Supervisor may suspend for fraud, &c.

SEC. 51. *And be it further enacted*, That from and after the passage of this act no assessor or collector shall be detailed or authorized to discharge any duty imposed by law on any other collector or assessor, but a supervisor of internal revenue may, within his territorial district, suspend any collector or assessor for fraud, or gross neglect of duty, or abuse of power, and shall immediately report his action to the Commissioner of Internal Revenue, with his reasons therefor in writing, who shall thereupon take such further action as he may deem proper.

Mar. 2, 1867.

No salary unless confirmed by Senate.

SEC. 1. * * * * *

That no assessor or collector shall be entitled to any portion of the salary pertaining to the office unless such assessor [or collector] shall have been confirmed by the Senate, except in cases of commissions to fill vacancies which may have happened by death or resignation during the recess of the Senate. (*Extract from an act making appropriations for the legislative, executive, and judicial expenses of the Government for the year ending thirtieth of June, eighteen hundred and sixty-eight, and for other purposes, approved March* 2, 1867. 14 *Stat., ch.* 166, *p.* 445.)

June 30, 1864.
July 13, 1866, § 9.
Fiscal year to be observed in adjusting accounts.

SEC. 26. *And be it further enacted, That in the adjustment of the accounts of assessors and collectors of internal revenue which shall accrue after the thirtieth of June, eighteen hundred and sixty-four, and in the payment of their compensation for services after that date, the fiscal year of the Treasury shall be observed; and where such compensation, or any part of it, shall be by commissions upon assessments or collections, and shall during any year, in consequence of a new appointment, be due to more than one assessor or collector in the same district, such commissions shall be apportioned between such assessors or collectors; but in no case shall a greater amount of the commissions be allowed to two or more assessors or collectors in the same district than is or may be authorized by law to be allowed to one assessor or collector. And the salary and commissions of assessors and collectors heretofore earned and accrued shall be adjusted, allowed, and paid in conformity to the provisions of this section, and not otherwise; but no payment shall be made to assessors or collectors on account of salaries or commissions without the certificate of the Commissioner of Internal Revenue that all reports required by law or regulation have been received, or that a satisfactory explanation has been rendered to him of the cause of the delay.*

Commissions to be apportioned in case of two or more officers in same year.
Salaries and commissions heretofore earned.
No payment of salary or commissions to be made without certificate of Commissioner.

July 20, 1868.
June 6, 1872, § 12.
Appointment of supervisors.
June 6, 1872, § 12.
Salary.

SEC. 49. *And be it further enacted,* That *the President may nominate, and, by and with the advice and consent of the Senate, appoint,* not exceeding *ten* officers to be called supervisors of internal revenue, each one of whom *shall be assigned by the Secretary of the Treasury, on the recommendation of the Commissioner of Internal Revenue, to duty in any part of the United States, and may be transferred from place to place, according to the exigency of the public service;* and shall receive in addition to expenses necessarily incurred by him and allowed and certified by the said Commissioner as a compensation for his services, such salary as the Commissioner of Internal Revenue may deem just and reasonable, not exceeding three thousand dollars per annum. It shall be the duty of every supervisor of internal revenue, under the direction of the Commissioner, to see that all laws and regulations relating to the collection of internal taxes are faithfully executed and complied with; to aid in the prevention, detection, and punishment of any frauds in relation thereto, and to examine into the efficiency and conduct of all officers of internal revenue; * and for such purposes he shall have power to examine all persons, books, papers, accounts, and premises, and to administer oaths and to summon any person to produce books and papers, or to appear and testify under oath before him, and to compel a compliance with such summons in the same manner as assessors may do. It shall be the duty of every supervisor of internal revenue as aforesaid to report in writing to the Commissioner of Internal Revenue any neglect of duty, incompetency, delinquency, or malfeasance in office of any internal-revenue officer * of which he may obtain knowledge, with a statement of all the facts in each case, and any evidence sustaining the same; and he shall have power to transfer any inspector, gauger, or store keeper from one distillery or other place of duty to another, or from one col-

Duties of supervisors.
June 6, 1872, § 12.
May summon and examine persons and papers.
Report to Commissioner.
June 6, 1872, § 12.
May transfer or suspend inspectors, gaugers, and store-keepers.

lection district to another,* and may, by notice in writing, suspend from duty any such inspector, gauger, or storekeeper, and in case of suspension shall immediately notify the collector of the proper district and the Commissioner of Internal Revenue, and within three days thereafter make report of his action, and his reasons therefor, in writing, to said Commissioner, who shall thereupon take such further action as he may deem proper.

June 6, 1872, § 12.

SEC. 50. *And be it further enacted*, That the Commissioner of Internal Revenue shall have power, whenever in his judgment the necessities of the service may require, to employ competent *agents*, not exceeding twenty-five in number at any one time, to be paid under the provisions of the seventh section of the "Act to amend existing laws relating to internal revenue, and for other purposes," approved March 2, 1867, and he may, at his discretion, assign any such *agent* to duty under the direction of any *officer* of internal revenue, or to such other special duty as he may deem necessary, and that from and after the passage of this act no general or special agent, or inspector, by whatever name or designation he may be known, of the Treasury Department in connection with the internal revenue, except inspectors of tobacco, snuff, and cigars, and except as provided for in this act, shall be appointed, commissioned, employed, or continued in office, and the term of office or employment of all such general or special agents or inspectors now authorized as aforesaid under employment at the time of the passage of this act shall expire ten days after this act shall take effect.

July 20, 1868.

Employment of agents.

June 6, 1782, § 12.

Ibid.

To be assigned to duty under any internal revenue officer.

No agents or inspectors to be appointed, &c., in connection with the internal revenue except as provided for in this act.

SEC. 1. * * * * *

May 8, 1872.

From and after the passage of this act the Secretary of the Treasury shall have power to employ not more than three persons to assist the proper officers of the Government in discovering and collecting any money belonging to the United States whenever the same shall be withheld by any person or corporation, upon such terms and conditions as he shall deem best for the interests of the United States; but no compensation shall be paid to such persons except out of the money and property so secured; and no person shall be employed under the provisions of this clause who shall not have fully set forth in a written statement, under oath, addressed to the Secretary of the Treasury, the character of the claim out of which he proposes to recover, or assist in recovering moneys for the United States, the laws by the violation of which the same have been withheld, and the name of the person, firm, or corporation having thus withheld such moneys; and if any person so employed shall receive or attempt to receive any money or other consideration from any person, firm, or corporation alleged thus to have withheld money from the United States, except in pursuance of the written contract made in relation thereto with the Secretary of the Treasury, such person shall be deemed guilty of a misdemeanor, and upon conviction thereof shall be fined not less than one thousand dollars or imprisoned not less than two years, or both, in the discretion of any court of the United States having jurisdiction;

Secretary of the Treasury authorized to employ three persons to assist the proper officers of the Government in discovering and collecting money belonging to the United States, without compensation except as provided.

Penalties relating thereto.

and the person so employed shall be required to make report of his proceedings under such contract at any time when required to do so by the Secretary of the Treasury. (*Extract from an act making appropriations for the legislative, executive, and judicial expenses of the Government for the year ending June thirtieth, eighteen hundred and seventy-three, and for other purposes. Approved May* 8, 1872. 17 *Stat., ch.* 140, *p.* 69.)

July 20, 1868.

Appointment of internal-revenue storekeepers.

SEC. 52. *And be it further enacted*, That there shall be appointed by the Secretary of the Treasury such number of internal revenue storekeepers as may be necessary, the compensation of each of whom shall be determined by the Commissioner of Internal Revenue, not exceeding five dollars per day, to be paid by the United States, one or more of whom shall be assigned by the Commissioner of Internal Revenue to every bonded or distillery warehouse established by law; and no such storekeeper shall be engaged in any other business while in the service of the United States without the written permission of the Commissioner of Internal Revenue. Every storekeeper shall take an oath faithfully to perform the duties of his office, and shall give a bond, to be approved by the Commissioner of Internal Revenue, for the faithful discharge of his duties, in such form and for such amount as the Commissioner may prescribe. Every storekeeper shall have charge of the warehouse to which he may be assigned, under the direction of the collector controlling the same, which warehouse shall be in the joint custody of such storekeeper and the proprietor thereof, and kept securely locked, and shall at no time be unlocked and opened, or remain open, unless in the presence of such storekeeper or other person who may be designated to act for him as hereinafter provided; and no article shall be received in or delivered from such warehouse except on an order or permit addressed to the storekeeper and signed by the collector having control of the warehouse. Every storekeeper shall keep a warehouse book, which shall at all times be open to the examination of any revenue officer, in which he shall enter an account of all articles deposited in the warehouse to which he is assigned, indicating in each case the date of the deposit, by whom manufactured or produced, the number and description of the packages and contents, the quantities therein, the marks and serial numbers thereon, and by whom gauged, inspected, or weighed, and if distilled spirits, the number of gauge or wine-gallons and of proof-gallons; and before delivering any article from the warehouse he shall enter in said book the date of the permit or order of the collector for the delivery of such articles, the number and description of the packages, the marks and serial numbers thereon, the date of delivery, to whom delivered, and for what purpose, which purpose shall be specified in the permit or order for delivery; and in case of delivery of any distilled spirits the number of gauge or wine-gallons, and of proof-gallons, shall also be stated; and such further particulars shall be entered in the warehouse books as may be prescribed or found necessary for the identification of the packages, to insure the correct delivery thereof and proper accountability

Salary.

To take oath and give bond.

To have charge of warehouse.

To keep a warehouse-book.

thereof [therefor.] A daily return shall be furnished by every storekeeper to the collector of the district of all articles received in and delivered from the warehouse during the day preceding that on which the return is made, a copy of which shall be mailed by him at the same time to the Commissioner of Internal Revenue; and each storekeeper shall, on the first Monday of every month, make a report in triplicate of the number of packages of all articles, with the several descriptions thereof respectively, as above provided, which remained in the warehouse at the date of his last report, and of all articles received therein and delivered therefrom during the preceding month, and of all articles remaining therein at the end of said month; one of which reports shall be by him delivered to the assessor of the district, to be recorded and filed in his office; one delivered to the collector having control of the warehouse, to be recorded and filed in his office; and one transmitted to the Commissioner of Internal Revenue, to be recorded and filed in his office. Any internal-revenue storekeeper may be transferred by the supervisor of the district or by the Commissioner of Internal Revenue from one warehouse to any other. In case of the absence of any internal-revenue storekeeper by sickness or from any other cause, the collector having control of the warehouse may designate a person to have temporary charge of such warehouse who shall, during such absence, perform the duties and receive the pay of the storekeeper for the time he may be so employed; and for any violation of the law he shall be subject to the same punishment as storekeepers. Any storekeeper or other person in the employment of the United States having charge of a bonded warehouse, who shall remove or allow to be removed any cask or other package therefrom without an order or permit of the collector, or which has not been marked or stamped in the manner required by law, or shall remove or allow to be removed any part of the contents of any cask or package deposited therein, shall be immediately dismissed from office or employment, and, on conviction, be fined not less than five hundred dollars, nor more than two thousand dollars, and imprisoned not less than three months nor more than two years.

Storekeeper to make daily return.

To make monthly report in triplicate.

May be transferred by Commissioner or supervisor.

Temporary storekeepers.

Penalties relating to storekeepers.

SEC. 53. *And be it further enacted*, That there shall be appointed by the Secretary of the Treasury, in every collection-district where the same may be necessary, one or more internal revenue gaugers, who shall each take an oath faithfully to perform his duties, and shall give his bond, with one or more sureties, satisfactory to the Commissioner of Internal Revenue, for the faithful discharge of the duties assigned to him by law or regulations; and the penal sum of said bond shall not be less than five thousand dollars, and said bond shall be renewed or strengthened as the Commissioner of Internal Revenue may require. The duties of every such gauger shall be performed under the supervision and direction of the collector of the district to which he may be assigned, or of the collector in charge of exports at any port of entry to which he may be assigned.* Every gauger shall, under such regulations as may be prescribed by the Com-

July 20, 1868.

Appointment of gaugers.

To give bond.

Duties to be performed under supervision of collector.

June 6, 1872, § 12.

To make daily return.

missioner of Internal Revenue, make a daily return, in duplicate; one to be delivered to the assessor and the other to the collector of his district, giving a true account, in detail, of all articles gauged and proved or inspected by him, and for whom, and the number and kind of stamps used by him. Any gauger who shall make any false or fraudulent inspection, gauging, or proof, shall pay a penalty of one thousand dollars, and, on conviction, shall be fined not less than five hundred dollars nor more than five thousand dollars, and imprisoned not less than three months nor more than three years.

Penalties relating to gaugers.

June 6, 1872.

Compensation of gaugers.

SEC. 14. That on and after the date when this act shall take effect, the compensation of internal-revenue gaugers shall be by fees dependent upon the quantity gauged, to be prescribed by the Commissioner of Internal Revenue, which, together with their actual and necessary traveling expenses, verified by the oath of the gauger, and the compensation of internal-revenue gaugers and store-keepers, shall be paid by the United States monthly, without requiring reimbursement by distillers.

June 30, 1864.

Inspectors of tobacco and cigars.

July 20, 1868, § 50.

SEC. 58. *And be it further enacted*, That there shall be appointed by the Secretary of the Treasury, in every collection district where the same may be necessary, one or more inspectors of * tobacco, cigars, * who shall take an oath faithfully to perform their duties, in such form as the Commissioner of Internal Revenue shall prescribe, and who shall be entitled to receive such fees as may be fixed and prescribed by said Commissioner, to be paid by the owner or manufacturer of the articles inspected. And any manufacturer of * tobacco, cigars, * which may by law be required to be inspected, who shall refuse to admit an inspector upon his premises, so far as it may be necessary for the performance of his duties, or who shall obstruct an inspector in the performance of his duties, shall forfeit the sum of one hundred dollars, to be recovered in the manner provided for other penalties imposed by this act.

July 20, 1868, § 50.

Manufacturer refusing to admit inspector on his premises.

Mar. 2, 1867.

All inspectors required to give bond in a sum not less than $5,000.

SEC. 31. *And be it further enacted*, That all inspectors appointed under the provisions of the act or acts of which this is amendatory shall be required to give bonds, with security, approved by the Secretary of the Treasury or assessor of the district, in a sum not less than five thousand dollars, conditioned for the faithful discharge of the duties of such inspector.

GENERAL DUTIES, POWERS, LIABILITIES, ETC., OF OFFICERS.

June 30, 1864.

July 20, 1868, § 50.
Mar. 3, 1865, § 1.

Assessors and their assistants, collectors and their deputies, and inspectors authorized to administer oaths.

SEC. 52. *And be it further enacted*, That all assessors and their assistants, all collectors and their deputies, * and all inspectors, are hereby authorized to administer oaths and take evidence touching any part of the administration of this law with which they are respectively charged, *or* where such oaths and evidence are by law authorized to be taken; and any perjury therein shall be punished in the like manner, and to the same degree, as in the case of perjury committed in proceedings in the courts of the United States.

SEC. 180. The authority to frank mail-matter is conferred upon and limited to the following persons: * * * * Seventh. Assessors and collectors and their assistants and deputies, for the interchange of official communications only. * * * * * * *

June 8, 1872.

Franking privilege of internal revenue officers.

[Sec. 65, July 13, 1866, is superseded by the above.]

SEC. 19. * * * * *

Mar. 2, 1867.

Any officer of internal revenue may be specially authorized by the Commissioner of Internal Revenue to seize any property which may by law be subject to seizure, and for that purpose such officer shall have all the power conferred by law upon collectors of internal revenue, and such special authority shall be limited in respect of time, place, and kind or class of property as the said Commissioner may specify.

July 20, 1868, § 37.

Commissioner may authorize any internal-revenue officer to seize property. But see July 20, 1868, § 51.

June 30, 1864.

SEC. 36. *And be it further enacted*, [That each and every collector, or his deputy, who shall be guilty of any extortion or willful oppression, under color of law, or shall knowingly demand other or greater sums than shall be authorized by law, or shall receive any fee, compensation, or reward, except as herein prescribed, for the performance of any duty, or shall willfully neglect to perform any of the duties enjoined by this act, shall, upon conviction, be subject to a fine of not exceeding one thousand dollars, or to be imprisoned for not exceeding one year, or both, at the discretion of the court, and be dismissed from office, and be forever thereafter incapable of holding any office under the Government; and one-half of the fine so imposed shall be for the use of the United States, and the other half for the use of the informer, who shall be ascertained by the judgment of the court; and the said court shall also render judgment against said collector or deputy collector for the amount of damages accruing to the party injured, to be collected by execution.][1] And each and every collector, or his deputies, shall give receipts for all sums by them collected.

Penalty upon collectors for extortion or oppression. Superseded by § 98, July 20, 1868.

Disposal of fines.

Receipt to be given by collector and deputy.

June 30, 1864.

SEC. 37. *And be it further enacted*, That a collector or deputy collector, assessor, assistant assessor, * or inspector, shall be authorized to enter, in the day-time, any brewery, distillery,[2] manufactory, building, or place where any property, articles, or objects, subject to duty or taxation under the provisions of this act, are made, produced, or kept, within his district, so far as it may be necessary for the purpose of examining said property, articles, or objects, or inspecting the accounts required by this act from time to time to be made or kept by any manufacturer or producer, relating to such property, articles, or objects. And every owner of such brewery, distillery,[2] manufactory, building, or place, or persons having the agency or superintendence of the same, who shall refuse to admit such officer, or to suffer him to examine said property, articles, or ob-

July 20, 1868, § 50.

Revenue officers may enter brewery, &c., in the day-time.

Penalty for refusing to admit officers.

[1] The portion of this section in brackets is retained because it is in force as being in effect a part of section 38, June 30, 1864, so far as it relates to penalties, although otherwise superseded by section 98, act July 20, 1868.

[2] See section 32, July 20, 1868.

jects, or to inspect said accounts, shall, for every such refusal, forfeit and pay the sum of five hundred dollars: *Provided, however*, That when such premises shall be open at night, such officers may enter while so open in the performance of their official duties.

Premises may be entered at night when open.

June 30, 1864.

SEC. 38. *And be it further enacted*, That if any person shall forcibly obstruct or hinder any assessor or assistant assessor, or any collector or deputy collector, * or inspector, in the execution of this act, or of any power and authority hereby vested in him, or shall forcibly rescue, or cause to be rescued, any property, articles, or objects, after the same shall have been seized by him, or shall attempt or endeavor so to do, the person so offending shall, upon conviction thereof, for every such offense, forfeit and pay the sum of five hundred dollars, or double the value of the property so rescued, or be imprisoned for a term not exceeding two years, at the discretion of the court: *Provided*, That if any such officer shall divulge to any party, or make known in any manner other than is provided in this act, the operations, style of work, or apparatus of any manufacturer or producer visited by him in the discharge of his official duties, he shall be subject to the penalties prescribed in section *thirty-six* of this act.

Penalty for obstructing revenue officer.

July 20, 1868, § 50.

See, however, last clause § 67, July 13, 1866, and § 32, July 20, 1868.

Penalty for officer divulging the operations of any person visited.

March 3, 1865, § 1.

June 30, 1864.

SEC. 21. *And be it further enacted*, That every assessor or assistant assessor who shall enter upon and perform the duties of his office *without having taken the oath or affirmation required by law*, * shall, upon conviction thereof in any circuit or district court of the United States having jurisdiction thereof, be subject to a fine not exceeding one thousand dollars, or to imprisonment for not exceeding one year, or both, at the discretion of the court, and shall be dismissed from office, and shall be forever disqualified from holding any office under the Government of the United States. And one-half of the fine so imposed shall be for the use of the United States, and the other half for the use of the informer, who shall be ascertained by the judgment of the court; and the said court shall also render judgment against the said assessor or assistant assessor for the amount of damages sustained in favor of the party injured, to be collected by execution.

July 13, 1866, § 9.
July 20, 1868, § 98.

Penalty for assessor or assistant failing to take the oath of office prescribed by law.

Disposition of penalties.

June 30, 1864.

SEC. 23. *And be it further enacted*, That if any assessor shall demand of, or receive directly or indirectly from, any assistant assessor, as a condition of his appointment to or continuance in, his said office of assistant assessor, any portion of the compensation herein allowed such assistant assessor, or any other consideration, such assessor so offending shall be summarily dismissed from office, and shall be liable to a fine of not less than five hundred dollars upon conviction of said offense in any district or circuit court of the United States of the district in which such offense may be committed.

Corruption by assessor in appointment of assistant assessor.

Penalty.

July 13, 1866.

SEC. 60. *And be it further enacted*, That every internal-revenue officer, whose payment, charges, salary, or compensation shall be composed, either wholly or in part, of fees, commissions, allowances, or rewards, from whatever source derived, shall be required to render to the Commissioner of

Internal revenue officers to make statement of fees, &c., when required

Internal Revenue, under regulations to be approved by the Secretary of the Treasury, a statement under oath setting forth the entire amount of such fees, commissions, emoluments, or rewards of whatever nature, or from whatever source received, during the time for which said statement is rendered; and any false statement knowingly and willfully rendered under the requirements of this section, or regulations established in accordance therewith, shall be deemed willful perjury, and punished, on conviction thereof, as provided in section forty-two of the act of June thirty, eighteen hundred and sixty-four, to which this act is an amendment; and any neglect or omission to render such statement when required shall be punished on conviction thereof by a fine of not less than two hundred dollars nor more than five hundred dollars, in the discretion of the court.

False statement to be deemed perjury.

Penalty for neglect, &c., to make statement when required.

SEC. 97. *And be it further enacted*, That any internal-revenue officer who shall be or become interested, directly or indirectly, in the manufacture of tobacco, snuff, or cigars, or in the production, rectification, or redistillation of distilled spirits, shall be dismissed from office; and any such officer who shall become so interested in any such manufacture or production, rectification, or redistillation, shall, on conviction, be fined not less than five hundred dollars nor more than five thousand dollars.

July 20, 1868.

Internal-revenue officer becoming interested in the manufacture or production of distilled spirits, tobacco, snuff, and cigars.

Penalty.

SEC. 59. *And be it further enacted*, That * any assessor, collector, inspector, * who shall hereafter become interested, directly or indirectly, in the production, by distillation or by other process, of * ale, or beer, or other fermented liquors, shall, on conviction before any court of the United States of competent jurisdiction, pay a penalty not less than five hundred dollars nor more than five thousand dollars, in the discretion of the court. And any such officer interested as aforesaid in any such manufacture at the time this act takes effect, who shall fail to divest himself of such interest within sixty days thereafter, shall be held and declared to have become so interested after this act takes effect.

July 13, 1866.

July 20, 1868, § 50.
July 20, 1868, § 97.

Internal-revenue officer becoming interested in the production of fermented liquors.

Penalty.

SEC. 98. *And be it further enacted*, That if any officer or agent appointed and acting under the authority of any revenue law of the United States shall be guilty of any extortion or willful oppression, under color of law; or shall knowingly demand other or greater sums than shall be authorized by law; or shall receive any fee, compensation, or reward for the performance of any duty except as by law prescribed; or shall willfully neglect to perform any of the duties enjoined on him by law; or shall conspire or collude with any other person to defraud the United States; or shall make opportunity for any person to defraud the United States; or shall do, or omit to do, any act with intent to enable any other person to defraud the United States; or shall negligently or designedly permit any violation of the law by any other person; or shall make or sign any false entry in any book, or make or sign any false certificate or return in any case where he is by law or regulation required to make any entry, certificate, or return; or having knowledge or information of the violation of any revenue law by any person, or of fraud committed by any

July 20, 1868.

Officer or agent acting under authority of any revenue law guilty of extortion, oppression, conspiracy, collusion, fraud, negligence, &c.

Having knowledge of violation of internal-revenue law and failing to report.

person against the United States under any revenue law of the United States, shall fail to report, in writing, such knowledge or information to his next superior officer, and to the Commissioner of Internal Revenue; or shall demand, or accept, or attempt to collect, directly or indirectly, as payment or gift or otherwise, any sum of money or other thing of value for the compromise, adjustment, or settlement of any charge or complaint for any violation or alleged violation of law, except as expressly authorized by law so to do, he shall be dismissed from office, and shall be held to be guilty of a misdemeanor, and shall, on conviction, be fined not less than one thousand dollars nor more than five thousand dollars, and imprisoned not less than six months nor more than three years. And one-half of the fine so imposed shall be for the use of the United States, and the other half for the use of the informer, who shall be ascertained by the judgment of the court; and the said court shall also render judgment against the said officer or agent for the amount of damages sustained in favor of the party injured, to be collected by execution.

Accepting gifts or payment in compromise.

Penalty.

March 2, 1867.

July 20, 1868, § 98.

Penalty for accepting any gift, &c., for the settlement of any charge of violation of law.

SEC. 26. *And be it further enacted*, That if any * district attorney, marshal, or * person[1] charged with the execution or supervision of the execution of any of the provisions of this act, or of the act to which this is amendatory, shall demand, or accept, or attempt to collect, directly or indirectly, as payment or gift or otherwise, any sum of money or other property of value for the compromise, adjustment, or settlement of any charge or complaint for any violation, or alleged violation of any of the said provisions, except as expressly authorized by law so to do, he shall be held to be guilty of a misdemeanor, and shall for every such offense be liable to indictment and trial in any court of the United States having competent jurisdiction, and on conviction thereof shall be fined in double the sum or value of the money or property received or demanded, and be imprisoned for a period of not less than one year nor more than ten years.

ASSESSMENT OF TAXES.

June 30, 1864.

Persons liable to taxation to make list or return.

Mar. 2, 1867, § 1.

Return to be made on oath.

Nature of return.

July 14, 1870, § 6.

SEC. 11. *And be it further enacted*, That it shall be the duty of any person, partnership, firm, association, or corporation, made liable to any duty, license,[2] stamp, or tax imposed by law, when not otherwise provided for, on or before the first Monday of *March* in each year, and in other cases before the day of levy, to make a list or return, verified by oath or affirmation, to the assistant assessor of the district where located, of * the articles or objects charged with a special duty or tax, the quantity of goods, wares, and merchandise made or sold, and charged with a specific or ad valorem duty or tax, the several rates and aggregate amount, according to the respective provisions of this act, and according to the forms and regulations to be prescribed

[1] But see § 98, act July 20, 1868, in which the words "officer or agent" probably include those who are intended to be embraced in the term "person."

[2] Wherever the word "license" occurs in this compilation it means "special tax."

by the Commissioner of Internal Revenue, under the direction of the Secretary of the Treasury, for which such person, partnership, firm, association, or corporation is liable to be assessed.

SEC. 12. *And be it further enacted*, That the instructions, regulations, and directions, as hereinbefore mentioned, shall be binding on each assessor and his assistants, and on each collector and his deputies, and on all other persons, in the performance of the duties enjoined by or under this act; pursuant to which instructions the said assessors shall, on the first Monday of *March* in each year, and from time to time thereafter, in accordance with this act, direct and cause the several assistant assessors to proceed through every part of their respective districts, and inquire after and concerning all persons being within the assessment districts where they respectively reside, owning, possessing, or having the care or management of any property, goods, wares, and merchandise, articles or objects liable to pay any duty, stamp, or tax, including all persons liable to pay a license or other duty, under the provisions of this act, and to make a list of the owners, and to value and enumerate the said objects of taxation, respectively, by reference to any lists of assessment or collection taken under the laws of the respective States, to any other records or documents, to the written list, schedule, or return required to be made out and delivered to the assistant assessor, and by all other lawful ways and means, in the manner prescribed by this act, and in conformity with the regulations and instructions before mentioned.

June 30, 1864.

Regulations of Commissioner binding on all persons.

See § 1, June 30, 1864.

Mar. 2, 1867, § 1.

Assistant assessors to canvass districts.

Duties of assistant assessors.

SEC. 13. *And be it further enacted*, That if any person liable to pay any duty or tax, or owning, possessing, or having the care or management of property, goods, wares, and merchandise, articles or objects liable to pay any duty, tax, or license, shall fail to make and exhibit a list or return required by law, but shall consent to disclose the particulars of any and all the property, goods, wares, and merchandise, articles and objects liable to pay any duty or tax, or any business or occupation liable to pay any license, as aforesaid, then, and in that case, it shall be the duty of the officer to make such list or return, which, being distinctly read, consented to, and signed and verified by oath or affirmation by the person so owning, possessing, or having the care and management as aforesaid, may be received as the list of such person.

June 30, 1864.

Assistant assessor to make list for person disclosing.

List to be read to and consented to by the person liable to tax.

To be signed and verified by oath or affirmation.

SEC. 14. *And be it further enacted, That in case any person shall be absent from his or her residence or place of business at the time an assistant assessor shall call for the annual list or return, and no annual list or return has been rendered by such person to the assistant assessor as required by law, it shall be the duty of such assistant assessor to leave at such place of residence or business, with some one of suitable age and discretion, if such be present, otherwise to deposit in the nearest post-office, a note or memorandum, addressed to such person, requiring him or her to render to such assistant assessor the list or return required by law within ten days from the date of such note or memorandum, verified by oath or affirma-*

June 30, 1864.

July 13, 1866, § 9.

Notice to be left for absent persons.

Persons neglecting to make return. *tion. And if any person, on being notified or required as aforesaid, shall refuse or neglect to render such list or return within the time required as aforesaid, or if any person without notice, as aforesaid, shall not deliver a monthly or other list or return at the time required by law, or if any person shall deliver or disclose to any assessor or assistant assessor any list, statement, or return which, in the opinion of the assessor, is* Or making fraudulent return. *false or fraudulent, or contains any understatement or under-* May be summoned before the assessor. *valuation, it shall be lawful for the assessor to summon such person, his agent, or other person having possession, custody, or care of books of account containing entries relating to the trade or business of such person, or any other person he may* Power of assessor. *deem proper, to appear before such assessor and produce such book, at a time and place therein named, and to give testimony or answer interrogatories under oath or affirmation respecting any objects liable to tax as aforesaid, or the lists, statements, or returns thereof, or any trade, business, or profession liable to any tax as aforesaid. And the assessor may summon, as aforesaid, any person residing or found within the State in in which his district is situated. And when the person intended to be summoned does not reside and cannot be found within such State, the assessor may enter any collection district where such person may be found, and there make the examination hereinbefore authorized. And to this end he shall there have and may exercise all the power and authority he has or may lawfully exercise in the district for which he is commissioned.*[1] Service of summons. *The summons authorized by this section shall in all cases be served by an assistant assessor of the district where the person to whom it is directed may be found, by an attested copy delivered to such person in hand or left at his last and usual place* Travel. *of abode, allowing such person at the rate of one day for each twenty-five miles he may be required to travel, computed from the place of service to the place of examination; and the certificate of service signed by such assistant assessor shall be evidence of the facts it states on the hearing of an application for* Summons to produce books. *an attachment; and when the summons requires the production of books, it shall be sufficient if such books are described with* Proceedings in case of failure to obey summons. *reasonable certainty. In case any person so summoned shall neglect or refuse to obey such summons, or to give testimony, or to answer interrogatories as required, it shall be lawful for the assessor to apply to the judge of the district court or to a commissioner of the circuit court of the United States for the district within which the person so summoned resides for an attach-* Authority and duty of judge or commissioner. *ment against such person as for a contempt. It shall be the duty of such judge or commissioner to hear such application, and, if satisfactory proof be made, to issue an attachment, directed to some proper officer, for the arrest of such person, and upon his being brought before him to proceed to a hearing of the case; and upon such hearing the judge or commissioner shall have power to make such order as he shall deem proper, not inconsistent with the provisions of existing laws for the punishment of contempts, to enforce obedience to the requirements of the summons and punish such person for his default* Assessors may enter premises. *or disobedience. It shall be the duty of the assessor or assistant assessor of the district within which such person shall have tax-*

[1] But see § 51, July 20, 1868.

*able property to enter into and upon the premises, if it be necessary, of such person so refusing or neglecting, or rendering a false or fraudulent list or return, and to make, according to the best information which he can obtain, including that derived from the evidence elicited by the examination of the assessor, and on his own view and information, such list or return, according to the form prescribed, of the property, goods, wares, and merchandise, and all articles or objects liable to tax, owned or possessed or under the care or management of such person, and assess the tax thereon, including the amount, if any, due for special * tax; and in case of the return of a false or fraudulent list or valuation, he shall add one hundred per centum to such tax; and in case of a refusal or neglect, except in cases of sickness or absence, to make a list or return, or to verify the same as aforesaid, he shall add fifty per centum to such tax; and in case of neglect occasioned by sickness or absence as aforesaid, the assessor may allow such further time for making and delivering such list or return as he may judge necessary, not exceeding thirty days; and the amount so added to the tax shall, in all cases, be collected by the collector at the same time and in the same manner as the tax; and the list or return so made and subscribed by such assessor or assistant assessor shall be taken and reputed as good and sufficient for all legal purposes.*

May make list or return.

July 14, 1870, § 6.

Penalties to be assessed.

In case of sickness or absence, further time.

Collection of assessed penalties.

Return of assessor sufficient.

SEC. 3. *And be it further enacted, That it shall be the duty of all persons required to make returns or lists of * articles or objects charged with an internal tax, to declare in such returns or lists whether the several rates and amounts therein contained are stated according to their values in legal-tender currency or according to their values in coined money; and in case of neglect or refusal so to declare to the satisfaction of the assistant assessor receiving such returns or lists, such assistant assessor is hereby required to make returns or lists for such persons so neglecting or refusing, as in cases of persons neglecting or refusing to make the returns or lists required by the acts aforesaid,*[1] *and to assess the tax thereon, and to add thereto the amount of penalties imposed by law in cases of such neglect or refusal. And whenever the rates and amounts contained in the returns or lists as aforesaid shall be stated in coined money, it shall be the duty of each assessor receiving the same to reduce such rates and amounts to their equivalent in legal-tender currency, according to the value of such coined money in said currency for the time covered by said returns. And the lists required by law to be furnished to collectors by assessors shall in all cases contain the several amounts of taxes assessed, estimated, or valued in legal-tender currency only.*

Mar. 10, 1866.

July 13, 1866, § 9, (bis.)
July 14, 1870, § 6.
Returns must show whether made in legal-tender currency or coined money.
Penalty for refusal or neglect.

Returns stated in coin to be reduced to legal-tender currency.

Lists returned to collectors to be in legal-tender currency.

SEC. 15.* *And be it further enacted,* That if any person shall deliver or disclose to any assessor or assistant assessor appointed in pursuance of law any false or fraudulent list, return, account, or statement, with intent to defeat or evade the valuation, enumeration, or assessment intended to be made, or if any person who being duly summoned to appear to testify, or to appear and produce such books as aforesaid,

June 30, 1864.

Penalty for making fraudulent return.

[1] In the amendatory section (9 *bis.*) of the act of July 13, 1866, the words "the acts aforesaid" referred to the acts of June 30, 1864, and March 10, 1866.

Or for neglecting to appear and produce books.

shall neglect to appear or to produce said books, he shall, upon conviction thereof before any circuit or district court of the United States, be fined in any sum not exceeding one thousand dollars, or be imprisoned for not exceeding one year, or both, at the discretion of the court, with costs of prosecution.

June 30, 1864.

Taxable property owned by non-resident.

SEC. 16. *And be it further enacted*, That whenever there shall be in any assessment district any property, goods, wares, and merchandise, articles or objects, not owned or possessed by, or under the care or management of, any person within such district, and liable to be taxed as aforesaid, and no list of which shall have been transmitted to the assistant assessor in the manner provided by this act, it shall be the duty of the assistant assessor for such district to enter into and upon the premises where such property is situated, and take such view thereof as may be necessary, and to make lists of the same, according to the form prescribed, which lists, being subscribed by the said assessor, shall be taken and reputed as good and sufficient lists of such property, goods, wares, and merchandise, articles or objects as aforesaid, for all legal purposes.

June 30, 1864.

Person having taxable property in another district may make return in the district where he resides.

SEC. 17. *And be it further enacted*, That any owner or person having the care or management of property, goods, wares, and merchandise, articles or objects, not lying or being within the assessment district in which he resides, shall be permitted to make out and deliver the list thereof required by this act (provided the assessment district in which the said objects of duty or taxation are situated is therein distinctly stated) at the time and in the manner prescribed to the assistant assessor of the assessment district wherein such person resides.

List to be transmitted to other district for examination.

And it shall be the duty of the assistant assessor who receives any such list to transmit the same to the assistant assessor where such objects of taxation are situate, who shall examine such list; and if he approves the same, he shall return it to the assistant assessor from whom he received it, with his approval thereof; and if he fails to approve the same, he shall make such alterations therein and additions thereto as he may deem to be just and proper, and shall then return the said list to the assistant assessor from whom it was received, who shall proceed, in making the assessment of the tax upon the list by him so received, in all respects as if the said list had been made out by himself.

June 30, 1864.

Annual, monthly, and special lists.

SEC. 18. *And be it further enacted*, That the lists aforesaid shall, where not otherwise specially provided for, be taken with reference to the day fixed for that purpose by this act, as aforesaid; and, where duties accrue at other and different times, the list shall be taken with reference to the time when said duties become due, and shall be denominated annual, monthly, and special lists. And the assistant assessors, respectively, after collecting the said lists, shall proceed to

Two general lists to be made.

Alphabetical list of residents.

arrange the same, and to make two general lists—the first of which shall exhibit, in alphabetical order, the names of all persons, firms, companies, or corporations liable to pay any duty, tax, or license under this act, residing within the assessment district, together with the value and assessment or enumeration, as the case may require, of the objects liable to duty or taxation within such districts for which each such person is liable, or for which any firm, company, or corporation is liable, with the amount of duty or tax payable thereon; and the second list shall exhibit, in alphabetical order, the names of all persons residing out of the collection district, who own property within the district, together with the value and assessment or enumeration thereof, as the case may be, with the amount of duty or tax payable thereon as aforesaid. The forms of the said general list shall be devised and prescribed by the assessor, under the direction of the Commissioner of Internal Revenue, and lists taken according to such forms shall be made out by the assistant assessors and delivered to the assessor within thirty days after the day fixed by this act as aforesaid, requiring lists from individuals; or where duties, licenses, or taxes accrue at other and different times, the lists shall be delivered from time to time as they become due.

And of non-residents.

Forms to be prescribed by Commissioner.

Lists to be returned by assistant assessor within thirty days.

Other lists to be delivered from time to time.

June 30, 1864.

July 13, 1866, § 9.

Annual assessments to be advertised.

SEC. 19. *And be it further enacted, That the assessor for each collection district shall give notice by advertisement in one newspaper published in each county within said district, and if there be none published in the district, then in a newspaper published in the collection district adjoining thereto, and shall post notices in at least four public places within each assessment district, and shall mail a copy of such notice to each postmaster in his district, to be posted in his office, stating the time and place within said collection district when and where appeals will be received and determined relative to any erroneous or excessive valuations, assessments, or enumerations by the assessor or assistant assessor returned in the annual list, and such notice shall be advertised and posted by the assessor and mailed as aforesaid at least ten days before the time appointed for hearing said appeals. And it shall be the duty of the assessor for each collection district, at the time fixed for hearing such appeals as aforesaid, to submit the proceedings of the assessor and assistant assessor, and the annual lists taken and returned as aforesaid, to the inspection of any and all persons who may apply for that purpose. And such assessor is hereby authorized at any time to hear and determine in a summary way, according to law and right, upon any and all appeals which may be exhibited against the proceedings of the said assessor or assistant assessors, and the office or principal place of business of the said assessor shall be open during the business hours of each day for the hearing of appeals by parties who shall appear voluntarily before him: Provided, That no appeal shall be allowed to any party after he shall have been duly assessed, and the annual list containing the assessment has been transmitted to the collector of the district. And all appeals to the assessor as aforesaid shall be made in writing, and shall specify the particular cause, matter, or thing respecting which a decision is requested, and shall, moreover, state the ground or principle of error complained of. And the assessor shall have power to re-examine and determine upon the assessments and valuations, and rectify the same as shall appear just and*

Assessor to hold appeals.

Lists to be submitted to the inspection of any and all persons.

Appeals to be made in writing.

Assessor to re-examine and correct assessments.

Assessment not to be increased without five days' notice.

equitable; but such valuation, assessment, or enumeration shall not be increased without a previous notice of at least five days to the party interested to appear and object to the same if he judge proper, which notice shall be in writing and left at the dwelling-house, office, or place of business of the party by such assessor, assistant assessor, or other person, or sent by mail to the nearest or usual post-office address of said party: Provided further, That on the hearing of appeals it shall be lawful for the assessor to require by summons the attendance of witnesses and the production of books of account in the same manner and under the same penalties as are provided in cases of refusal or neglect to furnish lists or returns. The costs for the attendance and mileage of said witnesses shall be taxed by the assessor and paid by the delinquent parties, or by the disbursing agent for the district, on certificate of the assessor, at the rates allowed to witnesses in the district courts of the United States.

Witnesses may be summoned.

Fees of witnesses.

June 30, 1864.

July 13, 1866, § 9.

Assessors to make lists.

SEC. 20. *And be it further enacted, That the assessor of each collection district shall, immediately after the expiration of the time for hearing appeals concerning taxes returned in the annual list, and from time to time, as taxes become liable to be assessed, make out lists containing the sums payable according to law upon every subject of taxation for each collection-district; which list shall contain the name of each person residing within the said district, or*[1] *owning or having the care or superintendence of property lying within the said district, or engaged in any business or pursuit which is liable to any tax, when such person or persons are known, together with the sums payable by each; and where there is any property within any collection district liable to tax, not owned or occupied by or under the superintendence of any person resident therein, there shall be a separate list of such property, specifying the sum payable, and the names of the respective proprietors when known. And the assessor making out any such separate list shall transmit to the assessor of the district where the persons liable to pay such tax reside, or shall have their principal place of business, copies of the list of property held by persons so liable to pay such tax, to the end that the taxes assessed under the provisions of this act may be paid within the collection district where the persons liable to pay the same reside, or may have their principal place of business. And in all other cases the said assessor shall furnish to the collectors of the several collection districts, respectively, within ten days after the time of hearing appeals concerning taxes returned in the annual list, and from time to time thereafter as required, a certified copy of such list or lists for their proper collection districts. And in case it shall be ascertained that the annual list, or any other list, which may have been, or which shall hereafter be, delivered to any collector, is imperfect or incomplete in consequence of the omission of the names of any persons or parties liable to tax, or in consequence of any omission, or understatement, or undervaluation, or false or fraudulent statement contained in any return or returns made by any persons or parties liable to tax, the said assessor may, from time to time or at any time within fifteen months from the*

Contents of lists.

List of property owned by non-residents.

To be transmitted to assessor of district where person liable resides or has his place of business.

Annual lists to be sent to collector within ten days after hearing appeals.

When list is imperfect or incomplete.

Re-assessment may be made within fifteen months.

[1] This word "or" cannot have been intended, although it is in the law.

time of the passage of this act or from the time of the delivery of the list to the collector as aforesaid, enter on any monthly or special list the names of such persons or parties so omitted, together with the amount of tax for which they may have been or shall become liable, and also the names of the persons or parties in respect to whose returns, as aforesaid, there has been or shall be any omission, undervaluation, understatement, or false or fraudulent statement, together with the amounts for which such persons or parties may be liable, over and above the amount for which they may have been or shall be assessed upon any return or returns made as aforesaid, and shall certify or return said list to the collector as required by law. And all provisions of law for the ascertainment of liability to any tax, or the assessment or collection thereof, shall be held to apply, as far as may be necessary to the proceedings herein authorized and directed. And wherever the word "duty" is used in this act, or the acts to which this is an amendment, it shall be construed to mean "tax," whenever such construction shall be necessary in order to effect the purposes of said acts.

Further proceedings regulated.

Word "duty" to mean tax when necessary.

COLLECTION OF TAXES, INCLUDING DISTRAINT, AND SEIZURE AND SALE OF REAL ESTATE.

June 30, 1864.

Collector to sign triplicate receipts of lists received from assessor.

SEC. 27. *And be it further enacted*, That each collector, on receiving, from time to time, lists and returns from the said assessors, shall subscribe three receipts: one of which shall be made upon a full and correct copy of each list or return, and be delivered by him to, and shall remain with, the assessor of his collection district, and shall be open to the inspection of any person who may apply to inspect the same; and the other two shall be made upon aggregate statements of the lists or returns aforesaid, exhibiting the gross amount of taxes to be collected in his collection district, one of which aggregate statements and receipts shall be transmitted to the Commissioner of Internal Revenue, and the other to the First Comptroller of the Treasury.

June 30, 1864.

July 13, 1866, § 9. See July 13, 1866, § 11.

Collectors to give notice to tax-payers within twenty days.

SEC. 28. *And be it further enacted, That each of said collectors shall, within twenty days after receiving his annual collection list from the assessors, give notice, by advertisement in one newspaper published in each county in his collection district, if there be any, and if not, then in a newspaper published in an adjoining county, and by notifications to be posted in at least four public places in each county in his collection-district, that the said taxes have become due and payable, and state the time and place within said county at which he or his deputy will attend to receive the same, which time shall not be less than ten days after the date of such notification, and shall send a copy of such notice by mail to each postmaster in the county, to be posted in his office. And if any person shall neglect to pay, as aforesaid, for more than ten days, it shall be the duty of the collector or his deputy to issue to such person a notice, to be left at his dwelling or usual place of business, or be sent by mail, demanding the payment of said taxes, stating the amount thereof, with a fee of twenty cents for the issuing and service of such notice, and with four cents for each mile actually and*

In case of neglect, collector to give notice personally or by mail.

If taxes are not paid within ten days after demand, penalty of five per cent., &c., to be added.

necessarily traveled in serving the same. And if such persons shall not pay the duties or taxes, and the fee of twenty cents and mileage as aforesaid, within ten days after the service or the sending by mail of such notice, it shall be the duty of the collector or his deputy to collect the said taxes and fee of twenty cents and mileage, with a penalty of FIVE PER CENTUM, TOGETHER WITH INTEREST AT THE RATE OF ONE PER CENTUM PER MONTH UPON SAID TAX FROM THE TIME THE SAME BECAME DUE, BUT NO INTEREST FOR ANY FRACTION OF A MONTH SHALL BE DEMANDED. *And with respect to all such taxes as are not included in the annual lists aforesaid, and all taxes the collection of which is not otherwise provided for in this act, it shall be the duty of each collector, in person or by deputy, to give notice and demand payment thereof, in the manner last mentioned, within ten days from and after receiving the list thereof from the assessor, or within twenty days from and after the expiration of the time within which such tax should have been paid; and if the annual or other taxes shall not be paid within ten days from and after such notice and demand, it shall be lawful for such collector, or his deputies, to proceed to collect the said taxes, with* FIVE *per centum additional thereto,* WITH INTEREST *as aforesaid, by distraint and sale of the goods, chattels, or effects, including stocks, securities, and evidences of debt, of the persons delinquent as aforesaid. And in case of distraint, it shall be the duty of the officer charged with the collection to make, or cause to be made, an account of the goods or effects distrained, a copy of which, signed by the officer making such distraint, shall be left with the owner or possessor of such goods or effects, or at his or her dwelling or usual place of business, with some person of suitable age and discretion, if any such can be found, with a note of the sum demanded, and the time and place of sale; and the said officer shall forthwith cause a notification to be published in some newspaper within the county wherein said distraint is made, if there is a newspaper published in said county, or to be publicly posted at the post office, if there be one within five miles, nearest to the residence of the person whose property shall be distrained, and in not less than two other public places, which notice shall specify the articles distrained, and the time and place for the sale thereof, which time shall not be less than ten nor more than twenty days from the date of such notification to the owner or possessor of the property and the publication or posting of such notice as herein provided, and the place proposed for sale shall not be more than five miles distant from the place of making such distraint. And said sale may be adjourned from time to time by said officer, if he shall think it advisable to do so, but not for a time to exceed in all thirty days. And if any person, bank, association, company, or corporation, liable to pay any tax, shall neglect or refuse to pay the same after demand, the amount shall be a lien in favor of the United States from the time it was due until paid, with the interest, penalties, and costs that may accrue in addition thereto, upon all property and rights to property belonging to such person, bank, association,*

Mar. 2, 1867, § 8.

Taxes not included in annual lists.

Collectors to demand payment when.

Upon non-payment, collector to make distraint.

March 2, 1867, § 8.

Proceedings in case of distraint.

Notice previous to sale.

Adjournment of sale.

Anything unpaid to be a lien from the time it was due.

company, or corporation; and the collector, after demand, may levy, or by warrant may authorize a deputy collector to levy, upon all property and rights to property belonging to such person, bank, association, company, or corporation, or on which the said lien exists, for the payment of the sum due as aforesaid, with interest and penalty for non-payment, and also of such further sum as shall be sufficient for the fees, costs and expenses of such levy. And in all cases of sale, as aforesaid, the certificate of such sale shall transfer to the purchaser all right, title and interest of such delinquent in and to the property sold; and where such property shall consist of stocks, said certificate shall be notice, when received, to any corporation, company, or association of said transfer, and shall be authority to such corporation, company, or association to record the same on their books and records, in the same manner as if transferred or assigned by the person or party holding the same, in lieu of any original or prior certificates, which shall be void, whether cancelled or not. And said certificates, where the subject of sale shall be securities or other evidences of debt, shall be good and valid receipts to the person holding the same, as against any person holding, or claiming to hold, possession of such securities or other evidences of debt. And all persons, and officers of companies or corporations, are required, on demand of a collector or deputy collector about to distrain, or having distrained on any property or rights of property, to exhibit all books containing evidence or statements relating to the subject or subjects of distraint, or the property or rights of property liable to distraint for the tax so due as aforesaid: Provided, That in any case of distraint for the payment of the taxes aforesaid, the goods, chattels, or effects so distrained shall and may be restored to the owner or possessor, if, prior to the sale, payment of the amount due shall be made to the proper officer charged with the collection, together with the fees and other charges; but in case of non-payment as aforesaid, the said officers shall proceed to sell the said goods, chattels, or effects at public auction, and shall retain from the proceeds of such sale the amount demandable for the use of the United States, and a commission of five per centum thereon for his own use, with the fees and charges for distraint and sale, rendering the overplus, if any there be, to the person who may be entitled to receive the same: Provided further, That there shall be exempt from distraint and sale, if belonging to the head of a family, the school-books and wearing apparel necessary for such family; also arms for personal use, one cow, two hogs, five sheep and the wool thereof, provided the aggregate market value of said sheep shall not exceed fifty dollars; the necessary food for such cow, hogs, and sheep for a period not exceeding thirty days; fuel to an amount not greater in value than twenty-five dollars; provisions to an amount not greater than fifty dollars; household furniture kept for use to an amount not greater than three hundred dollars; and the books, tools, or implements of a trade or profession to an amount not greater than one hundred dollars shall also be exempt; and the officer making the distraint shall summon three disinterested householders of the vicinity, who shall appraise and set apart to the owner the amount of property herein declared to be exempt.

Collector may distrain, upon what.

Effect of certificate of sale.

In case stocks are sold.

Books relating to subject of distraint.

Goods to be restored on payment before sale.

Otherwise to be sold.

Property exempt from distraint.

June 30, 1864.

Bill of sale given by collector to be prima facie evidence of right to make sale, and conclusive evidence of regularity of his proceedings.

SEC. 45. *And be it further enacted*, That in all cases of distraint and sale of goods or chattels for non-payment of taxes, duties, or licenses, as provided for, the bill of sale of such goods or chattels given by the officer making such sale, to the purchaser thereof, shall be prima facie evidence of the right of the officer to make such sale, and conclusive evidence of the regularity of his proceedings in selling the same.

July 13, 1866.

When monthly returns to be made.

When tax to be certified to collector.

Quarterly returns likewise.

When payable.

If not paid five per cent., &c., to be added.

Mar. 2, 1867, § 8.

But notice to be given.

Demand to be made.

SEC. 11. *And be it further enacted*, That all lists or returns required to be made monthly, by any person, firm, company, corporation, or party whatsoever, liable to tax, shall be made on or before the tenth day of each and every month, and the tax assessed or due thereon shall be certified or returned by the assessor to the collector on or before the last day of each and every month. And all lists or returns required to be made quarterly, and all other lists or returns, for which no provision is otherwise made, shall be made on or before the tenth day of each and every month in which said list or return is required to be made, or succeeding the time when the tax may be due and liable to be assessed, and the tax thereon shall be certified or returned as herein provided for monthly lists or returns. And the tax shall be due and payable on or before the last day of each and every month. And in case said tax is not paid on or before the last day of each and every month the collector shall add * * * * thereto *five per centum, together with interest at the rate of one per centum, per month upon said tax from the time the same became due, but no interest for any fraction of a month shall be demanded: Provided*, That notice of the time when said tax shall become due and payable shall be given in such manner as shall be prescribed by the Commissioner of Internal Revenue; and if said tax shall not be paid on or before the last day of the month as aforesaid, it shall be the duty of said collector to demand payment thereof, * * * * * * * *

Mar. 2, 1867, § 8.

Distraint.

In case of neglect.

in the manner prescribed by law, [*with*] *a penalty of five per centum, together with interest at the rate of one per centum per month upon said tax from the time the same became due, but no interest for any fraction of a month shall be demanded;* and if said tax and *five* per centum additional *with interest* are not paid within ten days from and after such demand thereof, it shall be lawful for the collector or his deputy to make distraint therefor, as provided by law; * * * * * and in all cases of neglect to make such lists or returns, or in case of false and fraudulent returns, the provisions of existing law, as amended by this act, shall be applicable thereto.

June 30, 1864.

July 13, 1866, § 9.

Property indivisible the whole to be sold.

Disposition of surplus proceeds.

SEC. 29. *And be it further enacted, That in all cases where property liable to distraint for taxes may not be divisible, so as to enable the collector by a sale of part thereof to raise the whole amount of the tax, with all costs, charges, and commissions, the whole of such property shall be sold, and the surplus of the proceeds of the sale, after satisfying the tax, costs, and charges, shall be paid to the person legally entitled to receive the same; or if he cannot be found, or refuse to receive the same, then such surplus shall be deposited in the Treasury of the*

United States, to be there held for the use of the person legally entitled to receive the same, until he shall make application therefor to the Secretary of the Treasury, who, upon such application and satisfactory proofs in support thereof, shall, by warrant on the Treasury, cause the same to be paid to the applicant. And if any of the property advertised for sale as aforesaid is of a kind subject to tax, and such tax has not been paid, and the amount bid for such property is not equal to the amount of such tax, the collector may purchase the same in behalf of the United States for an amount not exceeding the said tax. And in all cases where property subject to tax, but upon which the tax has not been paid, shall be seized upon distraint and sold, the amount of such tax shall, after deducting the expenses of such sale, be first appropriated out of the proceeds thereof to the payment of said tax. And if no assessment of tax has been made upon such property, the collector shall make a return thereof in the form required by law, and the assessor shall assess the tax thereon. And all property so purchased may be sold by said collector, under such regulations as may be prescribed by the Commissioner of Internal Revenue. And the collector shall render a distinct account of all charges incurred in the sale of such property to the Commissioner of Internal Revenue, who shall by regulation determine the fees and charges to be allowed in all cases of distraint and other seizures; or where necessary expenses for making such distraint or seizure have been incurred, and in case of sale, the said collector shall pay into the treasury the surplus, if any there be, after defraying such fees and charges.

Property may be purchased for the United States.

Taxes on property sold.

How assessed.

Property purchased by collector may be sold.

Fees, &c., in cases of seizures.

SEC. 30. *And be it further enacted, That in any case where goods, chattels, or effects sufficient to satisfy the taxes imposed by law upon any person liable to pay the same shall not be found by the collector or deputy collector whose duty it may be to collect the same, he is hereby authorized to collect the same by seizure and sale of real estate; and the officer making such seizure and sale shall give notice to the person whose estate is proposed to be sold, by giving him in hand, or leaving at his last or usual place of abode, if he has any such within the collection district where said estate is situated, a notice, in writing, stating what particular estate is proposed to be sold, describing the same with reasonable certainty, and the time when and the place where said officer proposes to sell the same; which time shall not be less than twenty nor more than forty days from the time of giving said notice. And the said officer shall also cause a notification to the same effect to be published in some newspaper within the county where such seizure is made, if any such there be, and shall also cause a like notice to be posted at the post-office nearest to the estate to be seized, and in two other public places within the county; and the place of said sale shall not be more than five miles distant from the estate seized, except by special order of the Commissioner of Internal Revenue. At the time and place appointed, the officer making such seizure shall proceed to sell the said estate at public auction, offering the same at a minimum price, including the expense of making such levy, and all charges for advertising and an officer's fee of ten dollars. And in case the real estate so seized, as aforesaid, shall consist of several distinct tracts or parcels, the officer making sale*

June 30, 1864.

July 13, 1866, § 9.

Personal property not sufficient, real estate may be seized and sold.

Notice.

Time of.

To be advertised.

Place of sale.

Mode of sale.

Mode of sale in case of several parcels.

thereof shall offer each tract or parcel for sale separately, and shall, if he deem it advisable, apportion the expenses, charges, and fees, aforesaid, to such several tracts or parcels, or to any of them, in estimating the minimum price aforesaid. [In a certain case, estate may be purchased for the United States.] *And if no person offers for said estate the amount of said minimum price, the officer shall declare the same to be purchased by him for the United States, and shall deposit with the district attorney of the United States a deed thereof, as hereinafter specified and provided; otherwise, the same shall be declared to be sold to the highest bidder.* [Adjournment.] *And said sale may be adjourned from time to time by said officer for not exceeding thirty days in all, if he shall think it advisable so to do.* [If amount bid not paid, estate to be resold.] *If the amount bid shall not be then and there paid, the officer shall forthwith proceed to again sell said estate in the same manner, and upon any sale and the payment of the purchase money shall give to the* [Certificate of purchase.] *purchaser a certificate of purchase, which shall set forth the real estate purchased, for whose taxes the same was sold, the name of the purchaser, and the price paid therefor;* [To be surrendered, and deed given, if estate not redeemed.] *and if the said real estate be not redeemed in the manner and within the time hereinafter provided, then the said collector or deputy collector shall execute to the said purchaser, upon his surrender of said certificate, a deed of the real estate purchased by him as aforesaid,* [Deed in accordance with State laws.] *reciting the facts set forth in said certificate, and in accordance with the laws of the State in which such real estate is situate upon the subject of sales of real estate under execution, which said deed shall be prima facie evidence of the facts therein stated;* [Effect of deed.] *and if the proceedings of the officer as set forth have been substantially in accordance with the provisions of law, shall be considered and operate as a conveyance of all the right, title, and interest the party delinquent had in and to the real estate thus sold at the time the lien of the United States attached thereto.* [Owner may redeem before sale.] *Any person, whose estate may be proceeded against as aforesaid, shall have the right to pay the amount due, together with the costs and charges thereon, to the collector or deputy collector at any time prior to the sale thereof, and all further proceedings shall cease from the time of such payment.* [After sale, when and how.] *The owners of any real estate sold as aforesaid, their heirs, executors, or administrators, or any person having any interest therein, or a lien thereon, or any person in their behalf, shall be permitted to redeem the land sold as aforesaid, or any particular tract thereof, at any time within one year after the sale thereof, upon payment to the purchaser, or, in case he cannot be found in the county in which the land to be redeemed is situate, then to the collector of the district in which the land is situate, for the use of the purchaser, his heirs or assigns, the amount paid by the said purchaser and interest thereon at the rate of twenty per centum per annum.* [Collector may seize and sell lands in any other district in the State.] *And any collector or deputy collector may, for the collection of taxes imposed upon any person or for which any person may be liable, and committed to him for collection, seize and sell the lands of such person situated in any other collection district within the State in which said officer resides; and his proceedings in relation thereto shall have the same effect as if the same were had in his proper collection district.* [Record of sales.] *And it shall be the duty of every collector to keep a record of all sales of land made in his collection district, whether by himself or his deputies, or by another collector, in which shall be set forth the tax for which any such sale was made, the dates of seizure and sale, the name of the party assessed, and all proceedings in making said sale, the amount of fees and expenses, the name of the purchaser, and the date of the deed; which record shall be certified by the officer making the sale. And it shall be the duty of any deputy making sale, as aforesaid, to return a statement of all his proceedings to the collector, and to certify the record thereof. And in case of the death or removal of the collector or the expiration of his term of office from any other cause, said record shall be delivered to his successor in office; and a copy of every such record, certified by the collector, shall be evidence in any court of the truth of the facts therein stated. And when any lands sold, as aforesaid, shall be redeemed as hereinbefore provided, the collector shall make an entry of the fact upon the record aforesaid, and the said entry shall be evidence of such redemption. And when any property, personal or real, seized and sold by virtue of the foregoing provisions, shall not be sufficient to satisfy the claim of the United States for which distraint or seizure may be made against any person whose property may be so seized and sold, the collector may, thereafter, and as often as the same may be necessary, proceed to seize and sell, in like manner, any other property liable to seizure of such person until the amount due from him, together with all expenses, shall be fully paid: Provided, That the word "county," wherever the same occurs in this act, or the acts of which this is amendatory, shall be construed to mean also a parish or any other equivalent subdivision of a State or Territory.*

Return by deputy.

Record to be delivered to successor.

To be evidence in any court.

Record of redemption.

Tax not satisfied, other property may be seized and sold.

Word "county" defined.

SEC. 106. *And be it further enacted*, That in any case where there has been a refusal or neglect to pay any tax imposed by the internal revenue laws, and where it is lawful and has become necessary to seize and sell real estate to satisfy the tax, the Commissioner of Internal Revenue may, if he deems it expedient, direct that a bill in chancery be filed, in a district or circuit court of the United States, to enforce the lien of the United States for tax upon any real estate, or to subject any real estate owned by the delinquent, or in which he has any right, title, or interest, to the payment of such tax. And all persons having liens upon the real estate sought to be subjected to the payment of any tax as aforesaid, or claiming any ownership or interest therein, shall be made parties to such proceedings, and shall be brought into court as provided in other suits in chancery in said courts. And the said courts shall have, and are hereby given, jurisdiction in all such cases, and shall at the term next after such time as the parties shall be duly notified of the proceedings, unless otherwise ordered by the court, proceed to adjudicate all matters involved therein, and to pass upon and finally determine the merits of all claims to and liens upon the real estate in question, and shall, in all cases where a claim or interest of the United States therein shall be established, decree a sale, by the proper officer of the court, of such real estate, and a distribution of the proceeds of such sale according to the findings of the court in respect to the interests of the parties and of the United States.

July 20, 1868.

Bill in chancery may be filed to enforce lien of United States on real estate.

All persons having liens shall be made parties.

Proceedings of court.

Mar. 2, 1867.

Commissioner to have charge of real estate.

SEC. 4. *And be it further enacted*, That the Commissioner of Internal Revenue shall have charge of all real estate which has been or shall be assigned, set off, or conveyed, by purchase or otherwise, to the United States, in payment of debts arising under the laws relating to internal revenue, and of all trusts created for the use of the United States, in payment of such debts due them; and, with the approval of the Secretary of the Treasury, may sell and dispose of, at public vendue, upon not less than twenty days' notice, lands assigned or set off to the United States in payment of such debts, or vested in them by mortgage or other security, for the payment of such debts; and in cases where real estate has already become the property of the United States by conveyance or otherwise, in payment of or as security for a debt arising under the laws relating to internal revenue, and such debt shall have been paid, together with the interest thereon, at the rate of one per centum per month, to the United States, within two years from the date of the acquisition of such real estate, it shall be lawful for the Commissioner of Internal Revenue, with the approval of the Secretary of the Treasury, to release by deed, or otherwise convey, such real estate to the debtor from whom it was taken, or to his heirs or other legal representatives.

May sell at auction.

In certain cases may release to debtor.

June 30, 1864.

Taxes returned against non-residents.

SEC. 31. *And be it further enacted*, That if any collector shall find, upon any list of taxes returned to him for collection, property lying within his district which is charged with any specific or ad valorem tax or duty, but which is not owned, occupied, or superintended by some person known to such collector to reside or to have some place of business within the United States, and upon which the duty or tax has not been paid within the time required by law, such collector shall forthwith take such property into his custody, and shall advertise the same, and the tax charged upon the same, in some newspaper published in his district, if any shall be published therein, otherwise in some newspaper in an adjoining district, for the space of thirty days; and if the taxes thereon, with all charges for advertising, shall not be paid within said thirty days, such collector shall proceed to sell the same, or so much as is necessary, in the manner provided for the sale of other goods distrained for the non-payment of taxes, and out of the proceeds shall satisfy all taxes charged upon such property, with the costs of advertising and selling the same. And like proceedings to those provided in the preceding section[1] for the purchase and resale of property which cannot be sold for the amount of duty or tax due thereon shall be had with regard to property sold under the provisions of this section. And any surplus arising from any sale herein provided for shall be paid into the Treasury, for the benefit of the owner of the property. And the Secretary of the Treasury is authorized, in any case where money shall be paid into the treasury for the benefit of any owner of property sold as aforesaid, to repay the same, on proper proof being furnished that the person applying therefor is entitled to receive the same.

How collected.

[1] Sec. 30, act June 30, 1864, as amended. Ante, page 29.

SEC. 32. *And be it further enacted*, That whenever a collector shall have on any list duly returned to him the name of any person not within his collection district who is liable to tax, or of any person so liable to tax who shall have, in the collection district in which he resides, no sufficient property subject to seizure or distraint from which the money due for duties or tax can be collected, it shall and may be lawful for such collector to transmit a copy or statement containing the name of the person liable to such duty or tax aforesaid, with the amount and nature thereof, duly certified under his hand, to the collector of any district to which said person shall have removed, or in which he shall have property, real or personal, liable to be seized and sold for duty or tax; and the collector of the district to whom the said certified copy or statement shall be transmitted shall proceed to collect the said duty or tax in the same way as if the name of the person and objects of tax contained in the certified copy or statement were on any list furnished to him by the assessor of his own collection district; and the said collector, upon receiving said certified copy or statement as aforesaid, shall transmit his receipt for it to the collector sending the same to him.

June 30, 1864.

Collector may transmit list to another district where person liable resides, or where he has property.

Duty of collector receiving such list.

COLLECTORS' ACCOUNTS, AND RESPONSIBILITY FOR PUBLIC MONEYS.

SEC. 33. *And be it further enacted*, That the several collectors shall, at the expiration of each and every month after they shall, respectively, commence their collections, transmit to the Commissioner of Internal Revenue a statement of the collections made by them, respectively, within the month,

* * * * * * *

and each of the said collectors shall complete the collection of all sums assigned to him for collection, as aforesaid, shall pay over the same into the Treasury, and shall render his acounts to the Treasury Department as often as he may be required. And the Secretary of the Treasury is authorized to designate one or more depositories in each State, for the deposit and safe-keeping of the moneys collected by virtue of this act; and the receipt of the proper officer of such depository to a collector for the money deposited by him shall be a sufficient voucher for such collector in the settlement of his accounts at the Treasury Department. * * *

June 30, 1864.

Collectors to transmit monthly statements of collections to Commissioner.

Mar. 3, 1865, § 3.

Accounts to be rendered as often as required.

Depositories.

Mar. 3, 1865, § 3.

SEC. 3. *And be it further enacted*, That from and after the thirtieth day of June, eighteen hundred and sixty-five, the gross amount of all duties, taxes, and revenues received or collected by virtue of the several acts to provide internal revenue to support the Government and to pay the interest on the public debt, and of any other act or acts that may now or hereafter be in force connected with the internal revenues, shall be paid by the officers, collectors, or agents receiving or collecting the same, daily into the Treasury of the United States, under the instructions of the Secretary of the Treasury, without any abatement or deduction on account of salary, compensation, fees, costs, charges, ex-

Mar. 3, 1865.

All taxes to be paid daily into the Treasury after June 30, 1865.

penses or claims of any description whatever, anything in any law to the contrary notwithstanding. And all moneys now directed by law to be paid to the Commissioner of Internal Revenue, including those derived from the sale of stamps, shall be paid into the Treasury of the United States by the party making such payment; and a certificate of such payment stating the name of the depositor and the specific account on which the deposit was made, signed by the Treasurer, assistant treasurer, designated depositary, or proper officer of a deposit bank, and transmitted to and received by the Commissioner of Internal Revenue, shall be deemed a compliance with the law requiring payment to be made to the Commissioner, any law to the contrary notwithstanding: *Provided*, That in districts where, from the distance of the officer, collector, or agent receiving or collecting such duties, taxes, and revenues from a proper government depository, the Secretary of the Treasury may deem it proper, he may extend the time for making such payment, not exceeding, however, in any case, a period of one month.

Certificate of deposit to be returned to Commissioner.

Secretary may extend time in certain cases.

June 30, 1864.

Section 16, act of August 6, 1846, applied to internal revenue officers.

SEC. 51. *And be it further enacted*, That the provisions of the sixteenth section of the act approved August sixth, eighteen hundred and forty-six, entitled "An act to provide for the better organization of the Treasury, and for the collection, safe-keeping, transfer, and disbursement of the public revenue," are hereby applied to, and shall be construed to include all officers of the internal revenue charged with the safe-keeping, transfer, or disbursement of the public moneys arising therefrom, and to all other persons having actual charge, custody, or control of moneys or accounts arising from the administration of the internal revenue.

August 6, 1846.

Entries to be made of the public moneys other than those of the Post Office Department.

Felony to use, loan, or deposit in a bank, &c., public money.

Evidence of embezzlement.

SEC. 16. *And be it further enacted*, That all officers and other persons, charged by this act, or any other act, with the safe-keeping, transfer, and disbursement, of the public moneys, other than those connected with the Post Office Department, are hereby required to keep an accurate entry of each sum received, and of each payment or transfer; and that if any one of the said officers, or of those connected with the Post Office Department, shall convert to his own use, in any way whatever, or shall use, by way of investment in any kind of property or merchandise, or shall loan, with or without interest, or shall deposit in any bank, or shall exchange for other funds, except as allowed by this act, any portion of the public moneys intrusted to him for safe-keeping, disbursement, transfer, or for any other purpose, every such act shall be deemed and adjudged to be an embezzlement of so much of the said moneys as shall be thus taken, converted, invested, used, loaned, deposited, or exchanged, which is hereby declared to be a felony; and any failure to pay over or to produce the public moneys intrusted to such person shall be held and taken to be *prima facie* evidence of such embezzlement; and if any officer charged with the disbursements of public moneys shall accept, or receive, or transmit to the Treasury Department to be allowed in his favor, any receipt or voucher from a creditor of the United States, without having paid to such creditor, in such funds as the said officer may have received for disbursement, or such other funds as he may be authorized by this act to take in exchange, the full amount specified in such receipt or voucher, every such act shall be deemed to be a conversion by such officer to his own use of the amount specified in such receipt or voucher; and any officer or agent of the United States, and all persons advising or participating in such act, being convicted thereof before any court of the United States of competent jurisdiction, shall be sentenced to imprisonment for a term of not less than six months nor more than ten years, and to a fine equal to the amount of the money embezzled. And upon the trial of any indictment against any person for embezzling public money under the provisions of this act, it shall be sufficient evidence, for the purpose of showing a balance against such person, to produce a transcript from the books and proceedings of the Treasury, as required in civil cases, under the provisions of the act entitled "An act to provide more effectually for the settlement of accounts between the United States and receivers of public money," approved March third, one thousand seven hundred and ninety-seven; and the provisions of this act shall be so construed as to apply to all persons charged with the safe-keeping, transfer, or disbursement, of the public money, whether such persons be indicted as receivers or depositaries of the same; and the refusal of such person, whether in or out of office, to pay any draft, order, or warrant, which may be drawn upon him by the proper officer of the Treasury Department, for any public money in his hands belonging to the United States, no matter in what capacity the same may have been received or may be held, or to transfer or disburse any such money promptly, upon the legal requirement of any authorized officer of the United States, shall be deemed and taken, upon the trial of any indictment against such person for embezzlement, as *prima facie* evidence of such embezzlement.

Payment in other funds to be deemed a conversion.

Punishment.

What shall be sufficient evidence to show a balance on a charge of embezzlement,

1797 ch. 20.

SEC. 1. *Be it enacted by the Senate and House of Representatives of the United States of America in Congress assembled*, That when any revenue officer, or other person accountable for public money, shall neglect or refuse to pay into the Treasury, the sum or balance reported to be due to the United States, upon the adjustment of his account, it shall be the duty of the Comptroller, and he is hereby required to institute suit for the recovery of the same, adding to the sum stated to be due on such account, the commissions of the delinquent, which shall be forfeited in every instance where suit is commenced and judgment obtained thereon, and an interest of six per cent. per annum, from the time of receiving the money, until it shall be repaid into the Treasury.

Mar. 3, 1797.

Revenue officer or other person not paying public money to be sued, to forfeit commissions, and to pay interest.

SEC. 2. *And be it further enacted*, That in every case of delinquency, where suit has been or shall be instituted, a transcript from the books and proceedings of the Treasury, certified by the Register, and authenticated under the seal of the Department, shall be admitted as evidence, and the

Mar. 3, 1797.

A transcript of the books of the Treasury to be evidence.

court trying the cause, shall be thereupon authorized to grant judgment, and award execution, accordingly. And all copies of bonds, contracts, or other papers relating to, or connected with the settlement of any account between the United States and an individual, when certified by the Register to be true copies of the originals on file, and authenticated under the seal of the Department, as aforesaid, may be annexed to such transcripts, and shall have equal validity, and be entitled to the same degree of credit, which would be due to the original papers, if produced and authenticated in court: *Provided*, That where suit is brought upon a bond, or other sealed instrument, and the defendant shall plead "*non est factum*," or upon motion to the court, such plea or motion being verified by the oath or affirmation of the defendant, it shall be lawful for the court to take the same into consideration, and (if it shall appear to be necessary for the attainment of justice) to require the production of the original bond, contract or other paper specified in such affidavit.

Original contract to be produced in certain cases.

Mar. 3, 1797.

Judgment to be rendered at return term, except in certain cases.

SEC. 3. *And be it further enacted*, That where suit shall be instituted against any person or persons indebted to the United States, as aforesaid, it shall be the duty of the court where the same may be pending, to grant judgment at the return term, upon motion, unless the defendant shall, in open court, (the United States attorney being present) make oath or affirmation, that he is equitably entitled to credits which had been, previous to the commencement of the suit, submitted to the consideration of the accounting officers of the Treasury, and rejected; specifying each particular claim, so rejected in the affidavit; and that he cannot then come safely to trial. Oath or affirmation to this effect being made, subscribed, and filed, if the court be thereupon satisfied, a continuance, until the next succeeding term, may be granted; but not otherwise, unless as provided in the preceding section.

Mar. 3, 1797.

No claim for credit to be admitted unless presented to the Treasury, or out of the power of the party to do it.

SEC. 4. *And be it further enacted*, That in suits between the United States and individuals, no claim for a credit shall be admitted, upon trial, but such as shall appear to have been presented to the accounting officers of the Treasury, for their examination, and by them disallowed, in whole or in part, unless it should be proved, to the satisfaction of the court, that the defendant is, at the time of trial, in possession of vouchers not before in his power to procure, and that he was prevented from exhibiting a claim for such credit, at the Treasury, by absence from the United States, or some unavoidable accident.

Mar. 3, 1797.

In all cases of insolvency, the debt due to the United States shall be first paid.

SEC. 5. *And be it further enacted*, That where any revenue officer, or other person hereafter becoming indebted to the United States, by bond or otherwise, shall become insolvent, or where the estate of any deceased debtor, in the hands of executors or administrators, shall be insufficient to pay all the debts due from the deceased, the debt due to the United States shall be first satisfied; and the priority hereby established shall be deemed to extend, as well to cases in which a debtor, not having sufficient property to pay all his debts, shall make a voluntary assignment thereof, or in which the estate and effects of an absconding, concealed, or absent debtor, shall be attached by process of law, as to cases in which an act of legal bankruptcy shall be committed.

March 3, 1797.

Writs of execution may be executed in any State.

SEC. 6. *And be it further enacted*, That all writs of execution upon any judgment obtained for the use of the United States, in any of the courts of the United States in one State, may run and be executed in any other State, or in any of the Territories of the United States, but shall be issued from, and made returnable to the court where the judgment was obtained, any law to the contrary notwithstanding.

March 3, 1797.

Prior legal remedies not to be impaired.

SEC. 7. *And be it further enacted*, That nothing in this act shall be construed to repeal, take away, or impair any legal remedy or remedies for the recovery of debts now due, or hereafter to be due, to the United States, in law or equity, from any person or persons whatsoever, which remedy or remedies might be used if this act was not in force.

June 30, 1864.

July 13, 1866, § 9.

Collectors shall be charged with what.

SEC. 34. *And be it further enacted, That each collector shall be charged with the whole amount of taxes, whether contained in lists delivered to him by the assessors, respectively, or delivered or transmitted to him by assistant assessors from time to time, or by other collectors, or by his predecessor in office, and with the additions thereto, with the par value of all stamps deposited with him, and with all moneys collected for passports, penalties, forfeitures, fees, or costs, and he shall be credited with all payments into the Treasury made as provided by law, with all stamps returned by him uncancelled to the Treasury, and with the amount of taxes contained in the lists transmitted in the manner above provided to other collectors, and by them receipted as aforesaid; and also with the amount of the taxes of such persons as may have absconded, or become insolvent, prior to the day when the tax ought, according to the provisions of law, to have been collected, and with all uncollected taxes transferred by him or by his deputy acting as collector to his successor in office: Provided, That it shall be proved to the satisfaction of the Commissioner of Internal Revenue that due diligence was used by the collector, who shall certify the facts to the First Comptroller of the Treasury. And each collector shall also be credited with the amount of all property purchased by him for the use of the United States, provided he shall faithfully account for and pay over the proceeds thereof upon a resale of the same as required by law. In case of the death, resignation, or removal of the collector, all lists and accounts of taxes uncollected shall be transferred to his successor in office as soon as such successor shall be appointed and qualified, and it shall be the duty of such successor to collect the same.*

Credited with what.

Lists & accounts of taxes uncollected to be transferr'd to successor for collection.

June 30, 1864.

Collectors failing to account for taxes due.

Duty of the First Comptroller thereon.

Solicitor of the Treasury to issue a warrant.

SEC. 35. *And be it further enacted*, That if any collector shall fail either to collect or to render his account, or to pay over in the manner or within the times hereinbefore provided, it shall be the duty of the First Comptroller of the Treasury, and he is hereby authorized and required, immediately after evidence of such delinquency, to report the same to the Solicitor of the Treasury, who shall issue a warrant of distress against such delinquent collector, directed to the marshal of the district, therein expressing the amount with which the said collector is chargeable, and the sums, if any, which have been paid over by him, so far as the same are ascertainable. And the said marshal shall, himself, or by his deputy, immediately proceed to levy and collect the sum which may remain due, with five per centum thereon, and all the expenses and charges of collection, by distress and sale of the goods and chattels, or any personal effects of the delinquent collector, giving at least five days' notice of the time and place of sale, in the manner provided by law for advertising sales of personal property on execution in the State wherein such collector resides. And the bill of sale of the officer of any goods, chattels, or other personal property, distrained and sold as aforesaid, shall be conclusive evidence of title to the purchaser, and prima facie evidence of the right of the officer to make such sale, and of the correctness of his proceedings in selling the same. And for want of goods and chattels, or other personal effects of such collector, sufficient to satisfy any warrant, of distress, issued pursuant to the preceding section[1] of this act, the lands and real estate of such collector, or so much thereof as may be necessary for satisfying the said warrant, after being advertised for at least three weeks in not less than three public places in the collection district, and in one newspaper printed in the county or district, if any there be, prior to the proposed time of sale, shall be sold at public auction by the marshal or his deputy, who, upon such sale, shall, as such marshal or deputy marshal, make and deliver to the purchaser of the premises so sold a deed of conveyance thereof, to be executed and acknowledged in the manner and form prescribed by the laws of the State in which said lands are situated, which said deeds so made shall invest the purchaser with all the title and interest of the defendant or defendants named in said warrant, existing at the time of the seizure thereof. And all moneys that may remain of the proceeds of such sale after satisfying the said warrant of distress, and paying the reasonable costs and charges of sale, shall be returned to the proprietor of the lands or real estate sold as aforesaid.

Marshal to levy on the property of the collector.

Bill of sale to be conclusive evidence of title, and prima facie evidence of right of officer to make sale.

Levy on real estate.

Notice of sale.

Marshal to execute deed.

Surplus to be returned to proprietor of lands sold.

July 20, 1868.

Collectors' bonded account.

SEC. 100. *And be it further enacted*, That every collector having charge of any warehouse in which distilled spirits, tobacco, or other articles, are stored in bond, shall render a monthly account of all such articles to the Commissioner of Internal Revenue, which account shall be examined and adjusted, monthly, by him, so as to exhibit a true statement of the liability and responsibility of every such collector on such account. In adjusting such account the collector shall be charged with all the articles which may have been deposited or received under the provisions of law, in any warehouse in his district and under his control, and shall be credited with all such articles shown to have been removed therefrom according to law, including transfers to other collectors and

[1] The words "section of this act" doubtless mean "provisions of this section."

to his successor in office, and also whatever allowances may have been made in accordance with law to any owner of such goods or articles for leakage or other losses. *And every collector of internal revenue from whose district any distilled spirits, tobacco, snuff, or cigars shall be shipped in bond, under the provisions of this act, shall render a monthly account of the same to the Commissioner of Internal Revenue, showing the amount of each article produced and shipped in bond, the amounts of which the exportation is completed according to law, and the amount remaining unaccounted for at the end of each month; also any excesses or deficiencies on the amounts originally reported as shipped.* June 6, 1872, § 31.

ABATEMENT AND REFUNDING OF TAXES.

June 30, 1864.

July 13, 1866, § 9.

SEC. 44. *And be it further enacted, That the Commissioner of Internal Revenue, subject to regulations prescribed by the Secretary of the Treasury, shall be, and is hereby, authorized, on appeal to him made, to remit, refund, and pay back all taxes erroneously or illegally assessed or collected, all penalties collected without authority, and all taxes that shall appear to be unjustly assessed or excessive in amount or in any manner wrongfully collected, and also repay to collectors or deputy collectors the full amount of such sums of money as shall or may be recovered against them, or any of them, in any court, for any internal taxes or licenses collected by them, with the costs and expenses of suit, and all damages and costs recovered against assessors, assistant assessors, collectors, deputy collectors, and inspectors, in any suit which shall be brought against them, or any of them, by reason of anything that shall or may be done in the due performance of their official duties; and all judgments and moneys recovered or received for taxes, costs, forfeitures, and penalties, shall be paid to the collector as internal taxes are required to be paid: Provided, that where a second assessment may have been made in case of a list, statement, or return which in the opinion of the assessor or assistant assessor was false or fraudulent, or contained any understatement or undervaluation, such assessment shall not be remitted, nor shall taxes collected under such assessment be recovered, refunded, or paid back, unless it is proved that said list, statement, or return was not false or fraudulent, and did not contain any understatement or undervaluation.*

Commissioner authorized to refund taxes illegally collected, &c.

See July 13, 1866, § 19; also June 6, 1872, § 44.

May repay to collectors and other officers money recovered of them for acts done in performance of duties.

Moneys recovered or received to be paid to collectors.

When second assessment may be set aside.

July 13, 1866.

SEC. 19. *And be it further enacted*, That no suit shall be maintained in any court for the recovery of any tax alleged to have been erroneously or illegally assessed or collected, until appeal shall have been duly made to the Commissioner of Internal Revenue according to the provisions of law in that regard, and the regulations of the Secretary of the Treasury established in pursuance thereof, and a decision of said Commissioner be had thereon, [unless such suit shall be brought within six months from the time of said decision, or within six months from the time this act takes effect: *Provided*, That if said decision shall be delayed more than six months from the date of such appeal, then said suit may be brought at any time within twelve months from the date

No suit to be maintained for illegal taxes until appeal is made to the Commissioner.

When to be brought.

No suit to restrain assessment,

&c., of tax to be maintained. Mar. 2, 1867, § 10. of such appeal,] [1] *and no suit for the purpose of restraining the assessment or collection of tax shall be maintained in any court.*

June 6, 1872. Suits for recovery of internal taxes, when to be brought. SEC. 44. That all suits and proceedings for the recovery of any internal tax alleged to have been erroneously assessed or collected, or any penalty claimed to have been collected without authority, or for any sum which it is alleged was excessive, or in any manner wrongfully collected, shall be brought within two years next after the cause of action accrued and not after; and all claims for the refunding of any internal tax or penalty shall be presented to the Commissioner of Internal Revenue within two years next after the cause of action accrued and not after: *Provided*, That actions for claims, which have accrued prior to the passage of this act, shall be commenced in the courts or presented to the Commissioner of Internal Revenue within one year from the date of said passage: *And provided further*, That where a claim shall be pending before said Commissioner the claimant may bring his action within one year after such decision and not after: *And provided further*, That no right of action barred by any statute now in force shall be revived by anything herein contained.

Claims for refunding, when to be presented.

Actions for claims, when to be commenced.

No right of action already barred to be revived.

April 10, 1869. Refunding of tax on tobacco, snuff, and cigars, in certain cases. SEC. 3. *And be it further enacted*, That any person having in his possession any tobacco, snuff, or cigars, manufactured and sold or removed from the manufactory, or from any place where tobacco, snuff, or cigars are made, since July twentieth, eighteen hundred and sixty-eight, or any person having in his possession cigars imported from foreign countries since July twentieth, eighteen hundred and sixty-eight, or withdrawn from a United States bonded warehouse since said date, such tobacco, snuff, and cigars, having been put up in packages, as prescribed in the act to which this act is an amendment, and all the other requirements of said act relating to tobacco, snuff, and cigars having been complied with, and who, on the first day of February, eighteen hundred and sixty-nine, filed with the assessor or assistant assessor of the district within which he resides, or has his place of business, the inventory required by the seventy-eighth and ninety-fourth sections of the act of July twentieth, eighteen hundred and sixty-eight, and who shall, prior to selling or offering such tobacco, snuff, or cigars for sale, affix and cancel proper internal revenue stamps, shall be entitled to have refunded to him an amount of tax previously paid thereon, equal to the value of the stamps affixed before sale as aforesaid; and the Commissioner of Internal Revenue shall be, and is hereby, authorized, on appeal to him made, to refund and pay back a sum of money equal to the value of the stamps so affixed, upon satisfactory evidence submitted to him that the tobacco and snuff were actually manufactured and removed from the place of manufacture, and that the cigars were so manufactured and removed, or imported and withdrawn from a United States bonded warehouse, and the several rates of tax imposed on such goods by the act of July twentieth, eighteen hundred

[1] The modification of the provisions in brackets by section 44 of the act of June 6, 1872, cannot be indicated otherwise than by reference to that section, immediately following.

and sixty-eight, as aforesaid assessed and paid, and that the claimant had in all respects complied with the internal revenue laws as far as they have been or may be applicable to such articles. The Commissioner of Internal Revenue is hereby authorized and empowered to prescribe such rules and regulations for carrying out the provisions of this section as in his judgment shall be deemed proper and necessary; and the Commissioner may in any case, at his discretion, allow snuff and smoking tobacco manufactured prior to the twentieth of July, eighteen hundred and sixty-eight, not in wooden packages, to be stamped and sold in the original packages; and the rate of duty on cigars imported prior to July twentieth, eighteen hundred and sixty-eight, and now remaining in bond, shall be the same as on cigars imported after that date.

Commissioner to make regulations.

Snuff and smoking tobacco manufactured prior to July 20, 1868.

Rate of duty on imported cigars.

May 27, 1872.

Secretary of Treasury authorized to abate or refund taxes on distilled spirits destroyed by accidental fire or other casualty.

Be it enacted by the Senate and House of Representatives of the United States of America in Congress assembled, That the Secretary of the Treasury be, and he is hereby, authorized, upon the production of satisfactory proof to him of the actual destruction by accidental fire or other casualty, and without any fraud, collusion, or negligence of the owner thereof, of any distilled spirits on which the tax at the time of the destruction of said spirits had not been paid and while the same remained in the custody of any officer of internal revenue in any distillery warehouse or bonded warehouse of the United States, to abate the amount of internal revenue taxes accruing thereon, and to cancel any warehouse bond, or enter satisfaction thereon, in whole or in part, as the case may be; and if such taxes have been collected since the destruction of said spirits, then the Secretary of the Treasury shall refund the same to the owners thereof out of any money in the Treasury not otherwise appropriated.

May 27, 1872.

When to take effect.

SEC. 2. That this act shall take effect in all cases of loss or destruction of distilled spirits as aforesaid which have occurred since the first day of January, eighteen hundred and sixty-eight: *Provided, however*, That when the owners of such distilled spirits, so destroyed as aforesaid, may be indemnified against said tax by a valid claim of insurance, said tax shall not be remitted to the extent of such insurance.

Insurance.

DRAWBACK.

June 30, 1864.

Drawback on certain manufactures exported.

Mar. 3, 1865, § 1. July 20, 1868, §§ 54 and 74, as amended June 6, 1872; Mar. 3, 1865, § 1.

SEC. 171. *And be it further enacted*, That from and after the date on which this act takes effect, there shall be an allowance or drawback on all articles on which any internal duty or tax shall have been paid, except [raw or manufactured cotton,[1]] *crude petroleum or rock-oil*, refined coal-oil, naphtha, benzine or benzole, * * * * *bullion, quicksilver, lucifer or friction matches, cigar lights, and wax tapers*, equal in amount to the duty or tax paid thereon, and no more, when exported, the evidence that any such duty or tax has been paid to be furnished to the satisfaction of the Commissioner of Internal Revenue by such

[1] See sec. 6, July 13, 1866, following.

person or persons as shall claim the allowance or drawback, and the amount to be ascertained under such regulations as shall, from time to time, be prescribed by the Commissioner of Internal Revenue, under the direction of the Secretary of the Treasury, and the same shall be paid by the warrant of the Secretary of the Treasury on the Treasurer of the United States, out of any money arising from internal duties not otherwise appropriated: *Provided*, That no allowance of drawback shall be made or had for any amount claimed or due less than ten dollars, anything in this act to the contrary notwithstanding: *And provided further*, That any certificate of drawback for goods exported, issued in pursuance of the provisions of law, may, under such regulations as may be prescribed by the Secretary of the Treasury, be received by the collector or his deputy in payment of duties under this act. And the Secretary of the Treasury may make such regulations with regard to the form of said certificates and the issuing thereof as, in his judgment, may be necessary*: *Provided also, That no claim for drawback on any articles of merchandise exported prior to June thirtieth, eighteen hundred and sixty-four, shall be allowed unless presented to the Commissioner of Internal Revenue within three months after this amendment takes effect.*

Method of payment.

No allowance to be less than $10.

Certificates of drawback receivable for duties.

Secretary may make regulations.

July 13, 1866, § 6,

Proviso of limitation. July 13, 1866, § 9.

July 13, 1866.

Drawback on articles manufactured of cotton.

SEC. 6. *And be it further enacted*, That upon articles manufactured exclusively from cotton, when exported, there shall be allowed as a drawback [an amount equal to the internal tax which shall have been assessed and paid upon such articles in their finished condition, and in addition thereto a drawback or allowance of[1]] as many cents per pound upon the pound of cotton cloth, yarn, thread, or knit fabrics, manufactured exclusively from cotton and exported, as shall have been assessed and paid in the form of an internal tax upon the raw cotton entering into the manufacture of said cloth or other article, the amount of such allowance or drawback to be ascertained in such manner as may be prescribed by the Commissioner of Internal Revenue, under the direction of the Secretary of the Treasury; and so much of section one hundred and seventy-one of the act of June thirty, eighteen hundred and sixty-four, "to provide internal revenue to support the Government, to pay interest on the public debt, and for other purposes," as now provides for a drawback on manufactured cotton, is hereby repealed.

Repeals former allowance.

Mar. 31, 1868.

No drawback allowed on any article on which there is no internal tax.

SEC. 3. *And be it further enacted*, That after the first day of June next, no drawback of internal taxes paid on manufactures shall be allowed on the exportation of any article of domestic manufacture on which there is no internal tax at the time of exportation; nor shall such drawback be allowed in any case unless it shall be proved by sworn evidence in writing, to the satisfaction of the Commissioner of Internal Revenue, that the tax had been paid, and that such articles of manufacture were, prior to the first day of April, eighteen hundred and sixty-eight, actually purchased or actually manufactured and contracted for, to be delivered

[1] The portion of this section relating to raw cotton is in force by virtue of the joint resolution of July 14, 1870, following, and the clause in brackets is retained to explain the subsequent text.

for such exportation; and no claim for such drawback, or for any drawback of internal tax on exportations made prior to the passage of this act, shall be paid unless presented to the Commissioner of Internal Revenue before the first day of October, eighteen hundred and sixty-eight.

Limitations as to time of exportation and presentation of claims.

But see joint resolution of July 14, 1870, following.

Be it resolved by the Senate and House of Representatives of the United States of America in Congress assembled, That the act of March thirty-first, eighteen hundred and sixty-eight, chapter forty-one, shall be held and construed not to prohibit the drawback provided for by section six of the act of July thirteenth, eighteen hundred and sixty-six, chapter one hundred and eighty-four, of as many cents per pound of cotton cloth, yarn, thread, or knit articles, manufactured exclusively from cotton and exported prior to May first, eighteen hundred and sixty-nine, as shall have been assessed and paid in form of an internal tax upon the raw cotton entering into the manufacture of said cloth or other article: *Provided*, That such drawbacks shall be limited to exportations made not more than six months after the date of Supplemental Regulations issued by the Commissioner of Internal Revenue, and approved by the Secretary of the Treasury May sixteen, eighteen hundred and sixty-eight.[1]

Joint resolution, July 14, 1870.

Drawback on raw cotton entering into the manufacture of cotton goods manufactured exclusively from cotton.

SEC. 54. *And be it further enacted, That distilled spirits upon which all taxes have been paid may be exported, with the privilege of drawback, in quantities of not less than one thousand gallons, and in distillers' original casks, containing not less than twenty wine gallons each, on application of the owner thereof to the collector of customs at any port of entries, and under such rules and regulations and after making such entry as may be prescribed by law and by the Secretary of the Treasury. The entry for such exportation shall be in triplicate, and shall contain the name of the person applying to export, the name of the distiller, and of the district in which the spirits were distilled, and the name of the vessel by which, and the name of the port to which, they are to be exported; and the form of the entry shall be as follows:*

July 20, 1868.

June 6, 1872, § 12.

Drawback on distilled spirits.

Regulations to be prescribed by Secretary.

"Export entry of distilled spirits entitled to drawback.

"Entry of spirits distilled by ——— ———, in ——— district, State of ———, to be exported by ——— ———, in the ———, whereof ——— ——— is master, bound to ———."

Form of entry for exportation.

And the entry shall specify the whole number of casks or packages, the marks and serial numbers thereon, the quality or kind of spirits as known in commerce, the number of gauge or wine gallons and of proof-gallons; and the amount of the tax on such spirits shall be verified by the oath or affirmation of the owner of the spirits, and that the tax has been paid thereon, and that they are truly intended to be exported to the port of ———, and not to be relanded within the limits of the United States. One bill of lading, duly signed by the master of the vessel, shall be deposited with said collector, to be filed at his office with the entry retained by him. One of said entries shall be, when the shipment is completed, transmitted to the Secretary

Bill of lading.

Entry to be transmitted to Secretary.

[1] By virtue of this proviso, November 16, 1868, has been held to be the date of limitation, although different from that fixed elsewhere in the section.

of the Treasury, to be recorded and filed in his office. The lading on board said vessel shall be only after the receipt of an order or permit signed by the collector of customs and directed to a customs gauger, and after each cask or package shall have been distinctly marked or branded by said gauger as follows: "For export from U. S. A.," and the tax-paid stamps thereon obliterated. The casks or packages shall be inspected and gauged alongside of or on the vessel by the gauger designated by said collector, under such rules and regulations as the Secretary of the Treasury may prescribe; and on application of the said collector it shall be the duty of the surveyor of the port to designate and direct one of the custom-house inspectors to superintend such shipment. And the gauger aforesaid shall make a full return of such inspection and gauging in such form as may be prescribed by the Secretary of the Treasury, showing by whom each cask of such spirits was distilled, the serial number of the cask, and of the tax-paid stamp attached thereto, the proof and quantity of such spirits as per the original gauge-mark on each cask, and the quantity in proof and wine gallons as per the gauge then made by him. And said gauger shall certify on such return that the shipment has been made, in his presence, on board the vessel named in the entry for export, which return shall be indorsed by said custom-house inspector certifying that the casks or packages have been shipped under his supervision on board said vessel, and the tax-paid stamps obliterated; and the said inspector shall make a similar certificate to the surveyor of the port, indorsed on or to be attached to the entry in possession of the custom-house. A drawback shall be allowed upon distilled spirits on which the tax has been paid and exported to foreign countries, under the provisions of this act, when exported as herein provided for. The drawback allowed shall include the taxes levied and paid upon the distilled spirits exported, at the rate of seventy cents per proof-gallon, as per last gauge of said spirits prior to exportation, and shall be due and payable only after the proper entries have been made and filed, and all other conditions complied with, as hereinbefore required, and on filing with the Secretary of the Treasury the proper claim, accompanied by the certificate of the collector of customs at the port of entry where the spirits are entered for export, that such spirits have been received into his custody and the tax-paid stamps thereon obliterated; and the Secretary of the Treasury shall prescribe such rules and regulations in relation thereto as may be necessary to secure the Treasury of the United States against frauds: Provided, That the drawback on spirits distilled prior to the passage of this act shall not exceed sixty cents per proof-gallon.

Duties of customs officers relative thereto.

Amount of drawback to be allowed, and evidence required.

July 20, 1868.

June 6, 1872, § 31.

Drawback on tobacco, snuff, and cigars.

SEC. 74. *And be it further enacted, That from and after the date on which this act takes effect*[1] *there shall be an allowance of drawback on tobacco, snuff, and cigars on which the internal tax has been paid by suitable revenue-stamps affixed to the same before removal from the place of manufacture, when the same are exported, equal in amount to the value of the stamps found to have been so af-*

[1] The amendments of the act of July 20, 1868, made by sec. 31 of the act of June 6, 1872, took effect July 1, 1872.

fixed, the evidence that the stamps were so affixed, and the amount of tax so paid, and of the subsequent exportation of the said tobacco, snuff, and cigars, to be ascertained under such rules and regulations as shall be prescribed by the Commissioner of Internal Revenue and approved by the Secretary of the Treasury. Any sum or sums found to be due under the provisions of this section shall be paid by the warrant of the Secretary of the Treasury on the Treasurer of the United States, out of any money arising from internal duties not otherwise appropriated: Provided, That no claim for an allowance of drawback shall be entertained or allowed for a sum less than fifty dollars, nor except upon evidence satisfactory to the Commissioner of Internal Revenue that the stamps affixed to the tobacco, snuff, or cigars alleged to have been exported were totally destroyed before the shipment thereof, and that the same have been landed in a foreign country or lost at sea, and have not been relanded within the limits of the United States. All tobacco and snuff now[1] *stored in any export bonded warehouse shall, on and after July first, eighteen hundred and seventy-two, be subject to the same tax as is provided by this act, and shall, within six months after the passage of this act, be withdrawn from such warehouse upon payment of the tax, or for export under the regulations of the Commissioner of Internal Revenue now in force concerning withdrawals of tobacco and snuff from bonded warehouses. And any tobacco or snuff remaining in any export bonded warehouse for a period of more than six months after the passage of this act shall be forfeited to the United States, and shall be sold or disposed of for the benefit of the same in such manner as shall be prescribed by the Commissioner of Internal Revenue under the direction of the Secretary of the Treasury.*

Regulations to be prescribed by Commissioner and approved by Secretary.

No claim less than fifty dollars allowed.

Evidence required.

Tobacco and snuff in export-bonded warehouse July 1, 1872, subject to the tax provided in the act of June 6, 1872, and to be withdrawn within six months.

When forfeited.

June 30, 1864.

Penalty for fraudulent claim for drawback.

SEC. 172. *And be it further enacted*, That if any person or persons shall fraudulently claim or seek to obtain an allowance or drawback on goods, wares, or merchandise, on which no internal duty shall have been paid, or shall fraudulently claim any greater allowance or drawback than the duty actually paid, as aforesaid, such person or persons shall forfeit triple the amount wrongfully or fraudulently claimed, or sought to be obtained, or the sum of five hundred dollars, at the election of the Secretary of the Treasury, to be recovered as in other cases of forfeiture provided for in the general provision of this act.[2]

SPECIAL TAXES.

June 30, 1864.

July 13, 1866, § 9.

Trades and occupations to pay a special tax.

SEC. 71. *And be it further enacted, That no person, firm, company, or corporation shall be engaged in, prosecute, or carry on any trade, business, or profession, hereinafter mentioned and described, until he or they shall have paid a special tax therefor in the manner hereinafter provided.*

June 30, 1864.

July 13, 1866, § 9.

Names, &c., to be registered.

SEC. 72. *And be it further enacted, That every person, firm, company, or corporation engaged in any trade, business, or profession, on which a special tax is imposed by law, shall register*

[1] The Attorney General has held that the word "now" relates to the date July 1, 1872.

[2] But see as to distilled spirits section 55, act July 20, 1868, as amended.

with the assistant assessor of the assessment district, first, his or their name or style, and in case of a firm or company, the names of the several persons constituting such firm or company, and their places of residence; second, the trade, business, or profession, and the place where such trade, business, or profession is to be carried on; third, if a rectifier, the number of

July 14, 1870, § 1. Tax to be paid and receipt given therefor.

barrels he designs to rectify.[1] **All of which facts shall be returned duly certified by such assistant assessor, to both the assessor and collector of the district; and the special tax shall be paid to the collector or deputy collector of the district as hereinafter provided for such trade, business, or profession, who shall give a receipt therefor.*

June 30, 1864. Mar. 2, 1867, § 9. Penalty for not paying special tax. July 20, 1868, § 44. June 6, 1872, § 32.

SEC. 73. *And be it further enacted, That any person who shall exercise or carry on any trade, business, or profession, or do any act hereinafter mentioned, for the exercising, carrying on, or doing of which a special tax is imposed by law, without payment thereof, as in that behalf required, shall, for every such offense, besides being liable to the payment of the tax, be subject to a fine or penalty of not less than ten nor more than five hundred dollars.*[2] * * *

June 6, 1872. Penalty for carrying on the business of manufacturer of tobacco, snuff, and cigars, dealer in manufactured tobacco, leaf-tobacco, and retail dealer in leaf-tobacco, without paying special tax.

SEC. 32. That any person, firm, company, or corporation who shall exercise or carry on the business of a manufacturer of tobacco, snuff, or cigars, dealer in manufactured tobacco, dealer in leaf-tobacco, or retail dealer in leaf-tobacco, without having paid a special tax therefor, as provided by law, shall, besides being liable to the payment of the tax, on conviction, be fined not more than five hundred dollars, or be imprisoned for a term of not more than one year, or both, at the discretion of the court.

June 30, 1864. July 13, 1866, § 9. Form of receipt. July 14, 1870, § 1.

SEC. 74. *And be it further enacted, That the receipt for the payment of any special tax shall contain and set forth the purpose, trade, business, or profession for which such tax is paid, and the name and place of abode of the person or persons paying the same; if by a rectifier,*[3] *the quantity of spirits intended to be rectified; * the time for which payment is made, the date or time of payment, and* * * * *

Proviso against carrying on business in any other place than described in receipt. July 14, 1870, § 1.

the place at which the trade, business, or profession for which the tax is paid shall be carried on: Provided, That the payment of the special tax herein imposed shall not exempt from an additional special tax the person or persons, or firm, company, or corporation doing business in any other place than that stated; but nothing herein contained shall require a special tax for the storage of goods, wares, or merchandise in other places than the place of business, nor for the sale by manufacturers or producers of their own goods, wares, and merchandise, at the place of production or manufacture and at their principal office or place of business, provided no goods, wares, or merchandise shall be kept except as samples, at said office or place*

Shall produce receipt on demand of officer.

of business. And every person exercising or carrying on any trade, business, or profession, or doing any act for which a

---

[1] But see section 59, July 20, 1868, as amended, as to rectifiers.

[2] But see sections 44, 59, 69, and 92, act July 20, 1868, as amended, and section 32, act June 6, 1872.

[3] But see section 59, July 20, 1868, as amended, as to rectifiers.

special tax is imposed, shall, on demand of any officer of internal revenue, produce and exhibit the receipt for payment of the tax, and unless he shall do so may be taken and deemed not to have paid such tax. And all such special taxes shall become due on the first day of May in each year, or on commencing any trade, business, or profession upon which such tax is by law imposed. In the former case the tax shall be reckoned for one year, and in the latter case, proportionately for that part of the year from the first day of the month in which the liability to a special tax commenced, to the first day of May following.* July 14, 1870, § 1. Special taxes due May 1, each year.

SEC. 75. *And be it further enacted, That upon the death of any person having paid the special tax for any trade, business or profession, it may and shall be lawful for the executors or administrators, or the wife or child, or the legal representatives of such deceased person to occupy the house or premises, and in like manner to exercise or carry on, for the residue of the term for which the tax shall have been paid, the same trade, business, or profession, as the deceased before exercised or carried on, in or upon the same houses or premises, without payment of any additional tax. And in case of the removal of any person or persons from the house or premises for which any trade, business, or profession was taxed, it shall be lawful for the person or persons so removing to any other place to carry on the trade, business, or profession specified in the tax-receipt at the place to which such person or persons may remove without payment of any additional tax: Provided, That all cases of death, change, or removal, as aforesaid, shall be registered with the assistant assessor, and with the collector, together with the name or names of the person or persons making such change or removal, or successor to any person deceased, under regulations to be prescribed by the Commissioner of Internal Revenue.* June 30, 1864. July 13, 1866, § 9. Executors, &c., may carry on business. Removals. Change or removal to be registered with the assistant assessor and collector.

SEC. 76. *And be it further enacted, That in every case where more than one of the pursuits, employments, or occupations, hereinafter described, shall be pursued or carried on in the same place by the same person at the same time, except as hereinafter provided, the tax shall be paid for each according to the rates severally prescribed.* * * * * June 30, 1864. July 13, 1866, § 9. Special tax to be paid for each pursuit, &c. July 14, 1870, § 1

SEC. 78. *And be it further enacted, That any number of persons,* * * * * * * *doing business in copartnership at any one place, shall be required to pay but one special tax for such copartnership.* June 30, 1864. July 13, 1866, § 9 July 14, 1870, § 1 Copartnerships.

SEC. 79. *And be it further enacted, That a special tax shall be, and hereby is, imposed as follows, that is to say:—* June 30, 1864. July 13, 1866, § 9 July 20, 1868, § 59 July 14, 1870, § 1

* * * * * * *

Brewers shall pay one hundred dollars. Every person, firm, or corporation who manufactures fermented liquors of any name or description, for sale, from malt, wholly or in part, or from any substitute therefor, shall be deemed a brewer: Provided, That any person, firm, or corporation, who manufactures less than five hundred barrels per year, shall pay the sum of fifty dollars. Brewers $100. Definition of. Brewers making less than 500 barrels per year, $50. July 20, 1868, § 5 July 14, 1870, § 1

* * * * * * *

SEC. 81. * * * * * June 30, 1864.

Provided, That the payment of any tax imposed by law shall not be held or construed to exempt any person carrying on any trade, business, or profession, from any penalty or punishment July 13, 1866, § 9 July 20, 1868, § 5 July 14, 1870, § 1

Payment of special tax does not exempt from penalty under State laws. *provided by the laws of any State for carrying on such trade, business or profession within such State, or in any manner to authorize the commencement or continuance of such trade, business, or profession contrary to the laws of such State, or in places prohibited by municipal law; nor shall the payment of* Payment of tax not to prevent State from taxing. *any tax herein provided be held or construed to prohibit or prevent any State from placing a duty or tax for State or other purposes on any trade, business, or profession, upon which a tax is imposed by law.*[1]

July 20, 1868. SEC. 59. *And be it further enacted,* That the following special taxes shall be, and are hereby, imposed, that is to say:

[Distillers producing one hundred barrels, or less, of distilled spirits, counting forty gallons of proof spirits to the barrel, within the year, shall each pay four hundred dollars; and if producing more than one hundred barrels, shall pay in addition four dollars for each such barrel produced in excess of one hundred barrels.][2] And * returns of the June 6, 1872, § 13. Distillers' returns. number of barrels of spirits, as before described, distilled by him, shall be * *furnished to the proper officers of internal revenue when demanded,* June 6, 1872, § 13. by each distiller. * Every person who Definition of distiller. produces distilled spirits, or who brews or makes mash, wort, or wash, fit for distillation or for the production of spirits, or who by any process of evaporization separates alcoholic spirit from any fermented substance, or who making or keeping mash, wort, or wash, has also in his possession or June 6, 1872, § 13. use a still, shall be regarded as a distiller. * * *

Rectifiers of distilled spirits, [rectifying, purifying, or re- Rectifier's special tax. fining two hundred barrels or less of distilled spirits, counting forty gallons of proof-spirits to the barrel, within the year,][3] shall each pay two hundred dollars. * And * re- June 6, 1872, § 13. Returns by rectifiers. turns of the quantity and proof of all the spirits purchased and of the number of barrels of spirits, as before described, rectified, purified, or refined by him, shall be *furnished* by each rectifier, * *to the proper officers of internal revenue when* June 6, 1872, § 13. *demanded.* * April 10, 1869, § 1. Definition of rectifier. *Every person who rectifies, purifies, or refines distilled spirits or wines by any process other than by original and continuous distillation from mash, wort, or wash, through continuous closed vessels and pipes, until the manufacture thereof is complete, and every wholesale or retail liquor-dealer who has in his possession any still or leach-tub, or who shall keep any other apparatus for the purpose of refining in any manner distilled spirits, and every person who, without rectifying, purifying, or refining distilled spirits, shall, by mixing such spirits, wine, or other liquor, with any materials, manufacture any spurious, imitation, or compound liquors, for sale, under the name of whisky, brandy, gin, rum, wine, spirits, cordials, or wine bitters, or any other name, shall be regarded as a rectifier, and as being engaged in the business of rectifying.* June 6, 1872, § 13. * * * * * * *

[1] This section now relates only to brewers; as to all other special taxes a similar provision will be found in section 59, act July 20, 1868, as amended.

[2] The clause in brackets is repealed, but is printed in order to explain the text following.

[3] The clause in brackets is in effect repealed, but is printed in order to explain the text following.

Provided, however, That nothing in this section shall be held to prohibit the purifying or refining of spirits in the course of original and continuous distillation through any material which will not remain incorporated with such spirits when the manufacture thereof is complete.

*Retail dealers in liquors shall pay twenty-five dollars. Every person who sells or offers for sale foreign or domestic distilled spirits [or] wines * in less quantities than five gallons at the same time, shall be regarded as a retail dealer in liquors.*

April 10, 1869, § 1. June 6, 1872, § 13. Retail dealer in liquors, special tax.

*Wholesale liquor-dealers shall each pay one hundred dollars. Every person who sells or offers for sale foreign or domestic distilled spirits [or] wines * in quantities of not less than five gallons at the same time, shall be regarded as a wholesale liquor-dealer.*

April 10, 1869, § 1. June 6, 1872, § 13. Wholesale liquor dealer's special tax.

[Dealers in liquors whose sales, including sales of all other merchandise, shall exceed twenty-five thousand dollars, shall each pay an additional tax at the rate of one dollar for every one hundred dollars of sales of liquors in excess of such twenty-five thousand dollars; and on every thousand dollars of sales of other merchandise shall pay at the same rate as a wholesale dealer; and][1] *such excess shall be returned * to the proper officers of internal revenue when demanded. But no distiller, * who has given the required bond, and who sells only distilled spirits * of his own production, at the place of manufacture, in the original casks or packages to which the tax stamps are affixed, shall be required to pay the special tax of a wholesale dealer on account of such sales.*

April 10, 1869, § 1. Dealers in liquor to make returns. June 6, 1872, § 13. Distiller not required to pay tax as wholesale dealer for certain sales. June 6, 1872, § 13.

* * * * * * *

Ibid.

Every person who sells or offers for sale malt liquors in larger quantities than five gallons at one time, but who does not deal in spirituous liquors, shall be regarded as a wholesale dealer in malt liquors, and not a wholesale liquor-dealer, and shall pay a special tax of fifty dollars.[2] *Every person who sells or offers for sale malt liquors in quantities of five gallons or less at one time, but who does not deal in spirituous liquors, shall be regarded as a retail dealer in malt liquors and not a retail liquor-dealer, and shall pay a special tax of twenty dollars.*

June 6, 1872, § 13. Special tax on wholesale dealer in malt liquors and retail dealer in malt liquors.

But the payment of any special tax imposed by this act shall not be held or construed to exempt any person carrying on any trade, business, or profession from any penalty or punishment therefor provided by the laws of any State; nor to authorize the commencement or continuance of any such trade, business, or profession, contrary to the laws of any State, or in places prohibited by municipal law; nor shall the payment of any such tax be held or construed to prohibit or prevent any State from placing a duty or tax on the same trade, business, or profession for State or other purposes.

Payment of special tax does not exempt from penalty under State laws. Payment of tax not to prevent State from taxing.

Manufacturers of stills shall each pay fifty dollars, and twenty dollars for each still or worm for distilling made by him. Any person who manufactures any still or worm to be used in distilling shall be deemed a manufacturer of stills.

Manufacturer of stills, special tax.

[1] The clause in brackets is repealed, but is printed in order to explain the text following.

[2] See proviso in sec. 17, June 6, 1872.

TOBACCO, SNUFF, AND CIGARS.

June 6, 1872, § 31.

Dealers in leaf-tobacco, special tax.

Dealers in leaf-tobacco, except retail dealers in leaf-tobacco, as hereinafter defined, shall each pay twenty-five dollars.

Definition of a dealer in leaf-tobacco.

Every person shall be regarded as a dealer in leaf-tobacco whose business it is, for himself or on commission, to sell, or offer for sale, or consign for sale on commission, leaf-tobacco; and payment of a special tax as dealer in tobacco, manufacturer of tobacco, manufacturer of cigars, or any other special tax, shall not exempt any person dealing in leaf-tobacco from the payment of the special tax therefor hereby required. But no farmer or planter shall be required to pay a special tax as a dealer in leaf-tobacco, for selling tobacco of his own production, or tobacco received by him as rent from tenants who have produced the same on his land. But nothing in this section shall be construed to exempt from a special tax any farmer or planter who shall, by peddling or otherwise, sell leaf-tobacco at retail directly to consumers, or who shall sell or assign, consign, transfer, or dispose of to persons other than those who have paid a special tax as leaf-dealers or manufacturers of tobacco, snuff, or cigars, or to persons purchasing leaf-tobacco for export.

Farmer or planter shall make statement on demand.

And it shall be the duty of every farmer or planter producing and selling leaf-tobacco, on demand of any internal-revenue officer, or other authorized agent of the Treasury Department, to furnish said officer or agent a true and correct statement, verified by oath or affirmation, of all his sales of leaf-tobacco, the number of hogsheads, cases, or pounds, with the name and residence, in each instance, of the person to whom sold, and the place to which it is shipped. And any such farmer or planter who shall willfully refuse to furnish such information, or who shall knowingly make false statements as to any of the facts aforesaid, shall be liable to a penalty not exceeding five hundred dollars.

Dealers in leaf-tobacco to sell only to certain specified persons.

Dealers in leaf-tobacco shall hereafter sell only to other dealers who have paid a special tax as such, and to manufacturers of tobacco, snuff, or cigars, and to such persons as are known to be purchasers of leaf-tobacco for export.

Retail dealers in leaf-tobacco, special tax.

Retail dealers in leaf-tobacco shall each pay five hundred dollars, and, if their annual sales exceed one thousand dollars, shall each pay, in addition thereto, fifty cents for every dollar in excess of one thousand dollars of their sales.

Definition.

Every person shall be regarded as a retail dealer in leaf-tobacco whose business it is to sell leaf-tobacco in quantities less than an original hogshead, case, or bale; or who shall sell directly to consumers, or to persons other than dealers in leaf-tobacco, who have paid a special tax as such; or to manufacturers of tobacco, snuff, or cigars who have paid a special tax; or to persons who purchase in original packages for export.

To keep books.

Retail dealers in leaf-tobacco shall also keep a book, and enter therein daily their purchases and sales, in a form and manner to be prescribed by the Commissioner of Internal Revenue, which book shall be open at all times for the inspection of any revenue officer.

Dealers in tobacco, special tax.

Dealers in tobacco shall each pay five dollars.

Definition of.

Every person whose business it is to sell, or offer for sale, manufactured tobacco, snuff, or cigars, shall be regarded as a dealer in tobacco, and the payment of a special tax as a wholesale or retail liquor-

dealer, or the payment of any other special tax, shall not relieve any person who sells manufactured tobacco and cigars from the payment of this tax: Provided, That no manufacturer of tobacco, snuff, or cigars shall be required to pay a special tax as dealer in manufactured tobacco and cigars for selling his own products at the place of manufacture.

Manufacturers of tobacco. Special tax. Definition of.

Manufacturers of tobacco shall each pay ten dollars. Every person whose business it is to manufacture tobacco or snuff for himself, or who shall employ others to manufacture tobacco or snuff, whether such manufacture shall be by cutting, pressing, grinding, crushing, or rubbing of any raw or leaf tobacco, or otherwise preparing raw or leaf tobacco, or manufactured or partially manufactured tobacco or snuff, or the putting up for use or consumption of scraps, waste, clippings, stems, or deposits of tobacco resulting from any process of handling tobacco, shall be regarded as a manufacturer of tobacco.

Manufacturers of cigars. Special tax. Definition of.

Manufacturers of cigars shall each pay ten dollars. Every person whose business it is to make or manufacture cigars for himself, or who shall employ others to make or manufacture cigars, shall be regarded as a manufacturer of cigars. No special-tax receipt shall be issued to any manufacturer of cigars until he shall have given the bond required by law. Every person whose business it is to make cigars for others, either for pay, upon commission, on shares, or otherwise, from material furnished by others, shall be regarded as a cigar-maker. Every cigar-maker shall cause his name and residence to be registered, without previous demand, with the assistant assessor of the division in which such cigar-maker shall be employed; and any manufacturer of cigars employing any cigar-maker who shall have neglected or refused to make such registry shall, on conviction, be fined five dollars for each day that such cigar-maker so offending, by neglect or refusal to register, shall be employed by him.

Cigar-makers to be registered.

Cigar-manufacturers employing cigar-makers not registered. Penalty.

Peddlers of tobacco. Classification and special tax of.

Peddlers of tobacco shall be classified and rated as follows, to wit: When traveling with more than two horses, mules, or other animals, the first class, and shall pay fifty dollars; when traveling with two horses, mules, or other animals, the second class, and shall pay twenty-five dollars; when traveling with one horse, mule, or other animal, the third class, and shall pay fifteen dollars; when traveling on foot or by public conveyance, the fourth class, and shall pay ten dollars. Any person who sells or offers to sell and deliver manufactured tobacco, snuff, or cigars, traveling from place to place, in the town or through the country, shall be regarded as a peddler of tobacco. Every peddler of tobacco, before commencing, or, if already commenced, before continuing to peddle tobacco, shall furnish to the collector of his district a statement accurately setting forth the place of his residence, and, if in a city, the street and number of the street where he resides; also the State or States through which he proposes to travel; the mode of travel, whether on foot, by public conveyance, or to travel with one, two, or more horses, mules, or other animals; to state also whether he proposes to sell his own manufactures or manufactures of others, and, if he sells for other parties, to name the person or persons for whom he sells. He shall also give a bond in the sum of two thousand dollars, to be approved by the col-

Definition of.

Shall furnish statement.

Bond.

lector of the district, that he will not engage in any attempt, by himself or by collusion with others, to defraud the Government of any tax on tobacco, snuff, or cigars; that he will neither sell, nor offer for sale any tobacco, snuff, or cigars, except in original and full packages, as the law requires the same to be put up and prepared by the manufacturer for sale, or for removal for sale or consumption, and except such packages of tobacco, snuff, and cigars as bear the manufacturer's label or caution-notice, and his legal marks and brands, and genuine internal-revenue stamps which have never before been used.

Peddler of tobacco to affix sign.

Every peddler of tobacco, snuff, or cigars, traveling with a wagon, shall affix and keep on the same, in a conspicuous place, a sign painted in oil-colors, or gilded, giving his full name, business, and collection-district, and shall obtain a certificate from the collector of the district, who is hereby authorized and directed to issue the same, giving the name of the peddler, his residence, the class of his special-tax receipt, and the fact of his having filed the required bond;

Collector to issue certificate.

Peddler of tobacco to exhibit certificate on demand of any officer of internal revenue.

and every person peddling tobacco shall, on demand of any officer of internal revenue, produce and exhibit said collector's certificate, and, unless he shall do so, may be taken and deemed not to have paid the special tax, nor otherwise to have complied with the law.

Seizure in case of refusal to exhibit receipt.

And in case any peddler shall refuse to exhibit his or her receipt as aforesaid, when demanded by any officer of internal revenue, said officer may seize the horse, or mule, wagon and contents, or pack, bundle, or basket of any person so refusing;

Proceedings under seizure.

and the assessor of the district in which the seizure has occurred may, on ten days' notice, published in any newspaper in the district, or served personally on the peddler, or at his dwelling-house, require such peddler to show cause, if any he has, why the horses or mules, wagon and contents, pack, bundle, or basket so seized shall not be forfeited; and in case no sufficient cause is shown the assessor may direct a forfeiture, and issue an order to the collector, or to any deputy collector of the district, for the sale of the property so forfeited; and the same, after payment of the expenses of the proceedings, shall be paid to the collector for the use of the United States;

Special taxes due on first of May in each year.

and all such special taxes shall become due on the first day of May in each year, or on commencing business; and if such peddler shall not have paid the special tax for the current year he shall pay the same within thirty days after the passage of this act. In the former case the tax shall be reckoned for one year, and in the latter case proportionately for that part of the year from the first day of the month in which the liability to a special tax commenced to the first day of May following.

Penalty for peddling tobacco, &c., in violation of law.

And any person who shall, after the passage of this act, be found peddling tobacco, snuff, or cigars, without having given the bond, or without having previously obtained the collector's certificate as herein provided, or who shall sell tobacco, snuff, or cigars otherwise than in original and full packages as put up by the manufacturer; or who shall have in his possession any internal revenue stamp or stamps which have been removed from any box or other package of tobacco, snuff, or cigars, or any empty or partially emptied box or other package which has been used for tobacco, snuff, or cigars, the stamp or stamps on which have not been destroyed; or shall fail to have affixed to his wagon, in a conspicuous place, a sign, painted in oil-colors, or gilded, giving his full name, business, and collection-district, shall, for each such offense, on conviction, be fined not less than one hundred dollars nor more than five hundred dollars, or imprisoned not less than six months nor more than one year, or both, at the discretion of the court.

July 20, 1868.

Re-adjustment of special taxes.

SEC. 60. *And be it further enacted*, That in every case where it becomes necessary to ascertain the amount of annual or monthly sales made by any person on whom a special tax is imposed by this act, or to ascertain the excess of such sales above a given amount, such amounts and excesses shall be ascertained and returned under such regulations and in such form as shall be prescribed by the Commissioner of Internal Revenue; and in any case where the amount of the tax has been increased by this act above the amount before paid by any person in that behalf, such person, except retail dealers, shall be again assessed and pay the amount of such increase from the taking effect of this act; and in any case where the amount of sales or receipts has been understated or under-estimated by any person, such person shall be again assessed for such deficiency, and shall be required to pay the same with any penalty or penalties that may by law have accrued or be chargeable thereon. * * * * * * * *

[*The remainder of this section relates exclusively to tobacco, snuff, and cigars, and will be found at* *post, p.* 91.]

DISTILLED SPIRITS.

AN ACT imposing taxes on distilled spirits and tobacco, and for other purposes, approved July 20, 1868, as amended.

(*The sections of this act are given in their consecutive order, either printed in full or accounted for.*)

July 20, 1868.

Tax on distilled spirits.

June 6, 1872, § 12.

Fractional gallons, how taxed.

June 6, 1872, § 12.

Who are liable for tax.

Tax to be a lien.

Be it enacted by the Senate and House of Representatives of the United States of America in Congress assembled, That there shall be levied and collected on all distilled spirits on which the tax prescribed by law has not been paid, a tax of *seventy* cents on each and every proof-gallon, to be paid by the distiller, owner, or person having possession thereof before removal from distillery warehouse; and the tax on such spirits shall be collected on the whole number of gauge or wine gallons when below proof, and shall be increased in proportion for any greater strength than the strength of proof spirit as defined in this act; and any fractional part of a gallon *amounting to one-half gallon or over* in a cask or package shall be taxed as a gallon, *and any fractional part of a gallon less than one-half gallon in any cask or package, shall be exempt from tax.* Every proprietor or possessor of a still, distillery, or distilling apparatus, and every person in any manner interested in the use of any such still, distillery, or distilling apparatus, shall be jointly and severally liable for the taxes imposed by law on the distilled spirits produced therefrom, and the tax shall be a first lien on the spirits distilled, the distillery used for distilling the same, the stills, vessels, fixtures, and tools therein, and on the lot or tract of land whereon the said distillery is situated, together with any building thereon, from the time said spirits are distilled until the said tax shall be paid.

Distilled spirits in bonded warehouse August 1, 1872.

June 6, 1872, § 12.

Refunding of special tax to distillers.

Provided, nevertheless, That distilled spirits lawfully deposited in a distillery bonded warehouse when this act shall take effect[1] *may be withdrawn therefrom on payment of the taxes thereon at the rate within the time and in the manner fixed by law at the time of such deposit: Provided further, That the special tax paid by distillers prior to the taking effect of this act, which has not been exhausted by the quantity of spirits distilled as provided by law, shall be refunded upon proper application out of any moneys arising from internal taxes not otherwise appropriated.*

July 20, 1868.

Standard of proof spirits.

SEC. 2. *And be it further enacted*, That proof spirit shall be held and taken to be that alcoholic liquor which contains one half its volume of alcohol of a specific gravity of seven thousand nine hundred and thirty-nine ten thousandths (.7939) at sixty degrees Fahrenheit; and the Commissioner of Internal Revenue, for the prevention and de-

[1] The act of June 6, 1872, so far as it relates to distilled spirits, took effect August 1, 1872, except where otherwise provided. See section 47 of said act.

tection of frauds by distillers of spirits, is hereby authorized to adopt and prescribe for use such hydrometers, saccharometers, weighing and gauging instruments, * or other means for ascertaining the quantity, gravity, and producing capacity of any mash, wort, or beer used or to be used in the production of distilled spirits, and the strength and quantity of spirits subject to tax, as he may deem necessary; and he may prescribe rules and regulations to secure a uniform and correct system of inspection, weighing, marking, and gauging of spirits. And in all sales of spirits hereafter made, a gallon shall be taken to be a gallon of proof spirit, according to the foregoing standard set forth and declared for the inspection and gauging of spirits throughout the United States. The tax on brandy made from grapes shall be the same and no higher than that upon other distilled spirits; and the Commissioner of Internal Revenue is hereby authorized, with the approval of the Secretary of the Treasury, to exempt distillers of brandy from apples, peaches, or grapes exclusively, from such other of the provisions of this act relating to the manufacture of spirits as in his judgment may seem expedient.

Hydrometers, saccharometers, &c. June 6, 1872, § 12.

Inspection, &c., of spirits.

Definition of gallon as used in sales.

Tax on brandy.

Brandy made from apples, peaches, or grapes, exclusively.

SEC. 3. *And be it further enacted, That the Commissioner of Internal Revenue is hereby authorized to order and require such changes of or additions to distilling apparatus, connecting pipes, pumps, or cisterns, or any machinery connected with or used in or on the distillery premises, or may require to be put on any of the stills, tubs, cisterns, pipes, or other vessels, such fastenings, locks, or seals as he may deem necessary.*

July 20, 1868. June 6, 1872, § 12.

Commissioner may require changes of, or additions to, distilling apparatus, &c.; also locks and seals.

SEC. 4. *And be it further enacted*, That distilled spirits, spirits, alcohol, and alcoholic spirit, within the true intent and meaning of this act, is that substance known as ethyl alcohol, hydrated oxide of ethyl, or spirit of wine, which is commonly produced by the fermentation of grain, starch, molasses, or sugar, including all dilutions and mixtures of this substance; and the tax shall attach to this substance as soon as it is in existence as such, whether it be subsequently separated as pure or impure spirit, or be immediately, or at any subsequent time, transferred into any other substance, either in the process of original production or by any subsequent process; and no mash, wort, or wash fit for distillation or the production of spirits or alcohol shall be made or fermented in any building or on any premises other than a distillery duly authorized according to law; and no mash, wort, or wash so made and fermented shall be sold or removed from any distillery before being distilled; and no person other than an authorized distiller shall by distillation, or by any other process, separate the alcoholic spirits from any fermented mash, wort, or wash; and no person shall use spirits or alcohol or any vapor of alcoholic spirits in manufacturing vinegar or any other article, or in any process of manufacture whatever, unless the spirits or alcohol so used shall have been produced in an authorized distillery and the tax thereon paid. Any person who shall violate any of the provisions of this section shall be fined, for every offense, not less than five hundred dollars, nor more than five thousand dollars, and imprisoned

July 20, 1868.

Definition of distilled spirits, &c.

When tax attaches.

Restrictions of production of mash, wort, or wash fit for distillation, or separating alcoholic spirits therefrom.

Manufacture of vinegar from spirits, &c.

Penalty.

Exception as to fermented liquors.

for not less than six months nor more than two years: *Provided*, That nothing in this section shall be construed to apply to fermented liquors.

Joint resolution March 3, 1871.

Fermented liquids used for the manufacture of vinegar exclusively.

Resolved by the Senate and House of Representatives of the United States of America in Congress assembled, That section four of the act of July twenty, eighteen hundred and sixty-eight, in relation to fermented liquors, be so amended as not to apply to the making of fermented liquids used for the manufacture of vinegar exclusively; but nothing in this resolution shall be construed to authorize the distillation of such fermented liquids except in an authorized distillery.

Joint resolution. Feb. 5, 1867.

Products of distillation containing spirits.

SEC. 1. * * * All products of distillation, by whatever name known, which contain distilled spirits or alcohol on which the tax imposed by law has not been paid, shall be considered and taxed as distilled spirits.

July 20, 1868.

Registry of stills, &c.

SEC. 5. *And be it further enacted*, That every person having in his possession or custody, or under his control, any still or distilling apparatus set up, shall register the same with the assistant assessor of the division in which said still or distilling apparatus shall be, by filing with him duplicate statements, in writing, subscribed by such person, setting forth the particular place where such still or distilling apparatus is set up, the kind of still and its cubic contents, the owner thereof, his place of residence, and the purpose for which said still or distilling apparatus has been or is intended to be used; one of which statements shall be retained and preserved by the assistant assessor and the other transmitted to the assessor of the district. Stills and distilling apparatus now set up shall be so registered within sixty days from the time this act takes effect, and those hereafter set up shall be so registered immediately upon their being set up. Any still or distilling apparatus not so registered, together with all personal property in the possession, or custody, or under the control of such person and found in the building, or in any yard or enclosure connected with the building, in which the same shall be set up, shall be forfeited. And any person having in his possession or custody, or under his control, any still or distilling apparatus set up which is not so registered, shall pay a penalty of five hundred dollars, and on conviction shall be fined not less than one hundred dollars nor more than one thousand dollars, and imprisoned for not less than one month nor more than two years.

Penalty for not registering.

July 20, 1868.

Notice of intention to carry on the business of distiller or rectifier.

SEC. 6. *And be it further enacted*, That every person engaged in, or intending to be engaged in, the business of a distiller or rectifier, shall give notice in writing, subscribed by him, to the assessor of the district within which such business is to be carried on, stating his name and place of residence, and if a company or firm, the name and place of residence of each member thereof, the place where said business is to be carried on, and whether of distilling or rectifying. And if such business be carried on in a city, the residence and place of business shall be indicated by the name of the street and number of the building. In case of a distiller, the notice shall also state the kind of stills, and the cubic contents thereof, the number and kind of boilers, the number of mash tubs and fermenting tubs, and the cubic contents of each tub, the number of receiving cisterns, and the cubic contents of each cistern, together with a particular description of the lot, or tract of land, on which the distillery is situated, with the size and description of the buildings thereon, and of what material constructed. The notice shall also state the number of hours in which the distiller will ferment each tub of mash or beer, the estimated quantity of distilled spirits which the apparatus is capable of distilling every twenty-four hours, and the names and residence of every person interested or to be interested in the business, and that said distillery and the premises connected therewith are not within six hundred feet of any premises authorized to be used for rectifying or refining distilled spirits by any process. In case of a rectifier, the notice shall state the precise location of the premises where such business is to be carried on, the name and residence of every person interested or to be interested in the business, by what process the applicant intends to rectify, purify, or refine distilled spirits, the kind and cubic contents of any still used or to be used for such purpose, and the estimated quantity of spirits which can be rectified, purified, or refined every twenty-four hours in such establishment, and that said rectifying establishment is not within six hundred feet of the premises of any distillery registered for the distillation of spirits. In case of any change in the location, form, capacity, ownership, agency, superintendency, or in the persons interested in the business of such distillery or rectifying establishment, or in the time of fermenting the mash or beer, notice thereof, in writing, shall be given to the said assessor or to the assistant assessor of the division within twenty-four hours of said change. And any assistant assessor receiving such notice shall immediately transmit the same to the assessor of the district. Every notice required by this section shall be in such form and shall contain such additional particulars as the Commissioner of Internal Revenue may from time to time prescribe. Any person failing or refusing to give such notice shall pay a penalty of one thousand dollars, and on conviction shall be fined not less than one hundred dollars nor more than two thousand dollars, and any person giving a false or fraudulent notice shall, on conviction, in addition to such penalty or fine, be imprisoned not less than six months nor more than two years.

July 20, 1868.

Distiller to give bond.

SEC. 7. *And be it further enacted*, That every distiller shall, on filing his notice of intention to continue or commence business, with the assessor before proceeding with such business, after the passage of this act and on the first day of May of each succeeding year, make and execute a bond in form prescribed by the Commissioner of Internal Revenue, with at least two sureties, to be approved by the assessor of the district. The penal sum of said bond shall not be less than double the amount of tax on the spirits that can be distilled in his distillery during a period of fifteen days. * * * * The condition of the bond shall be that the principal shall faithfully comply with all the provisions of law

June 6, 1872, § 12.

in relation to the duties and business of distillers, and will pay all penalties incurred or fines imposed on him for a violation of any of the said provisions; that he will not suffer the lot or tract of land on which the distillery stands, or any part thereof, or any of the distilling apparatus, to be encumbered by mortgage, judgment, or other lien during the time in which he shall carry on said business. The assessor may refuse to approve said bond when, in his judgment, the situation of the distillery is such as would enable the distiller to defraud the United States; and in case of such refusal, the distiller may appeal to the Commissioner of Internal Revenue, whose decision in the matter shall be final. A new bond may be required in case of the death, insolvency, or removal of either of the sureties, and in any other contingency, at the discretion of the assessor or Commissioner of Internal Revenue. Any person failing or refusing to give the bond hereinbefore required, or to renew the same, or giving any false, forged, or fraudulent bond, shall forfeit the distillery, distilling apparatus, and all real estate and premises connected therewith, and on conviction shall be fined not less than five hundred dollars, nor more than five thousand dollars, and imprisoned not less than six months nor more than two years.

July 20, 1868.

Distiller must be owner in fee-simple, or have written consent of owner, &c.

SEC. 8. *And be it further enacted*, That no bond of a distiller shall be approved unless he is the owner in fee, unencumbered by any mortgage, judgment, or other lien, of the lot or tract of land on which the distillery is situated, or unless he files with the assessor, in connection with his notice, the written consent of the owner of the fee, and of any mortgagee, judgment creditor, or other person having a lien thereon, duly acknowledged, that the premises may be used for the purpose of distilling spirits, subject to the provisions of law, and expressly stipulating that the lien of the United States for taxes and penalties shall have priority of such mortgage, judgment, or other encumbrance, and that in case of the forfeiture of the distillery premises, or any part thereof, the title of the same shall vest in the United States discharged from any such mortgage, judgment, or other encumbrance. In any case where the owner of a distillery or distilling apparatus, erected prior to the passage of this act, has an estate, for a term of years only, in the lot or tract of land on which the distillery is situated, the lease or other evidence of title to which shall have been duly recorded prior to the passage of this act, the value of such lot or tract of land, together with the building and distilling apparatus, shall be appraised in the manner to be prescribed by the Commissioner of Internal Revenue; and the assessor is hereby authorized to accept, in lieu of the said written consent of the owner of the fee, the bond of said distiller with not less than two sureties, who shall be residents of the collection district or county, or an adjoining county in the same State, in which the distillery is situated, and shall be the owners of unencumbered real estate in said district or county, or adjoining county, equal to such appraised value. The penal sum of said bond shall be equal to the appraised value of said lot or tract of land, together

Bond in lieu of written consent of owner of fee to be accepted in certain cases.

with the buildings and distilling apparatus, and such bond shall be conditioned that in case the distillery, distilling apparatus, or any part thereof, shall, by final judgment, be forfeited for the violation of any of the provisions of law, the obligors will pay the amount stated in said bond. Said bond shall be in such form as the Commissioner of Internal Revenue shall prescribe.

That section eight be amended so that in case of a distiller[y] or distilling apparatus erected prior to the twentieth of July, eighteen hundred and sixty-eight, on a tract or lot of land held under a lease or other evidence of title less than fee-simple, which was not required by the laws of the State to be recorded in order to be valid at the time of its execution, or in any case where the title was then and has continued to be in litigation, or where the owner is possessed of the fee but encumbered with a mortgage executed and duly recorded prior to the said twentieth of July, eighteen hundred and sixty-eight, and not due, or where the fee is held by a femme covert, minor, person of unsound mind, or other person incapable of giving consent as required by said act, a bond may be taken at the discretion of the Commissioner, as provided for in said section for a distillery erected on land the lease or other evidence of title to which was duly recorded prior to the passage of this act: Provided, That nothing herein contained shall be so construed as to apply to any distillery or distilling apparatus not erected prior to the twentieth of July, eighteen hundred and sixty-eight. Apr. 10, 1869, § 1. Modification of the foregoing.

Provided further, That in case of distilleries sold at judicial and other sales in favor of the United States, a bond may be taken at the discretion of the Commissioner of the Internal Revenue in lieu of the written consent required by such section, and the person giving such bond may be allowed to operate such distillery during the existence of the right of redemption from such sale, on complying with all the other provisions of law. June 6, 1872, § 13.

SEC. 9. *And be it further enacted*, That every distiller and person intending to engage in the business of a distiller shall, previous to the approval of his bond, cause to be made, under the direction of the assessor of the district, an accurate plan and description, in triplicate, of the distillery and distilling apparatus, distinctly showing the location of every still, boiler, doubler, worm tub, and receiving cistern, the course and construction of all fixed pipes used or to be used in the distillery, and of every branch thereof, and of every cock, or joint thereof, and of every valve therein, together with every place, vessel, tub, or utensil from and to which any such pipe shall lead, or with which it communicates. Such plan and description shall also show the number and location and cubic contents of every still, mash tub, and fermenting tub, together with the cubic contents of every receiving cistern, and the color of each fixed pipe, as required in this act. One copy of said plan and description shall be kept displayed in some conspicuous place in the distillery; two copies shall be furnished to the assessor of the district, one of which shall be kept by him and the other transmitted to the Commissioner of Internal Revenue. The accuracy of every such plan and description shall be verified by the assessor, the draughts- July 20, 1868. Plan of distillery.

man, and the distiller; and no alteration shall be made in such distillery without the consent, in writing, of the assessor, which alteration shall be shown on the original or by a supplemental plan and description, and a reference thereto noted on the original, as the asssessor may direct; and any supplemental plan and description shall be executed and preserved in the same manner as the original.

July 20, 1868. | June 6, 1872, § 12.

Survey of distillery.

SEC. 10. *And be it further enacted, That on the receipt of notice that any person wishes to commence the business of distilling, the assessor shall proceed, at the expense of the United States, with the aid of an assistant designated for the purpose by the Commissioner of Internal Revenue, to make a survey of such distillery for the purpose of estimating and determining its true spirit-producing capacity for a day of twenty-four hours, a written report of which survey shall be made in triplicate, one copy of which shall be delivered to the distiller, and shall take effect on and after the date of such delivery, one copy retained by the assessor, and the other transmitted to the Commissioner of Internal Revenue. In all surveys made under this act forty-five gallons of mash or beer brewed or fermented from grain shall represent not less than one bushel of grain, and seven gallons of mash or beer brewed or fermented from molasses shall represent not less than one gallon of molasses, except in distilleries operating on the sour-mash principle, in which distilleries sixty gallons of beer brewed or fermented from grain shall represent not less than one bushel of grain. If the Commissioner of Internal Revenue shall at any time be satisfied that such report of the capacity of any distillery is in any respect incorrect or needs revision, he shall direct the assessor to make, in like manner, another survey of said distillery, the report of said survey to be made in triplicate and deposited as hereinbefore provided.*

July 20, 1868. | June 6, 1872, § 12.

Distillers not to carry on business until law is complied with.

SEC. 11. *And be it further enacted,* That after the passage of this act it shall not be lawful for * any distiller * to *commence or* continue the business of distilling until such distiller shall have given the bond required by this act, and shall have complied with the provisions of law having reference to the registration and survey of distilleries, and having reference to the arrangement and construction of distilleries, and the premises connected therewith, in manner and as required by this act; nor shall it be lawful for any *person to engage in the business of* distilling on any premises distant less than six hundred feet, *in a direct line,* from any premises used for rectifying, nor shall any assessor assess or collector collect any special tax for rectifying distilled spirits on any premises distant less than six hundred feet, *in a direct line,* from any distillery when the distillery and rectifying establishments are occupied and used by different persons; nor shall the processes of distillation and rectification both be carried on within the distance of six hundred feet, *in a direct line.* In all cases where a distillery and rectifying establishment, distant the one from the other less than six hundred feet, *in a direct line,* are occupied and used by the same person, said person shall have the right to elect which business shall be discontinued at that place. In all cases where rectifying or distilling shall be discon-

Distilling and rectifying not to be carried on within six hundred feet of each other in a direct line.

tinued under the provisions of this section, and the time for which the special tax for rectifying or distilling was paid remains unexpired, the Secretary of the Treasury is hereby authorized to refund out of any money in the Treasury not otherwise appropriated, on requisition of the Commissioner of Internal Revenue, a proportionate part of any sum originally paid for special tax therefor, which shall be in such ratio to the whole sum paid as the unexpired time for which special tax was paid shall bear to the whole term for which the same was paid. Any collector or assessor of internal revenue who shall fail to perform any duty imposed by this section, or shall assess or collect any special tax in violation of its provisions, shall be liable to a penalty of five thousand dollars for each offense.

July 20, 1868.

Distilling on certain premises forbidden.

SEC. 12. *And be it further enacted*, That no person shall use any still, boiler, or other vessel for the purpose of distilling in any dwelling-house, nor in any shed, yard, or enclosure connected with any dwelling-house, nor on board of any vessel or boat, nor in any building or on any premises where beer, lager beer, ale, porter, or other fermented liquors, vinegar or ether are manufactured or produced, or where sugars or sirups are refined, or where liquors of any description are retailed, or where any other business is carried on, nor within six hundred feet, *in a direct line*, from any premises authorized to be used for rectifying; and every person who shall use any still, boiler, or other vessel for the purpose of distilling, as aforesaid, in any building or other premises where the above-specified articles are manufactured, produced, refined, or retailed, or other business is carried on, or on board of any vessel or boat, or in any dwelling-house, or other place as aforesaid, or shall aid or assist therein, or who shall cause or procure the same to be done, shall, on conviction, be fined one thousand dollars and imprisoned for not less than six months nor more than two years, in the discretion of the court: *Provided*, That saleratus may be manufactured, or meal or flour ground from grain, in any building or on any premises where spirits are distilled; but such meal or flour only to be used for distillation on the premises. *Provided further*, That any boiler used in generating steam or heating water to be used in such distillery may be located in any other building or on any other premises to be connected with such still or boiling tubs, by suitable pipes or other apparatus, or the steam from such boiler in the distillery may be conveyed to other premises to be used for manufacturing or other purposes.

June 6, 1872, § 12.

Penalty.

Proviso to § 25, act July 13, 1866.

Boiler used in generating steam or heating water for use of distillery.

SEC. 13. *Repealed by section* 12, *act June* 6, 1872.

July 20, 1868

Manufacturer of still, &c., to give notice.

SEC. 14. *And be it further enacted*, That any person who shall manufacture any still, boiler, or other vessel, to be used for the purpose of distilling, shall, before the same is removed from the place of manufacture, notify in writing the assessor of the district in which such still, boiler, or other vessel is to be used or set up, by whom it is to be used, its capacity, and the time when the same is to be removed from the place of manufacture; and no such still, boiler, or other vessel shall be set up without the permit in

Setting up still, &c., without permit; penalty.

writing of the said assessor for that purpose; and any person who shall set up any such still, boiler, or other vessel, without first obtaining a permit from the said assessor of the district in which such still, boiler, or other vessel is intended to be used, or who shall fail to give such notice, shall pay in either case the sum of five hundred dollars, and shall forfeit the distilling apparatus thus removed or set up in violation of law.

July 20, 1868.

Distillery warehouse.

June 6, 1872, § 12.

Tax on spirits to be paid before removal.

SEC. 15. *And be it further enacted*, That every distiller shall provide, at his own expense, a warehouse, to be situated on and to constitute a part of his distillery premises, to be used only for the storage of distilled spirits, of his own manufacture, *until the tax thereon shall have been paid;* but no dwelling-house shall be used for such purpose, and no door, window, or other opening shall be made or permitted in the walls of such warehouse leading into the distillery or into any other room or building; and such warehouse, when approved by the Commissioner of Internal Revenue, on report of the collector, is hereby declared to be a bonded warehouse of the United States, to be known as a distillery warehouse, and shall be under the direction and control of the collector of the district, and in charge of an internal revenue storekeeper, assigned thereto by the Commissioner of Internal Revenue; and the tax on the spirits stored in such warehouse shall be paid before removal from such warehouse.

July 13, 1866, § 43.

Spirits not to remain on distillery premises after tax has been paid.

* * * * * No distilled spirits on which the tax has been paid shall be stored or allowed to remain on any distillery premises, under the penalty of a forfeiture of all spirits so found. * * *

July 20, 1868.

Receiving-cisterns in distilleries.

SEC. 16. *And be it further enacted*, That the owner, agent, or superintendent of any distillery, established as hereinbefore provided, shall erect, in a room or building to be provided and used for that purpose, and for no other, and to be constructed in the manner to be prescribed by the Commissioner of Internal Revenue, two or more receiving cisterns, each to be at least of sufficient capacity to hold all the spirits distilled during the day of twenty-four hours, into which shall be conveyed all the spirits produced in said distillery; and each of such cisterns shall be so constructed as to leave an open space of at least three feet between the top thereof and the floor or roof above, and of not less than eighteen inches between the bottom thereof and the floor below, and shall be so situated that the officer can pass around the same, and shall be connected with the outlet of the worm or condenser by suitable pipes or other apparatus so constructed as always to be exposed to the view of the officer, and so connected and constructed as to prevent the abstraction of spirits while passing from the outlet of the worm or condenser back to the still or doubler, or forward to the receiving cistern; such cisterns and the room in which they are contained shall be in charge of and under the lock and seal of the internal revenue gauger designated for that duty; and on the third day after the spirits are conveyed into such cisterns the same shall be drawn off into casks under the supervision of such gauger in the presence of the storekeeper, and be removed directly to the distillery warehouse; and on special application to the assessor or assistant assessor by the owner, agent, or superintendent of any distillery, the spirits may be drawn off from the said cisterns under the supervision of the gauger at any time previous to the third day. All locks and seals required by law shall be provided by the Commissioner of Internal Revenue *at the expense of the United States from and after the passage of this act;* and the keys shall be in charge of the collector or such gauger as he may designate.

Locks and seals.

June 6, 1872, § 12.

July 20, 1868.

SEC. 17. *And be it further enacted,* That the door of the furnace of every still or boiler used in any distillery shall be so constructed that it may be securely fastened and locked. The fermenting tubs shall be so placed as to be easily accessible to any revenue officer, and each tub shall have distinctly painted thereon in oil colors its cubic contents in gallons, and the number of the tub. There shall be a clear space of not less than one foot around every wood still, and not less than two feet around every doubler and worm tank. The doubler and worm tanks shall be elevated not less than one foot from the floor; and every fixed pipe to be used by the distiller, except for conveyance of water, or of spent mash or beer only, shall be so fixed and placed as to be capable of being examined by the officer for the whole of its length or course, and shall be painted, and kept painted, as follows; that is to say: Every pipe for the conveyance of mash or beer shall be painted of a red color; every pipe for the conveyance of low wines back into the still or doubler shall be painted blue; every pipe for the conveyance of spirits shall be painted black; and every pipe for the conveyance of water shall be painted white. If any fixed pipe shall be used by any distiller which shall not be painted or kept painted as herein directed, or which shall be painted otherwise than as herein directed, he shall forfeit the sum of one thousand dollars. No assessor shall approve the bond of any distiller until all the requirements of the law and all regulations made by the Commissioner of Internal Revenue in relation to distilleries, in pursuance thereof, shall have been complied with. Any assessor who shall violate the provisions of this section shall forfeit and pay two thousand dollars, and shall be dismissed from office.

Doors of furnaces, tubs, doublers, worm-tanks, &c.

Pipes, how painted, &c.

Bond not to be approved until law and regulations are complied with; assessor violating these provisions to pay penalty.

July 20, 1868.

Apr. 10, 1869, § 1.

SEC. 18. *And be it further enacted,* That every person engaged in distilling or rectifying spirits, and every wholesale liquor dealer, * shall place and keep conspicuously on the outside of his distillery, rectifying establishment, or place of business, a sign, in plain and legible letters, not less than three inches in length, painted in oil-colors or gilded, and of a proper and proportionate width, the name or firm of the distiller, rectifier, [or] wholesale dealer, * with the words: "Registered distillery," "rectifier of spirits," [or] "wholesale liquor-dealer," * as the case may be; and no fence or wall of a height greater than five feet shall be erected or maintained around the premises of any distillery, so as to prevent easy and immediate access to said distillery; and every

Signs to be put up by distillers, rectifiers, and wholesale liquor-dealer.

Distillery fences.

Distiller to furnish keys of gates and doors. distiller shall furnish to the assessor of the district as many keys of the gates and doors of the distillery as may be required by the assessor, from time to time, for any revenue officer or other person who may be authorized to make survey or inspections of the premises or of the contents thereof; and said distillery shall be kept always accessible to any officer or other person having any such key. Any person Penalties. who shall violate any of the foregoing provisions of this section by negligence or refusal, or otherwise, shall pay a penalty of five hundred dollars. Any person *other than a* June 6, 1872, § 12. *rectifier or wholesale liquor dealer who has paid the special tax, or a distiller who has given the bond*, as required by law, who shall put up *or keep up* the sign required by this section, or any sign indicating that he may lawfully carry on the business Apr. 10, 1869, § 1. of a distiller, rectifier, [or] wholesale liquor dealer, * shall forfeit and pay one thousand dollars, and, on conviction, shall be imprisoned not less than one month nor more than six months; and any person who shall work in any distillery, rectifying establishment, [or] wholesale liquor-store, * on which no sign shall be placed and kept as here- Ibid. inbefore provided, and any person who shall knowingly receive at, carry, or convey, any distilled spirits to or from any such distillery, rectifying establishment, warehouse, or store, or who shall knowingly carry and deliver any grain, molasses, or other raw material to any distillery on which such sign shall not be placed and kept, shall forfeit all horses, carts, drays, wagons, or other vehicle or animal used in carrying or conveying of such property aforesaid, and, on conviction, shall be fined not less than one hundred dollars nor more than one thousand dollars, or be imprisoned not less than one month nor more than six months.

July 20, 1868. SEC. 19. *And be it further enacted*, That every person Distiller's books, entries. making or distilling spirits, or owning any still, boiler, or other vessel used for the purpose of distilling spirits, or having such still, boiler, or other vessel so used under his superintendence, either as agent or owner, or using any such still, boiler, or other vessel, shall, from day to day, make, or cause to be made, true and exact entry in a book or books, to be kept by him, in such form as the Commissioner of Internal Revenue may prescribe, of the kind of materials, and the quantity in pounds, bushels, or gallons purchased by him for the production of spirits, from whom and when purchased, and by what conveyance delivered at said distillery, together with the amount paid therefor, the kind and quantity of fuel purchased for use in the distillery, and from whom purchased, the amount paid for ice or water for use in the distillery, the repairs placed on said distillery or distilling apparatus, the cost thereof, and by whom and when made, and the name and residence of each person employed in or about the distillery, and in what capacity employed; and in another book shall make like entry [of] the quantity of grain or other material used for the production of spirits, the time of day when any yeast or other composition is put into any mash or beer for the purpose of exciting fermentation, the quantity of mash in each tub, designating the same by the number of the tub, the number of dry inches, that is to say, the number of inches between the top of each tub and the surface of the mash or beer therein at the time of yeasting, the gravity and temperature of the beer at the time of yeasting, and on every day thereafter its quantity, gravity and temperature at the hour of twelve meridian; also, the time when any fermenting tub is emptied of ripe mash or beer, the number of gallons of spirits distilled, the number of gallons placed in warehouse, and the proof thereof, and the number of gallons sold or removed, with the proof thereof, and the name, place of business and residence of the person to whom sold; and every fermenting tub shall be emptied at the end of the fermenting period, and shall remain empty for a period of twenty-four hours. On the first * days of each month, or within five days thereafter, respectively, every distiller shall render to the assistant assessor an account in duplicate, taken from his books, stating the quantity and kind of materials used for the production of spirits each day, and the number of wine gallons and of proof gallons of spirits produced and placed in warehouse. And the distiller or the principal manager of the distillery shall make and subscribe the following oath, to be attached to said return:—

June 6, 1872, § 12.

Distiller's monthly return.

"I, ——— ———, distiller, (or principal manager, as the case may be,) of the distillery at ———, do solemnly swear that, since the date of the last return of the business of said distillery, dated ——— day of ——— to ——— day of ———, both inclusive, there was produced in said distillery, and withdrawn and placed in warehouse, the number of wine gallons and proof gallons of spirits, and there were actually mashed and used in said distillery, and consumed in the production of spirits therein, the several quantities of grain, sugar, molasses, and other materials, respectively, hereinbefore specified, and no more."

The said book shall always be kept at the distillery, and be always open to the inspection of any revenue officer, and, when filled up, shall be preserved by the distiller for a period not less than two years thereafter, and whenever required shall be produced for the inspection of any revenue officer. * * And if any * false entry shall be made, or any entry shall be omitted therefrom with intent to defraud or to conceal from the revenue officers any fact or particular required to be stated and entered in either of said books, or to mislead in reference thereto, or if any distiller as aforesaid shall omit or refuse to provide either of said books, or shall cancel, obliterate, or destroy any part of either of such books, or any entry therein, with intent to defraud, or shall permit the same to be done, or such books, or either of them, be not produced when required by any revenue officer, the distillery, distilling apparatus, and the lot or tract of land on which it stands, and all personal property of every kind and description on said premises used in the business there carried on, shall be forfeited to the United States. And any person making such false entry or omitting to make any entry hereinbefore required to be made, with the intent aforesaid, or who shall cause or procure the same to be done, or who shall fraudulently cancel, obliterate, or destroy any

Book to be always kept at distillery, and open to inspection and preserved two years.

June 6, 1872, § 12.

False entries, omitting or refusing to provide books or produce the same, &c.

Penalty.

part of said books, or any entry therein, or who shall wilfully fail to produce such books or either of them, on conviction, shall be fined not less than five hundred dollars nor more than five thousand dollars, and imprisoned not less than six months nor more than two years.

July 20, 1868.

June 6, 1872, § 13.

Assessment for deficiencies.

SEC. 20. *And be it further enacted, That on the receipt of the distiller's return in each month, the assessor shall inquire and determine whether the distiller has accounted for all the grain or molasses used, and all the spirits produced by him in the preceding month. If the assessor is satisfied that the distiller has reported all the spirits produced by him, and the quantity so reported shall be found to be less than eighty per centum of the producing capacity of the distillery as estimated under the provisions of this act, an assessment shall be made for such deficiency at the rate of seventy cents for every proof gallon. In determining the quantity of grain used, fifty-six pounds shall be accounted as a bushel; and if the assessor finds that the distiller has used any grain or molasses in excess of the capacity of his distillery as estimated under the provisions of this act, an assessment shall be made against the distiller at the rate of seventy cents for every proof gallon of spirits that should have been produced from the grain or molasses so used in excess, which assessment shall be made whether the quantity of spirits reported is equal to or exceeds eighty per centum of the producing capacity of the distillery. If the assessor finds that the distiller has not accounted for all the spirits produced by him, he shall, from all the evidence he can obtain, determine what quantity of spirits was actually produced by such distiller, and an assessment shall be made for the difference between the quantity reported and the quantity shown to have been actually produced, at the rate of seventy cents for every proof gallon: Provided, That the actual product shall be assumed to be in no case less than eighty per centum of the producing capacity of the distillery as estimated under the provisions of this act, or under the act to which this is an amendment. Any and all assessments made under this section shall be a lien on all distilled spirits on the distillery premises, the distillery used for distilling the same, the stills, vessels, fixtures, and tools therein, and on the tract of land whereon the said distillery is located, together with any building thereon, from the time such assessment is made until the same shall have been paid.*

Assessment to be a lien on distillery, &c.

July 20, 1868.

Store-keeper to have charge of distillery.

Store-keeper's record of distillery operations.

SEC. 21. *And be it further enacted*, That the storekeeper assigned to any distillery warehouse shall also have charge of the distillery connected therewith; and, in addition to the duties required of him as a storekeeper in charge of a warehouse, shall keep in a book to be provided for that purpose, and in the manner to be prescribed by the Commissioner of Internal Revenue, a daily account of all the meal and vegetable productions or other substances brought into said distillery, or on said premises, to be used for the purpose of producing spirits, from whom purchased, and when delivered at said distillery, the kind and quantity of all fuel used, and from whom purchased, and of all repairs made on said distillery, and by whom and when made, the names and places of residence of all persons employed in or about the distillery, of the materials put into the mash tub, or otherweis used for the production of spirits, the time when any fermenting tub is emptied of ripe mash or beer, recording the same by the number painted on said tub, and of all spirits drawn off from the receiving cistern, and the time when the same were drawn off. Any distiller or person employed in any distillery who shall use, cause, or permit to be used any material for the purpose of making mash, wort, or beer, or for the production of spirits, or shall remove any spirits in the absence of the storekeeper or person designated to act as said storekeeper, shall forfeit and pay double the amount of taxes on the spirits so produced, distilled, or removed, and, in addition thereto, be liable to a penalty of one thousand dollars.

July 20, 1868.

Production of distilled spirits, when deemed to have commenced.

SEC. 22. *And be it further enacted*, That every distiller, at the hour of twelve meridian, on the third day after that on which his bond shall have been approved by the assessor, shall be deemed to have commenced and thereafter to be continuously engaged in the production of distilled spirits in his distillery, except in the intervals when he shall have suspended work, as hereinafter authorized or provided. Any distiller desiring to suspend work in his distillery may give notice in writing to the assistant assessor of his division, stating when he will suspend work; and on the day mentioned in said notice said assistant assessor shall, at the expense of the distiller, proceed to fasten securely the door of every furnace of every still or boiler in said distillery, by locks and otherwise, and shall adopt such other means as the Commissioner of Internal Revenue shall prescribe to prevent the lighting of any fire in such furnace or under such stills or boilers. The locks and seals, and other materials required for such purpose, shall be furnished to the assessor of the district by the Commissioner of Internal Revenue, to be duly accounted for by said assessor. Such notice by any distiller, and the action taken by the assistant assessor in pursuance thereof, shall be immediately reported to the assessor of the district, and by him transmitted to the Commissioner of Internal Revenue. No distiller, after having given such notice, shall, after the time stated therein, carry on the business of a distiller on said premises until he shall have given another notice in writing to said assessor, stating the time when he will resume work; and at the time so stated for resuming work the assistant assessor shall attend at the distillery to remove said locks and other fastenings; and thereupon, and not before, work may be resumed in said distillery, which fact shall be immediately reported to the assessor of the district, and by him transmitted to the Commissioner of Internal Revenue. Any distiller, after the time fixed in said notice declaring his intention to suspend work, who shall carry on the business of a distiller on said premises, or shall have mash, wort, or beer in his distillery, or on any premises connected therewith, or who shall have in his possession or under his control any mash, wort, or beer, with intent to distill the same on said premises, shall incur the forfeitures and be subject to the same punishment as provided for persons who carry on the business of a distiller without *having given the bond*

Notice of suspension of work.

Locks and seals to be furnished to assessor.

Notice of resumption of work.

Penalties.

June 6, 1872, § 12. Exception as to suspensions caused by unavoidable accident.

required by law: Provided, That nothing in this section shall be held to apply to suspensions caused by unavoidable accident; and the Commissioner of Internal Revenue shall prescribe rules and regulations to govern in such cases of involuntary suspension.

July 20, 1868. Drawing off, gauging, and removal of spirits to warehouse.

SEC. 23. *And be it further enacted*, That all distilled spirits shall be drawn from the receiving cisterns into casks, each of not less capacity than twenty gallons wine measure, and shall thereupon be gauged, proved, and marked by an internal revenue gauger, by cutting on the cask containing such spirits, in a manner to be prescribed by the Commissioner of Internal Revenue, the quantity in wine gallons, and in proof gallons, of the contents of such cask, and shall be immediately removed into the distillery warehouse, and the gauger shall, in presence of the storekeeper of the warehouse, place upon the head of the cask an engraved stamp, which shall be signed by the collector of the district and the storekeeper and gauger, and shall have written thereon the number of proof gallons contained therein, the name of the distiller, the date of the receipt in the warehouse, and the serial number of each cask, in progressive order, as the same shall be received from the distillery. Such serial number for every distillery shall begin with number one (No. 1) with the first cask deposited therein after this act takes effect, and no two or more casks warehoused at the same distillery shall be marked with the same number. The said stamp shall be as follows:—

Distillery-warehouse stamp.

Distillery warehouse stamp No. ——.

Issued by —— ——, collector, —— district, State of ——. Distillery warehouse of ——, 18—. Cask No. ——, contents —— gallons, proof spirit.

—— ——,
United States Storekeeper.

Attest:

—— ——,
United States Gauger.

June 6, 1872, § 12. Entry for deposit in distillery warehouse.

And the distiller or owner of all spirits so removed to the distillery warehouse shall on the first * *day* of each month, or within five days thereafter, enter the same for deposit in such warehouse, under such rules and regulations, not inconsistent herewith, as the Commissioner of Internal Revenue may prescribe; and said entry shall be in triplicate, and shall contain the name of the person making the entry, the designation of the warehouse in which the deposit is made, and the date thereof, and [shall] be in form as follows:

Entry for deposit in distillery warehouse.

Entry of distilled spirits deposited by —— ——, in distillery warehouse ——, in the —— district, State of ——, on the —— day of ——, anno Domini ——.

And the entry shall specify the kind of spirits, the whole number of casks, the marks and serial numbers thereon, the number of gauge or wine gallons and of proof gallons, and the amount of the tax on the spirits contained in them; all of which shall be verified by the oath or affirmation of the distiller or owner of the same attached to the entry; and the said distiller or owner shall give his bond in duplicate, with one or more sureties satisfactory to the collector of the district, conditioned that the principal named in said bond will pay the tax on the spirits, as specified in the entry, or cause the same to be paid, before removal from said distillery warehouse, and within one year from the date of said bond; and the penal sum of such bond shall not be less than double the amount of the tax on such distilled spirits. One of said entries shall be retained in the office of the collector of the district, one sent to the storekeeper in charge of the warehouse, to be retained and filed in the warehouse, and one sent with the duplicate of the bond to the Commissioner of Internal Revenue, to be filed in his office.

Bond for payment of tax.

SEC. 24. *And be it further enacted*, That any distilled spirits may, on payment of the tax thereon, be withdrawn from warehouse on application to the collector of the district in charge of such warehouse, on making a withdrawal entry, in duplicate, and in form as follows:—

July 20, 1868.

Withdrawal from warehouse, entry for.

Entry for withdrawal of distilled spirits from warehouse.
Tax paid.

Entry of distilled spirits to be withdrawn, on payment of the tax, from —— warehouse by —— ——, deposited on the —— day of ——, anno Domini ——, by —— ——, in said warehouse.

And the entry shall specify the whole number of casks with the marks and serial numbers thereon, the number of gauge or wine gallons, and of proof gallons, and the amount of the tax on the distilled spirits contained in them; all of which shall be verified by the oath or affirmation of the person making such entry; and on payment of the tax the collector shall issue his order to the storekeeper in charge of the warehouse for the delivery. One of said entries shall be filed in the office of the collector, and the other transmitted by him to the Commissioner of Internal Revenue.

SEC. 25. *And be it further enacted*, That whenever an order is received from the collector for the removal from any distillery warehouse of any cask of distilled spirits, on which tax has been paid, it shall be the duty of the gauger by whom the same is gauged and inspected, in presence of the storekeeper, before such cask has left the warehouse, to place upon the head thereof, in such manner as to cover no portion of any brand or mark prescribed by law already placed thereon, a stamp, on which shall be engraved the number of proof gallons contained in said cask on which the tax has been paid, and which shall be signed by the collector of the district, storekeeper, and gauger, and which shall state the serial number of the cask, the name of the person by whom the tax was paid, and the person to whom and the place where it is to be delivered; which stamp shall be as follows:—

July 20, 1868.

Gauger to mark and stamp spirits removed from warehouse.

Tax-paid stamp.

Tax-paid stamp No. ——.

Received —— —— 18—, from —— ——, tax on

—— gallons proof spirit, cask No. —, ——— warehouse at ——, for delivery to ——— at ———.

——— ———,
Collector —— *District, State of* ——.

Attest:

——— ———,
U. S. Storekeeper.

——— ———,
U. S. Gauger.

And at the time of affixing the tax-paid stamp or stamps, the gauger shall, in the presence of the storekeeper, cut or burn upon each cask the name of the distiller, the district, the date of the payment of [the] tax, the number of proof gallons, and the number of the stamp, which cutting or burning shall be erased when such cask is emptied, by cutting or burning a canceling line across such marks or brands. Whenever any cask or package of rectified spirits shall be filled for shipment, sale, or delivery, on the premises of any rectifier, who shall have paid the special tax required by law, it shall be the duty of a United States gauger to gauge and inspect the same and place thereon an engraved stamp, which shall be signed by the collector of the district and the said gauger, and state the date when affixed, and the number of proof gallons, which stamp shall be as follows:—

Gauging and stamping rectified spirits.

Stamp for rectified spirits.

Stamp for rectified spirits No. ——.

Issued by ——— ———, collector, —— district, State of ———.

——— ———, rectifier of spirits in the —— district, State of ———, ——— ———, 18—. —— proof gallons.

——— ———,
U. S. Gauger.

Gauging and stamping of spirits on premises of wholesale liquor dealer.
April 10, 1869, § 1.

Whenever any cask or package of distilled spirits shall be filled for shipment, sale, or delivery on the premises of any wholesale liquor-dealer, * it shall be the duty of a United States gauger to gauge and inspect the same, and place thereon an engraved stamp, signed by the collector of the district and the said gauger, stating the name of the * dealer and the date when affixed, and the number of proof gallons, which stamp shall be as follows:—

Ibid.

Wholesale liquor-dealer's stamp.

Wholesale liquor dealer's stamp No. ——.

Issued by ——— ———, collector —— district, State of ———.

——— ———, wholesale liquor dealer, of ———, —— district, State of ———, ——— ———, 18—. —— proof gallons.

——— ———,
U. S. Gauger, ——— *District, State of* ———.

Affixing and cancellation of stamps above designated.

All blanks in any of the above forms shall be duly filled in accordance with the facts in each case. And the stamps above designated shall be affixed so as to fasten the same securely to the cask or package and duly canceled, and shall then be immediately covered with a coating of transparent varnish or other substance, so as to protect them from removal or damage by exposure; and such affixing, cancellation, and covering shall be done in such manner as the Commissioner of Internal Revenue shall by regulation prescribe; but such stamps shall in every case be affixed to a smooth surface of the cask or other package, which surface shall not have been previously painted or covered with any substance.

July 20, 1868.

Stamps, how issued.

SEC. 26. *And be it further enacted*, That all stamps required for distilled spirits shall be engraved in their several kinds in book form, and shall be issued by the Commissioner of Internal Revenue to any collector, upon his requisition, in such numbers as may be necessary in the several districts. Each stamp shall have an engraved stub attached thereto with a number thereon corresponding with an engraved number on the stamp, and the stub shall not be removed from the book. And there shall be entered on the corresponding stub such memoranda of the contents of every stamp as shall be necessary to preserve a perfect record of the use of such stamp when detached.

Stubs.

July 20, 1868.

Stamps, form of.

SEC. 27. *And be it further enacted*, That every stamp for the payment of tax on distilled spirits shall have engraved thereon words and figures representing a decimal number of gallons, and a similar number of gallons shall be engraved on the stub corresponding to such stamp, and between the stamp and the stub, and connecting them, shall be engraved nine coupons, which, beginning next to the stamp, shall indicate in succession the several numbers of gallons between the number named in the stamp and the decimal number next above. And whenever any collector shall receive the tax on the distilled spirits contained in any cask, he shall detach from the book a stamp representing the denominate quantity nearest to the quantity of proof spirits in such cask, as shown by the gauger's return, with such number of the coupons attached thereto as shall be necessary to make up the whole number of proof gallons in said cask, and any *fractional part of a gallon amounting to one-half gallon or over* in addition to the number of full gallons * shall be regarded as a full gallon; *and any fractional part of a gallon less than one-half gallon in any cask or package shall be exempt from tax;* and all unused coupons shall remain attached to the marginal stub; and no coupon shall have any value or significance whatever when detached from the stamp and stub. And the tax-paid stamps with the coupons may denote such number of gallons, not less than twenty, as the Commissioner of Internal Revenue may deem advisable.

How used.

Coupons.

June 6, 1872, § 12.

Ibid.

July 20, 1868.

Accountability for stamp-books.

SEC. 28. *And be it further enacted*, That the books of tax-paid stamps issued to any collector shall be charged to his account at the full value of the tax on the number of gallons represented on the stamps and coupons contained in said books; and every collector shall make a monthly return to the Commissioner of Internal Revenue of all tax-paid stamps issued by him to be affixed to any cask or package containing distilled spirits, on which the tax has been paid, and account for the amount of the tax collected; and when the

Monthly return to be made.

Books of stubs to be returned to Commissioner.

said collector shall return to the Commissioner of Internal Revenue any book of marginal stubs, which it shall be his duty to do as soon as all the stamps contained in the book, when issued to him from the office of internal revenue, have been used, and shall have accounted for the tax on the number of gallons represented on the stamps and coupons that were contained in said book, there shall be allowed a commission of half of one per centum on the amount of the tax on spirits distilled after the passage of this act, in addition to any other commission by law allowed, which shall be equally divided between the collector receiving the tax and the assessor of the district in which the distilled spirits were produced.

Distilled-spirit stamps, other than tax-paid, value 10 cents.

June 6, 1872, § 12.

Books of stamps may be intrusted to gauger by collector.

All stamps relating to distilled spirits other than the tax-paid stamps shall be charged to collectors as representing the value of *ten* cents for each stamp; and the books containing such stamps may be intrusted by any collector to the gauger of the district, who shall make a daily report to the assessor and collector of all such stamps used by him, and for whom used, and from these reports the assessor of the district shall assess the person for whom they were used, and the collector shall thereupon

June 6, 1872, § 12.

collect the amount due for such stamps at the rate of *ten* cents for each stamp issued during the month; and when all the stamps contained in any such book shall have been issued, the gauger of the district shall return the book to the collector with all the marginal stubs therein.

June 6, 1872.

Restamping distilled spirits on which stamps have been lost or destroyed.

SEC. 15. That the Commissioner of Internal Revenue is hereby authorized, under regulations to be by him prescribed, with the approval of the Secretary of the Treasury, to issue tax-paid stamps for the restamping of distilled spirits upon which the tax shall have been duly paid but from which the stamps have been lost or destroyed by unavoidable accident.

July 20, 1868.

Officer using, or issuing, or permitting the use of stamps contrary to law; penalty.

SEC. 29. *And be it further enacted*, That any revenue officer who shall affix or cancel, or cause or permit to be affixed or canceled, any stamp relating to distilled spirits required or provided for in this act in any other manner or in any other place, or who shall issue the same to any other person than as provided by law, or regulation made in pursuance thereof, or who shall knowingly affix or permit to be affixed any such stamp to any cask or package of spirits of which the whole or any part has been distilled, rectified, compounded, removed, or sold, in violation of law, or which has in any manner escaped payment of tax due thereon, shall, for every such offense, be fined not less than five hundred dollars nor more than three thousand dollars, and be imprisoned for not less than six months nor more than three years.

July 20, 1868.

Reduction of capacity of distillery.

SEC. 30. *And be it further enacted*, That if any distiller shall desire to reduce the producing capacity of his distillery, he shall give notice of such intention in writing to said assessor, stating the quantity of spirits which he desires thereafter to manufacture or produce every twenty-four hours, and thereupon said assessor shall proceed, at the expense of the distiller, to reduce and limit the producing capacity of the distillery to the quantity stated in said notice, by placing upon a sufficient number of the fermenting tubs close-fitting covers, which shall be securely fastened by nails, seals, and otherwise, and in such manner as to prevent the use of such tubs without removing said covers or breaking said seals, and shall adopt such other precautions as shall be prescribed by the Commissioner of Internal Revenue to reduce the capacity of said distillery. And any person who shall break, injure, or in any manner tamper with any lock, seal, or other fastening applied to any furnace, still, or fermenting tub, or other vessel, in pursuance of the provisions of this act, or who shall open or attempt to open any door, tub, or other vessel which shall have been locked or sealed, or otherwise closed or fastened as herein provided, or who shall use any furnace, still, or fermenting tub, or other vessel which shall be so locked, sealed, or fastened, shall be deemed guilty of a felony, and, on conviction, shall be fined not less than one thousand dollars, nor more than five thousand dollars, and imprisoned for not less than one year nor more than three years.

Breaking, injuring, tampering with locks, seals, &c.

Using any furnace, still, &c., which shall be locked.

Penalty.

SEC. 31. *And be it further enacted*, That whenever any officer shall require that the water contained in any worm-tub in a distillery, at any time when the still shall not be at work, shall be drawn off, and the tub and worm cleansed, the water shall forthwith be drawn off, and the tub and worm cleansed by the distiller or his workmen accordingly; and the water shall be kept and continued out of such worm tub for the space of two hours, or until the officer has finished his examination thereof; and for any refusal or neglect to comply with the requisition of the officer in this behalf, or the provision in this clause contained, the distiller shall forfeit the sum of one thousand dollars, and it shall be lawful for the officer to draw off such water, or any portion of it, and to keep the same drawn off for so long a time as he shall think necessary.

July 20, 1868.

Drawing off water, cleansing worm-tub, &c., when required by officer.

Penalty for refusal or neglect to comply.

SEC. 32. *And be it further enacted*, That it shall be lawful for any revenue officer, at all times, as well by night as by day, to enter into any distillery, or building, or place, used for the business of distilling, or in connection therewith, for storage or other purposes, and to examine, gauge, measure, and take an account of every still or other vessel or utensil of any kind, and of all low wines, and of the quantity and gravity of all mash, wort, or beer, and of all yeast, or other compositions for exciting or producing fermentation in any mash or beer, and of all spirits and of all materials for making or distilling spirits, which shall be in any such distillery or premises, or in the possession of the distiller; and if any revenue officer, or any person called by him to his aid, shall be hindered, obstructed, or prevented by any distiller or by any workman, or other person acting for such distiller or in his employ from entering into any such distillery, or building, or place as aforesaid; or if any such officer shall be by the distiller, or his workman, or any person in his employ, prevented or hindered from, or opposed, or obstructed, or molested in the performance of his duty under this act, in any respect, the distiller shall forfeit the sum of one thousand dollars. If any officer, having de-

July 20, 1868.

Power of revenue officers to enter and examine distilleries; penalty for obstructing.

manded admittance into a distillery or premises of a distillery, and having declared his name and office, shall not be admitted into such distillery or premises by the distiller or other person having charge of the same, it shall be lawful for such officer, at all times, as well by night as by day, to break open by force any of the doors or windows, or to break through any of the walls of such distillery or premises necessary to be broken open or through, to enable him to enter the said distillery or premises; and the distiller shall forfeit the sum of one thousand dollars.

July 20, 1868.

April 10, 1869, § 1.

Distillers and rectifiers to furnish facilities for examination.

SEC. 33. *And be it further enacted*, That on the demand of any revenue officer, every distiller, [or] rectifier, * shall furnish strong, safe, and convenient ladders of sufficient length to enable the officer to examine and gauge any vessel or utensil in such distillery or premises; and shall, at all times when required, supply all assistance, lights, ladders, tools, staging, or other things necessary for inspecting the premises, stock, tools, and apparatus belonging to such person, and shall open all doors, and open for examination all boxes, packages, and all casks, barrels, and other vessels not under the control of a revenue officer in charge, under a penalty of five hundred dollars for every refusal or neglect so to do.

Penalty.

July 20, 1868.

Officers to break up ground or walls in order to examine

April 10, 1869, § 1.

SEC. 34. *And be it further enacted*, That it shall be lawful for any revenue officer, and any person acting in his aid to break up the ground on any part of the distillery or premises of a distiller, [or] rectifier, * or any ground adjoining or near to such distillery or premises, or any wall or partition thereof, or belonging thereto, or other place, to search for any pipe, cock, private conveyance, or utensil; and upon finding any such pipe or conveyance leading therefrom or thereto, he may break up any ground, house, wall, or other place through or into which such pipe or other conveyance shall lead, and break or cut away such pipe or other conveyance, and turn any cock, or examine whether such pipe or other conveyance may convey or conceal any mash, wort, or beer, or other liquor which may be used for distillation of low wines or spirits from the sight or view of the officer, so as to prevent or hinder him from taking a true account thereof.

July 20, 1868.

No process for mashing or distilling between 11 p. m. of Saturday and 1 a. m. of Monday.

SEC. 35. *And be it further enacted*, That no malt, corn, grain, or other material shall be mashed, nor any mash, wort, or beer brewed or made, nor any still used by a distiller at any time between the hour of eleven in the afternoon of any Saturday and the hour of one in the forenoon of the next succeeding Monday; and any person who shall violate the provisions of this section shall be liable to a penalty of one thousand dollars.

July 20, 1868.

Spirits unlawfully removed from distillery or warehouse forfeited.

SEC. 36. *And be it further enacted*, That all distilled spirits found elsewhere than in a distillery or distillery warehouse, not having been removed therefrom according to law, shall be forfeited to the United States. And in case of the seizure of any distilled spirits found elsewhere than in a distillery, distillery warehouse, or other warehouse for distilled spirits authorized by law, or in the store or place of

April 10, 1869, § 1.

business of a rectifier, or of a wholesale liquor-dealer, * or in transit from any one of said places; and in case of the seizure of any distilled spirits found in any one of the places aforesaid, or in transit therefrom, which shall not have been received into or sent out therefrom in conformity to law, or in regard to which any of the entries required by law to be made in the books of the owner of such spirits or of the storekeeper, wholesale dealer, [or] rectifier, * have not been made at the time or in the manner required, or in respect to which the owner or person having possession, control, or charge of said spirits shall have omitted to do any act required to be done, or shall have done or committed any act prohibited in regard to said spirits, the burden of proof shall be upon the claimant of said spirits to show that no fraud has been committed, and that all the requirements of the law in relation to the payment of the tax have been complied with. And any person who shall remove or shall aid or abet in the removal of any distilled spirits on which the tax has not been paid, to a place other than the distillery warehouse provided by law, or who shall conceal or aid in the concealment of any spirits so removed, or who shall remove or shall aid or abet in the removal of any distilled spirits from any distillery warehouse, or other warehouse for distilled spirits authorized by law, in any manner other than is provided by law, or who shall conceal or aid in the concealment of any spirits so removed, shall be liable to a penalty of double the tax imposed on such distilled spirits so removed or concealed, and shall, on conviction, be fined not less than two hundred dollars nor more than five thousand dollars, and imprisoned not less than three months nor more than three years.

Burden of proof, in case of seizure upon claimant.

Apr. 10, 1869, § 1.

Removal of spirits on which tax has not been paid, contrary to law, concealment of removal; aiding, &c.; penalty.

Provided, That the tax upon any spirits distilled and removed from the place where the same were distilled, and not deposited in bonded warehouse as required by law, shall, at any time, upon knowledge of such fact obtained by the assessor or assistant assessor of the district where such spirits were distilled, be assessed by him upon the distiller of the same, and certified or returned to the collector, who shall immediately demand payment of such tax, and upon the neglect or refusal of payment by the distiller, shall proceed to collect the same by distraint. But this provision shall not exclude any other remedy or proceeding provided by law.

Proviso, § 14, March 2, 1867.

Assessment of tax on spirits removed without deposit in warehouse, as required by law.

Provided further, That any person who shal ship, transport or remove any spirituous or fermented liquors or wines, under any other than the proper name or brand known to the trade as designating the kind and quality of the contents of the casks or packages containing the same, or who shall cause the same to be done, shall forfeit the same, and shall, on conviction thereof, be subject to and pay a fine of five hundred dollars.

Proviso, July 13, 1866, § 29.

Shipping spirituous or fermented liquors or wines under false name or brand.

SEC. 37. *And be it further enacted*, That no person shall remove any distilled spirits at any other time than after sun-rising and before sun-setting, in any cask or package containing more than ten gallons from any premises or building in which the same may have been distilled, redistilled, recti-

July 20, 1868.

Distilled spirits not to be removed at any other time than after sunrising and before sunsetting.

fied, compounded, manufactured, or stored, and every person who shall violate this provision shall be liable to a penalty of one hundred dollars for each cask, barrel, or package of spirits so removed; and said spirits, together with any vessel containing the same, and any horse, cart, boat, or other conveyance used in the removal thereof, shall be forfeited to the United States.

July 20, 1868.

Adding substances to create fictitious proof.

SEC. 38. *And be it further enacted*, That any person who shall add or cause to be added any ingredient or substance to any distilled spirits, before the tax imposed by law shall have been paid thereon, for the purpose of creating a fictitious proof, shall, on conviction, be fined not less than one hundred dollars nor more than one thousand dollars for each cask or package so adulterated, and imprisoned not less than three months nor more than two years, and every such cask or package, with its contents, shall be forfeited to the United States.

July 20, 1868.

Evading payment of the tax on spirits.

Changing mark or brand on any cask, &c.

Fraudulent use of cask or package.

SEC. 39. *And be it further enacted*, That any person who shall evade or attempt to evade the payment of the tax on any distilled spirits, in any manner whatever, shall forfeit and pay double the amount of the tax so evaded or attempted to be evaded; and any person who shall change or alter any stamp, mark or brand on any cask or package containing distilled spirits, or who shall put into any cask or package spirits of greater strength than is indicated by the inspection mark thereon, or who shall fraudulently use any cask or package having any inspection mark or stamp thereon for the purpose of selling other spirits or spirits of quantity or quality different from the spirits previously inspected therein, shall forfeit and pay the sum of two hundred dollars for every cask or package on which the stamp or mark is so changed or altered, or which is so fraudulently used, and, on conviction, shall be fined for each such offence not less than one hundred dollars nor more than one thousand dollars, and imprisoned not less than one month nor more than one year.

July 20, 1868.

Using false weights, &c., in ascertaining materials; using unregistered materials for distillation.

SEC. 40. *And be it further enacted*, That any person who shall knowingly use any false weights or measures in ascertaining, weighing, or measuring the quantities of grain, meal, or vegetable materials, molasses, beer, or other substances to be used for distillation, or who shall destroy, break, injure, or tamper with any lock or seal which may be placed on any cistern-room or building, by the duly authorized officers of the revenue, or shall open said lock or seal, or the door to such cistern-room or building, or shall in any manner gain access to the contents therein in the absence of the proper officer, shall, on conviction, be fined not less than five hundred dollars nor more than five thousand dollars, and imprisoned not less than one year nor more than three years; and any person who shall use any molasses, beer, or other substance, whether fermented on the premises or elsewhere, for the purpose of producing spirits, before an account for the same shall have been registered in the proper record-book provided for that purpose, shall forfeit and pay the sum of one thousand dollars for each and every offense so committed.

SEC. 41. *And be it further enacted*, That it shall be lawful for any internal-revenue officer to detain any cask or package containing, or supposed to contain, distilled spirits, when such officer has reason to believe the tax imposed by law upon the same has not been paid, or that the same is being removed in violation of law; and every such cask or package may be held by such officer at a safe place until it shall be determined whether the property so detained is liable by law to be proceeded against for forfeiture; but such summary detention shall not continue in any case longer than forty-eight hours, without process of law or intervention of the officer to whom such detention is to be reported.

July 20, 1868.

Power of officers to detain packages of spirits for forty-eight hours on suspicion.

SEC. 42. *And be it further enacted*, That no distillery nor distilling apparatus seized for any violation of law shall be released to the claimant or any intervening party before judgment, except in case of a distillery for which *bond has been given*, and which has a registered producing capacity of one hundred and fifty proof gallons, or more, per day, on showing by sufficient affidavits that there are hogs or other live stock, not less than fifty head in number, depending for their feed on the products of said distillery which would suffer injury if the business of such distillery is stopped; such distillery in that case may be released to the claimant, or any other intervening party, at the discretion of the court, on a bond to be given and approved in open court with two or more sureties for the full appraised value of all the property seized, which value shall be ascertained by three competent appraisers to be designated and appointed by the court. In case of the seizure of and judgment of forfeiture against any distillery used or fit for use in the production of distilled spirits having a registered producing capacity of less than one hundred and fifty gallons per day, or of any distillery *because no bond has been given*, the still, stills, doubler, worm, worm tub, and all mash tubs and fermenting tubs shall be so destroyed as to prevent the use of the same or any part thereof for the purpose of distilling; and the materials shall be sold as in case of other forfeited property.

July 20, 1868.

Release of distillery, &c., seized, before judgment, in what cases.

June 6, 1872, § 12.

Stills, &c., to be destroyed in certain cases of forfeiture.

June 6, 1872, § 12.

SEC. 43. *And be it further enacted*, That it shall be the duty of every person who empties or draws off, or causes to be emptied or drawn off, any distilled spirits from a cask or package bearing any mark, brand, or stamp required by law, at the time of emptying such cask or package, to efface and obliterate said mark, stamp, or brand. *And the Commissioner of Internal Revenue may make such change in stamps and may prescribe such instruments, or other means for attaching, protecting, and canceling stamps for tobacco, snuff, cigars, distilled spirits, and fermented liquors, or either of them, as he and the Secretary of the Treasury shall approve, such instruments to be furnished by the United States to the persons using the stamps to be affixed therewith, under such regulation as the Commissioner of Internal Revenue may prescribe.* Any such cask or package from which said mark, brand, and stamp is not so effaced and obliterated, as herein required, shall be forfeited to the United States, and may be seized by any

July 20, 1868.

Stamps, marks, &c., to be effaced at time of emptying casks.

June 6, 1872, § 1[illegible]

Commissioner may make change in stamps and prescribe instruments for attaching, protecting, and canceling the same.

Penalty for transporting, &c., in violation of this section.

officer of internal revenue wherever found. Any railroad company or other transportation company, or person, who shall receive or transport, or have in possession with intent to transport, or with intent to cause or procure to be transported, any such empty cask or package, or any part thereof, having thereon any brand, mark, or stamp, required by law to be placed on any cask or package containing distilled spirits, shall forfeit three hundred dollars for each such cask or package, or any part thereof, so received or transported, or had in possession with the intent aforesaid; and any boat, railroad car, cart, dray, wagon, or other vehicle, and all horses or other animals used in carrying or transporting the same, shall be forfeited to the United States.

Penalty for failing to efface marks, stamps, &c.

Any person who shall fail or neglect to efface and obliterate said mark, stamp, or brand, at the time of emptying such cask or package, or who shall receive any such cask or package, or any part thereof, with the intent aforesaid, or who shall transport the same, or knowingly aid or assist therein, or who shall remove any stamp provided by this act from any cask or package containing or which had contained distilled spirits, without defacing and destroying the same at the time of such removal, or who shall aid or assist therein, or who shall have in his possession any such stamp so removed, as aforesaid, or have in his possession any canceled stamp or any stamp which has been used, or which purports to have been used, upon any cask or package of distilled spirits, shall be deemed guilty of a felony, and, on conviction, shall be fined not less than five hundred dollars nor more than ten thousand dollars, and imprisoned not less than one year nor more than five years.

Having in possession canceled stamps, &c.

July 13, 1866.

SEC. 38. * * * * *

Buying or selling with inspection marks thereon spirit casks which have been used.

Any person who shall knowingly purchase or sell, with inspection marks thereon, any cask or package, after the same has been used for distilled spirits, * shall forfeit and pay the sum of two hundred dollars for every cask so purchased or used.

* * * * * *

July 20, 1868.

June 6, 1872, § 12.

April 10, 1869, § 1.

Rectifier, wholesale liquor-dealer, retail liquor-dealer, manufacturer of stills, carrying on business without payment of special tax.

Distiller not giving bond, or engaging in the business with intent to defraud the United States.

SEC. 44. *And be it further enacted*, That any person who shall carry on the business of a * rectifier, * wholesale liquor dealer, retail liquor dealer, or manufacturer of stills, without having paid the special tax, as required by law, or who shall carry on the business of a distiller without having given bond as required by law, or who shall engage in or carry on the business of a distiller, with intent to defraud the United States of the tax on the spirits distilled by him, or any part thereof, shall, for every such offense, be fined not less than one thousand dollars nor more than five thousand dollars, and imprisoned not less than six months nor more than two years. And all distilled spirits or wines, and all stills or other apparatus, fit or intended to be used for the distillation or rectification of spirits or for the compounding of liquors, owned by such person, wherever found, and all distilled spirits or wines and personal property found in the distillery or rectifying establishment, * or in any building, room, yard, or enclosure connected therewith, and used with or constituting a part of the premises; and all the right,

April 10, 1869, § 1.

title, and interest of such person in the lot or tract of land on which such distillery is situated, and all right, title, and interest therein of every person who knowingly has suffered or permitted the business of a distiller to be there carried on, or has connived at the same; and all personal property owned by or in possession of any person who has permitted or suffered any building, yard, or enclosure, or any part thereof, to be used for purposes of ingress or egress to or from such distillery which shall be found in any such building, yard, or enclosure, and all the right, title, and interest of every person in any premises used for ingress or egress to or from such distillery, who has knowingly suffered or permitted such premises to be used for such ingress or egress, shall be forfeited to the United States.

SEC. 5. *And be it further enacted*, That every person engaged in carrying on the business of a distiller who shall defraud or attempt to defraud the United States of the tax on the spirits distilled by him, or any part thereof, shall forfeit the distillery and distilling apparatus used by him, and all distilled spirits and all raw materials for the production of distilled spirits found in the distillery and on the distillery premises, and shall, on conviction, be fined not less than five hundred dollars, nor more than five thousand dollars, and be imprisoned not less than six months nor more than three years.

March 31, 1868.

Distiller defrauding or attempting to defraud the United States of tax on spirits.

SEC. 45. *And be it further enacted*, That every rectifier [and] wholesale liquor-dealer * shall provide himself with a book, to be prepared and kept in such form as shall be prescribed by the Commissioner of Internal Revenue, and shall, on the same day on which he receives any spirits, and before he shall draw off any part thereof, or add water or anything thereto, or in any respect alter the same, enter in such book, and in the proper columns respectively prepared for the purpose, the date when, the name of the person or firm from whom, and the place whence the spirits were received, by whom distilled, rectified, or compounded, and when and by whom inspected, and, if in the original package, the serial number of each package, the number of wine gallons and proof gallons, the kind of spirit, and the number and kind of adhesive stamps thereon; and every such rectifier * and wholesale dealer shall, at the time of sending out of his stock or possession any spirits, and before the same shall be removed from his premises, enter, in like manner, in the said book, the day when, and the name and place of business of the person or firm to whom such spirits are to be sent, the quantity and the kind or quality of such spirits, and also the number of gallons and fractions of a gallon at proof; and, if in the original packages in which they were received, he shall enter the name of the distiller and the serial number of the package. And every such book shall be at all times kept in some public or open place on the premises of such rectifier [or] wholesale dealer, * respectively, for inspection; and any revenue officer may make an examination of such book and take an abstract therefrom; and every such book, when it has been filled up as aforesaid, shall be preserved by such rectifier, [or] whole-

July 20, 1868.

April 10, 1869, § 1.

Rectifier's and wholesale liquor-dealer's book.

April 10, 1869, § 1.

Ibid.

April 10, 1869, § 1. sale liquor-dealer * for a period not less than two years; and during such time it shall be produced by him to every revenue officer demanding the same; and if any rectifier, [or]

Ibid. wholesale dealer * shall refuse or neglect to provide such book or to make entries therein as aforesaid, or shall cancel, alter, obliterate, or destroy any part of such book, or any entry therein, or make any false entry therein, or hinder or obstruct any revenue officer from examining such book or making an entry therein, or taking any abstract therefrom; or if such book shall not be preserved or not produced by

Ibid. any rectifier, or wholesale dealer, * as hereinbefore directed, he shall pay a penalty of one hundred dollars, and, on conviction, shall be fined not less than one hundred dollars nor more than five thousand dollars, and imprisoned not less than three months nor more than three years.

July 20, 1868.

April 10, 1869, § 1.

Purchase of quantities greater than twenty gallons from one person.

SEC. 46. *And be it further enacted*, That it shall not be lawful for any rectifier of distilled spirits, * liquor dealer, wholesale or retail liquor dealer, to purchase or receive any distilled spirits in quantities greater than twenty gallons from any person other than an authorized rectifier of dis-

April 10, 1869, § 1. tilled spirits, * distiller, or wholesale liquor dealer. Any person violating this section shall forfeit and pay one thousand dollars: *Provided*, That this shall not be held to apply to judicial sales nor to sales at public auction made by an auctioneer [who has paid a special tax as such.][1]

July 20, 1868.

Spirits drawn into new packages containing ten gallons or more to be gauged and branded.

SEC. 47. *And be it further enacted*, That all distilled spirits drawn from any cask or other package, and placed in any other cask or package containing not less than ten gallons, and intended for sale, shall be again inspected and gauged, and the cask or package into which it is so transferred shall be marked or branded, and such marking and branding shall distinctly indicate the name of the gauger, the time and place of inspection, the proof of the spirits, the particular name of such spirits as known to the trade, together with the name and place of business of the dealer, [or] rec-

Apr. 10, 1869, § 1. tifier, * as the case may be; and in all cases, except where such spirits have been rectified or compounded, the name also of the distiller, and the distillery where such spirits were produced, and the serial number of the original pack-

June 6, 1872, § 12. age, *or in case such spirits shall have been rectified, the name of the rectifier and the serial number of the rectifier's stamp;*

Penalty. and the absence of such mark or brand shall be taken and held as sufficient cause and evidence for the forfeiture of such unmarked packages of spirits.

July 20, 1868.

June 6, 1872, § 12.

Tax on imitation wines.

SEC. 48. *And be it further enacted, That on all wines, liquors, or compounds known or denominated as wine, and made in imitation of sparkling wine or champagne, but not made from grapes grown in the United States, and on all liquors, not made from grapes, currants, rhubarb, or berries grown in the United States, but produced by being rectified or mixed with distilled spirits or by the infusion of any matter in spirits, to be sold as wine, or as a substitute for wine, there shall be levied and collected a tax of ten cents per bottle or package containing not more than one pint, or of twenty cents per bottle or package*

[1] The special tax here referred to was repealed by § 1, act July 14, 1870.

containing more than one pint and not more than one quart, and at the same rate for any larger quantity of such merchandise, however the same may be put up, or whatever may be the package; and the Commissioner of Internal Revenue shall cause to be prepared suitable and special stamps denoting the tax herein imposed, to be affixed to each bottle or package containing such merchandise, by the person manufacturing, compounding, or putting up the same, before removal from the place of manufacture, compounding, or putting up; said stamps to be affixed and canceled in such manner as the Commissioner of Internal Revenue may prescribe; and the absence of such stamp from any bottle or package containing such merchandise shall be prima-facie evidence that the tax thereon has not been paid, and such merchandise shall be forfeited to the United States. Any person counterfeiting, altering, or re-using said stamps shall be subject to the same penalties as are imposed for the same offences in relation to proprietary stamps.

How to be stamped.

SEC. 49. See *Officers.*
SEC. 50. See *Officers.*
SEC. 51. See *Officers.*
SEC. 52. See *Officers.*
SEC. 53. See *Officers.*
SEC. 54. See *Drawback.*

July 20, 1868.
June 6, 1872, § 12.
Exportation of spirits withdrawn from bonded warehouse without payment of tax.

SEC. 55. *And be it further enacted, That distilled spirits may be withdrawn from distillery bonded warehouses, at the instance of the owner of the spirits, for exportation in the original casks, in quantities of not less than one thousand gallons, without the payment of tax, under such rules and regulations, and after making such entries and executing and filing with the collector of the district from which the removal is to be made such bonds and bills of lading, and giving such other additional security as may be prescribed by the Commissioner of Internal Revenue, with the approval of the Secretary of the Treasury: Provided, That bonds given under this section shall be canceled under such regulations as the Secretary of the Treasury shall prescribe.*

All distilled spirits intended for export, as aforesaid, before being removed from the distillery warehouse shall be marked as the Commissioner of Internal Revenue may prescribe, and shall have affixed to each cask an engraved stamp indicative of such intention, to be provided and furnished by the several collectors as in the case of other stamps, and to be charged to them and accounted for in the same manner, and for the expense attending the providing and affixing such stamps twenty-five cents for each package so stamped shall be paid to the collector on making the entry for such transportation. When the owner of the spirits shall have made the proper entries, filed the bonds, and otherwise complied with all the requirements of the law and regulations as herein provided, the collector shall issue to him a permit for the removal and transportation of said spirits to the collector of the port from which the same are to be exported, accurately describing the spirits to be shipped, the amount of tax thereon, the State and district from which the same is to be shipped, the name of the distiller by whom distilled, the port to which the same are to be transported, the name of the collector of the port to whom the spirits are to be consigned, and the route or routes over which they are to be sent to the port of shipment. Such shipment shall be made over bonded routes whenever practicable. The collector of the port shall receive such spirits, and permit the exportation thereof under the same rules and regulations as are prescribed for the exportation of spirits upon which the tax has been paid. Fraudulent claim for drawback. *And if any person shall fraudulently claim, or seek, or obtain an allowance of drawback on any distilled spirits, or shall fraudulently claim any greater allowance or drawback than the tax actually paid thereon, such person shall forfeit and pay to the Government of the United States triple the amount wrongfully and fraudulently sought to be obtained, and, on conviction, shall be imprisoned not more than ten years; and any owner, agent, or master of any vessel or any other person who shall knowingly aid or abet in the fraudulent collection or fraudulent attempt to collect any drawback upon, or shall knowingly aid or permit any fraudulent change in the spirits so shipped, shall, on conviction,* Penalty for. *be fined not exceeding five thousand dollars and imprisoned not more than one year, and the ship or vessel on board of which such shipment was made or pretended to be made shall be forfeited to the United States, whether a conviction of the master or owner be had or otherwise, and proceedings may be had in admiralty by libel for such forfeiture.*

Relanding spirits which have been shipped for exportation.

Any person who shall intentionally reland within the jurisdiction of the United States any distilled spirits which have been shipped for exportation under the provisions of this act, or who shall receive such relanded distilled spirits, and every person who shall aid or abet in such relanding or receiving of such spirits, shall, on conviction, be fined not exceeding five thousand dollars, and imprisoned not more than three years; and all distilled spirits so relanded, together with the vessel from which the same were relanded within the jurisdiction of the United States, and all boats, vehicles, horses, or other animals used in relanding and removing such distilled spirits, shall be forfeited to the United States.

July 20, 1868.

When a warehouse becomes unsafe, &c.

SEC. 56. *And be it further enacted*, That * * * [1] whenever in the opinion of the Commissioner of Internal Revenue any distillery or other warehouse shall become unsafe or unfit for use, or the merchandise therein shall for any reason be liable to loss or great wastage, the Commissioner may discontinue such warehouse, and require that the merchandise therein shall be transferred to such other warehouse as may be designated by him within such time as he shall prescribe. Such transfer shall be made under the supervision of the collector, or such other officer as may be designated by the Commissioner; and the expense thereof shall be paid by the owner of the merchandise; and if the owner of such merchandise shall fail to make such transfer within the time prescribed, or to pay the just and proper expense of such transfer, as ascertained and determined by the Commissioner, such merchandise may be seized and sold

[1] The portion of this section omitted related only to distilled spirits in bonded warehouse July 20, 1868, and has ceased to be operative by the withdrawal of the spirits within the time limited.

by the collector, in the same manner as goods are sold upon distraint for taxes, and the proceeds of such sale shall be applied to the payment of the taxes due thereon and the costs and expenses of such sale and removal, and the balance paid over to the owner of such merchandise.

July 20, 1868.

Stock on hand.

SEC. 57. *And be it further enacted*, That any person owning, or having in his possession, any distilled spirits intended for sale, exceeding in quantity fifty gallons, and not in a bonded warehouse at the time when this act takes effect, shall immediately make a return, under oath, to the collector of the district wherein such spirits may be held, stating the number and kind of packages, together with the marks and brands thereon, and the place where the same are stored, together with the quantity of spirits, as nearly as the owner can determine the same. Upon the receipt of such return the collector, being first satisfied that the tax on said spirits has been paid, shall immediately cause the same to be gauged and proved by an internal revenue gauger, who shall mark, by cutting, the contents and proof on each cask or package containing five wine gallons or more, and shall affix and cancel an engraved stamp thereon, which stamp shall be as follows:

Stamp for stock on hand.

Stamp for stock on hand. No. —.

Issued by ——— ———.

——— ———,

Collector of ——— *district, State of* ———.

Distilled spirits. Tax paid prior to (here engrave the date when this act takes effect.) ——— proof-gallons. Gauged ———, 18 —.

——— ———, *Gauger.*

All distilled spirits owned or held by any person, as aforesaid, shall be included in the same return, and the gauging shall be continuous until all the spirits owned or held by such person are gauged or stamped, as aforesaid, and a report thereof in duplicate shall immediately be made by the gauger to the collector and assessor of the district showing the number of packages, contents, and proof of each package gauged and stamped, and one of said reports shall be transmitted by the collector to the Commissioner of Internal Revenue. No such spirits shall be gauged or stamped in any cistern or other stationary vessel. Any person owning, or having in possession, such spirits and refusing or neglecting to make such return shall forfeit the same; and all distilled spirits found, after thirty days from the time this act takes effect, in any cask or package containing * five gallons *or more*, without having thereon each mark and stamp required therefor by this act, shall be forfeited to the United States. Any person who shall gauge, mark or stamp any cask or package of distilled spirits under the provisions of this section, or who shall cause or procure the same to be done, knowing that the same were manufactured or removed from warehouse subsequent to the taking effect of this act, or that the taxes thereon have not been paid, shall, on conviction, be fined not less than five hundred dollars nor more than five thou-

Penalty for failure to mark and stamp packages.

June 6, 1872, § 12.

sand dollars, and imprisoned not less than six months nor more than three years. All stamps required by this section shall be prepared, issued, and affixed upon casks and packages and canceled in the same manner as provided for other stamps for distilled spirits in this act, and shall be charged at the rate of twenty-five cents for each stamp.

July 20, 1868.

Spirits sold under judicial process, or distraint.

SEC. 58. *And be it further enacted*, That all distilled spirits forfeited to the United States sold by order of court or under process of distraint shall be sold subject to tax; and the purchaser shall immediately, and before he takes possession of said spirits, pay the tax thereon. And any distilled spirits condemned before the passage of this act, and in the possession of the United States, shall be sold as herein provided. And if any tax-paid stamps are affixed to any cask or package so condemned, such stamps shall be obliterated and destroyed by the collector or marshal after forfeiture and before such sale.

Stamp to be destroyed before sale.

SEC. 59. See *Special Taxes*.

July 13, 1866.

Forfeited boilers, stills, &c., to be sold at public auction.

SEC. 44. *And be it further enacted*, That all boilers, stills, or other vessels, tools, and implements, used in distilling or rectifying, and forfeited under any of the provisions of this act, and all condemned material, together with any engine or other machinery connected therewith, and all empty barrels, and all grain or other material suitable for distillation, shall, under the direction of the court in which the forfeiture is recovered, be sold at public auction, and the proceeds thereof, after deducting the expenses of sale, shall be disposed of according to law. And all spirits or spirituous liquors which may be forfeited under the provisions of this act, unless herein otherwise provided, shall be disposed of by the Commissioner of Internal Revenue as the Secretary of the Treasury may direct. * And any word or word in any and all parts of this act, and of all acts to which this act is additional, indicating or referring to person or persons, shall be taken to include partnerships, firms, associations, bodies corporate or politic, or any other party whatsoever, when not otherwise designated, or manifestly incompatible with the intent thereof. * * *

Forfeited liquors to be disposed of by Commissioner.

July 20, 1868, § 2.

Words person or persons to include partnerships, &c.

July 20, 1868, § 42.

TOBACCO AND SNUFF.[1]

SEC. 60. [*The first portion of this section relates to special taxes and will be found under that head. The second portion is printed succeeding section* 71, *post, p.* 91.]

SEC. 61. *And be it further enacted*, That upon tobacco and snuff which shall be manufactured and sold, or removed for consumption or use, there shall be assessed and collected the following taxes: July 20, 1868. Tax on tobacco and snuff.

On snuff, manufactured of tobacco or any substitute for tobacco, ground, dry, damp, pickled, scented, or otherwise, of all descriptions, when prepared for use, a tax of thirty-two cents per pound. And snuff flour, when sold, or removed for use or consumption, shall be taxed as snuff, and shall be put up in packages and stamped in the same manner as snuff. Tax on snuff.

On all chewing and smoking tobacco, fine-cut, cavendish, plug, or twist, cut or granulated, of every description; on tobacco twisted by hand or reduced into a condition to be consumed, or in any manner other than the ordinary mode of drying and curing, prepared for sale or consumption, even if prepared without the use of any machine or instrument, and without being pressed or sweetened; and on all fine-cut shorts and refuse scraps, clippings, cuttings, and sweepings of tobacco, a tax of twenty cents per pound. June 6, 1872, § 31. Tax on chewing and smoking tobacco.

SEC. 62. *And be it further enacted*, That from and after the passage of this act all manufactured tobacco shall be put up and prepared by the manufacturer for sale, or removal for sale or consumption, in packages of the following description, and in no other manner: July 20, 1868. Tobacco and snuff, how put up.

All snuff in packages containing one, two, four, six, eight, and sixteen ounces, or in bladders, *and* in jars containing not exceeding twenty pounds. June 6, 1872, § 31.

All fine-cut chewing tobacco, and all other kinds of tobacco not otherwise provided for, in packages containing * one, two, four, eight, and sixteen ounces, except that fine-cut chewing tobacco may, at the option of the manufacturer, be put up in wooden packages containing ten, twenty, forty, and sixty pounds each. Ibid.

All smoking tobacco, *and all cut and granulated tobacco other than fine-cut chewing, and shorts, the refuse of fine-cut chewing*, all fine-cut shorts which has passed through a Ibid.

---

[1] Section 31 of the act of June 6, 1872, provides as follows:

"That on and after the first day of July next the act entitled 'An act imposing taxes on distilled spirits and tobacco, and for other purposes,' approved July twentieth, eighteen hundred and sixty-eight, be, and the same is hereby, amended as follows:"

The sections of said act following, relating to tobacco, snuff, and cigars, are printed as thus amended.

riddle of thirty-six meshes to the square inch, and all refuse scraps, *clippings*, *cuttings*, and sweepings of tobacco, in packages containing two, four, eight, and sixteen ounces each.

June 6, 1872, § 31.

All cavendish, plug, and twist tobacco in wooden packages not exceeding two hundred pounds net weight.

Ibid.

And every such wooden package shall have printed or marked thereon the manufacturer's name and place of manufacture * and the registered number of the manufactory, and the gross weight, the tare, and the net weight of the tobacco in each package: *Provided*, That these limitations and descriptions of packages shall not apply to tobacco and snuff transported in bond for exportation and actually exported.

Ibid.

Shorts, refuse scraps, clippings, cuttings, and sweepings of tobacco may be sold in bulk, as material, &c., without payment of tax, under restrictions, &c.

And provided further, That fine-cut shorts, the refuse of fine-cut chewing-tobacco, refuse scraps, clippings, cuttings, and sweepings of tobacco may be sold in bulk as material, and without the payment of tax, by one manufacturer directly to another manufacturer, or for export, under such restrictions, rules, and regulations as the Commissioner of Internal Revenue may prescribe: And provided further, That wood, metal, paper, or other materials may be used separately or in combination for packing tobacco, snuff, and cigars, under such regulations as the Commissioner of Internal Revenue may establish.

Wood, metal, paper, &c., may be used in packing.

July 20, 1868.

SEC. 63. *And be it further enacted*, That every person before commencing, or, if already commenced, before continuing the manufacture of tobacco or snuff, shall, in addition to a compliance with all other provisions of law, furnish, without previous demand therefor, to the assessor or assistant assessor of the district where the manufacture is to be carried on, a statement, in duplicate, subscribed under oath or affirmation, accurately setting forth the place, and if in a city, the street and number of the street, where the manufacture is to be carried on; the number of cutting machines, presses, snuff mills, hand mills, or other machines; the name, kind, and quality of the article manufactured, or proposed to be manufactured; and, if the same shall be manufactured for, or to be sold and delivered to, any other person, as agent, or under a special contract, the name and residence and business or occupation of the person for whom the said article is to be manufactured, or to whom it is to be delivered; and shall give a bond in conformity with the provisions of this act, to be approved by the collector of the district, in the sum of two thousand dollars, with an addition to said sum of three thousand dollars for each cutting machine kept for use, of one thousand dollars for each screw-press kept for use in making plug or pressed tobacco, of five thousand dollars for each hydraulic press kept for use, of one thousand dollars for each snuff mill kept for use, and of one thousand dollars for each hand mill, or other mill or machine, kept for the grinding, cutting, or crushing of tobacco; that he will not engage in any attempt, by himself or by collusion with others, to defraud the Government of any tax on his manufactures; that he will render truly and correctly all the returns, statements, and inventories prescribed by law or regulations; that whenever he shall add to the number of cutting machines, presses, snuff mills, hand mills, or other mills or machines as aforesaid, he will

Manufacturer's statement.

Bond.

immediately give notice thereof to the collector of the district; that he will stamp, in accordance with law, all tobacco and snuff manufactured by him before he removes any part thereof from the place of manufacture; that he will not knowingly sell, purchase, expose, or receive for sale any manufactured tobacco or snuff which has not been stamped as required by law; and that he will comply with all the requirements of law relating to the manufacture of tobacco or snuff. *Additional sureties may be required by the collector, from time to time, but the penal sum of said bond shall not be computed by him in excess of the sum of twenty thousand dollars, except under special instructions of the Commissioner of Internal Revenue.* And every manufacturer shall obtain a certificate from the collector of the district, who is hereby authorized and directed to issue the same, setting forth the kind and number of machines, presses, snuff mills, hand mills, or other mills and machines, as aforesaid, for which the bond has been given, which certificate shall be posted in a conspicuous place within the manufactory. And any tobacco manufacturer who shall neglect or refuse to obtain such certificate, or to keep the same posted as hereinbefore provided, shall, on conviction, be fined not less than one hundred dollars nor more than five hundred dollars. And any person manufacturing tobacco or snuff of any description without first giving bond as herein required, shall, on conviction, be fined not less than one thousand dollars nor more than five thousand dollars, and imprisoned for not less than one year nor more than five years. And the working or preparation of any leaf tobacco, or tobacco stems, scraps, clippings, or waste, by sifting, twisting, screening, or any other process, shall be deemed manufacturing.[1]

June 6, 1872, § 31.

Certificate.

Penalties.

What deemed madufacturing.

July 20, 1868.

Sign to be put up by manufacturer of tobacco and snuff.

SEC. 64. *And be it further enacted*, That within thirty days after the passage of this act every manufacturer of tobacco and snuff shall place and keep on the side or end of the building within which his business is carried on, so that it can be distinctly seen, a sign, with letters thereon not less than three inches in length, painted in oil colors, or gilded, giving his full name and business. Any person neglecting to comply with the requirements of this section shall, on conviction, be fined not less than one hundred dollars nor more than five hundred dollars.

July 20, 1868.

Record of manufacturers of tobacco and snuff.

SEC. 65. *And be it further enacted*, That it shall be the duty of every assistant assessor to keep a record, in a book or books to be provided for the purpose, to be open to the inspection of any person, of the name and residence of every person engaged in the manufacture of tobacco or snuff in his division, the place where such manufacture is carried on, and the number of the manufactory; and the assistant assessor shall enter in said record, under the name of each manufacturer, a copy of every inventory required by this act to be made by such manufacturer, and an abstract of his monthly returns; and each assessor shall keep a similar record for the district, and shall cause the several manu-

[1] See definition of manufacturer of tobacco, in section 59, July 20, 1868, as amended. See ante, p. 51.

Manufactories to be numbered.

factories of tobacco or snuff in his district to be numbered consecutively, which numbers shall not thereafter be changed.

July 20, 1868.

Inventory and books of tobacco and snuff manufacturer.

SEC. 66. *And be [it] further enacted*, That every person, now or hereafter engaged in the manufacture of tobacco or snuff, shall make and deliver to the assistant assessor of the division a true inventory, in such form as shall be prescribed by the Commissioner of Internal Revenue, of the quantity of each of the different kinds of tobacco, snuff-flour, snuff, stems, scraps, clippings, waste, tinfoil, licorice, sugar, gum, and other materials held or owned by him on the first day of January of each year, or at the time of commencing and at the time of concluding business, if before or after the first of January, setting forth what portion of said goods and materials, and what kinds, were manufactured or produced by him, and what was purchased from others; which inventory shall be verified by his oath or affirmation; and the assistant assessor shall make personal examination of the stock sufficient to satisfy himself as to the correctness of the inventory, and shall verify the fact of such examination by oath or affirmation taken before the assessor, to be indorsed on or affixed to the inventory; and every such person shall keep a book or books, the forms of which shall be prescribed by the Commissioner of Internal Revenue, and enter therein daily an accurate account of all the articles aforesaid purchased by him, the quantity of tobacco, snuff, and snuff-flour, stems, scraps, clippings, waste, tinfoil, licorice, sugar, gum, and other materials, of whatever description, whether manufactured, (and if plug tobacco the number of net pounds of lumps made in the lump-room, and the number of packages and pounds produced in the press-room each day,) sold, consumed, or removed for consumption or sale, or removed from the place of manufacture in bond, and to what district; and shall, on or before the tenth day of each and every month, furnish to the assistant assessor of the division a true and accurate abstract from such book of all such purchases, sales, and removals, made during the month next preceding, which abstract shall be verified by his oath or affirmation; and in case of refusal or wilful neglect to deliver the inventory, or keep the account, or furnish the abstract aforesaid, he shall, on conviction, be fined not less than five hundred dollars nor more than five thousand dollars, and imprisoned not less than six months nor more than three years. And it shall be the duty of any dealer in leaf tobacco, or in any material used in manufacturing tobacco or snuff, on demand of any officer of internal revenue, to render a true and correct statement, verified by oath or affirmation, of the quantity and amount of such leaf tobacco or materials sold or delivered to any person named in such demand; and in case of refusal or neglect to render such statement, or if there is cause to believe such statement to be incorrect or fraudulent, the assessor shall make an examination of persons, books, and papers, in the same manner as provided in this act in relation to frauds and evasions.

Abstract from book to be furnished by manufacturer.

Penalties.

Dealers in leaf-tobacco to render statement of sales when demanded.

July 20, 1868.

SEC. 67. *And be it further enacted*, That the Commissioner of Internal Revenue shall cause to be prepared suitable and special revenue stamps for payment of the tax on tobacco and snuff, which stamps shall indicate the weight and class of the article on which payment is to be made, and shall be affixed and canceled in the mode prescribed by the Commissioner of Internal Revenue, and stamps when used on any wooden package shall be canceled by sinking a portion of the same into the wood with a steel die; also such *export* stamps as are required by this act, which stamps shall be furnished to the collectors of internal revenue requiring the same, who shall each keep at all times a supply equal in amount to three months' sales thereof, and shall sell the same only to the manufacturers of tobacco and snuff in their respective districts who have given bonds as required by law, to owners or consignees of tobacco or snuff, upon the requisition of the proper custom-house officer having the custody of such tobacco or snuff, and to persons required by law to affix the same to tobacco or snuff on hand on the first day of January, anno Domini eighteen hundred and sixty-nine; and every collector shall keep an account of the number, amount, and denominate value of stamps sold by him to each manufacturer, and to other persons above described.

Stamps for tobacco and snuff to be prepared, furnished, and sold; mode of affixing and cancellation.

June 6, 1872, § 31.

Collector to keep an account of stamps sold.

[Provided,] *That such stamps as may be required to stamp tobacco, snuff, or cigars, sold under distraint by any collector of internal revenue, or for stamping any tobacco, snuff, or cigars which may have been abandoned, condemned, or forfeited, and sold by order of court or of any government officer for the benefit of the United States, may, under such rules and regulations as the Commissioner of Internal Revenue shall prescribe, be used by the collector making such sale, or furnished by a collector to a United States marshal, or to any other government officer making such sale for the benefit of the United States, without making payment for said stamps so used or delivered; and any revenue collector using or furnishing stamps in manner as aforesaid, on presenting vouchers satisfactory to the Commissioner of Internal Revenue, shall be allowed credit for the same in settling his stamp account with the department: And provided further, That in case it shall appear that any abandoned, condemned, or forfeited tobacco, snuff, or cigars, when offered for sale, will not bring a price equal to the tax due and payable thereon, such goods shall not be sold for consumption in the United States; and upon application made to the Commissioner of Internal Revenue, he is authorized and hereby directed to order the destruction of such tobacco, snuff, or cigars by the officer in whose custody and control the same may be at the time, and in such manner and under such regulations as the Commissioner of Internal Revenue may prescribe.*

June 6, 1872, § 31.

Stamps for tobacco, snuff, and cigars sold under distraint, abandoned, condemned, forfeited, or sold by order of court, &c.

Abandoned, condemned, or forfeited tobacco, snuff, and cigars not to be sold for consumption in the United States for a price not equal to the tax, but may be destroyed.

SEC. 68. *And be it further enacted*, That every manufacturer of tobacco or snuff shall, in addition to all other requirements of this act relating to tobacco, print on each package or securely affix, by pasting on each package containing tobacco or snuff manufactured by or for him, a label on which shall be printed, together with the proprietor's or manufacturer's name, the number of the manufactory, and the district and state in which it is situated, these words:

July 20, 1868.

Label on packages of tobacco and snuff.

"NOTICE.—The manufacturer of this tobacco has complied with all the requirements of law. Every person is cautioned, under the penalties of law, not to use this package for tobacco again."

Penalty.

Any manufacturer of tobacco who shall neglect to print on or affix such label to any package containing tobacco made by or for him, or sold or offered for sale by or for him; or any person who shall remove any such label so affixed from any such package, shall, on conviction, be fined fifty dollars for each package in respect to which such offence shall be committed.

July 20, 1868.

Removing unlawfully, selling without stamps or payment of tax, or giving bond, making false entries, &c.

June 6, 1872, § 31.

SEC. 69. *And be it further enacted*, That any manufacturer of tobacco or snuff who shall remove otherwise than as provided by law, or sell any tobacco or snuff without the proper stamps denoting the tax thereon, or without having paid the special tax, or given bond as required by law, or who shall make false or fraudulent entries of manufactures or sales of tobacco or snuff, or who shall make false or fraudulent entries of the purchases or sales of leaf tobacco, tobacco stems, or other material, or who shall affix any false, forged, fraudulent, spurious, or counterfeit stamp, or imitation of any stamp required by this act, *or any stamp or stamps which have been previously used*, to any box or package containing any tobacco or snuff, shall, in addition to the penalties elsewhere provided in this act for such offences, forfeit to the United States all the raw material and manufactured or partly manufactured tobacco and snuff, and all machinery, tools, implements, apparatus, fixtures, boxes and barrels, and all other materials which shall be found in the possession of such person, in the manufactory of such person, or elsewhere.

July 20, 1868.

Absence of stamp to be notice and evidence of non-payment.

SEC. 70. *And be it further enacted*, That the absence of the proper stamp on any package of manufactured tobacco or snuff shall be notice to all persons that the tax has not been paid thereon, and shall be prima facie evidence of the non-payment thereof. And such tobacco or snuff shall be forfeited to the United States.

July 20, 1868.

Removing, except in proper packages, or without stamp, selling unlawfully, &c.

June 6, 1872, §31.

Ibid.

Ibid.

SEC. 71. *And be it further enacted*, That any person who shall remove from any manufactory, or from any place where tobacco or snuff is made, any manufactured tobacco or snuff without the same being put up in proper packages, or without the proper stamp for the amount thereon being affixed and canceled, as required by law; or, if intended for export, without the proper * [export] stamp being affixed; or shall use, sell, or offer for sale, or have in possession, except in the manufactory, *or while in transfer, under bond or a collector's permit, from any manufactory, store, or warehouse, to a vessel for exportation to a foreign country*, any manufactured tobacco or snuff, without proper stamps being affixed and canceled; or shall sell, or offer for sale, for consumption in the United States, or use, or have in possession, except in the manufactory, *or while in transfer under bond or a collector's permit, from any manufactory, store, or warehouse, to a vessel for exportation to a foreign country*, any manufactured tobacco or snuff on which only the * stamp marking the same for export has been affixed, shall, on conviction thereof for each such offence, respectively, be fined not less than one thousand dollars nor more than five thousand dollars, and be imprisoned not less than six months nor more than two years. And any person who shall affix to any package containing tobacco or snuff any false, forged, fraudulent, spurious, or counterfeit stamp, or a stamp which has been before used, shall be deemed guilty of a felony, and on conviction shall be fined not less than one thousand dollars nor more than five thousand dollars, and imprisoned not less than two years nor more than five years.

Penalty for affixing stamp which is false, fraudulent, &c.

SEC. 60. * * * *And if any manufacturer of tobacco, snuff, or cigars shall sell, or remove for sale or consumption, any tobacco, snuff, or cigars upon which a tax is required to be paid by stamps, without the use of the proper stamps, in addition to the other penalties imposed by law for such sale or removal, it shall be the duty of the proper assessor or assistant assessor, or any internal-revenue officer detailed by the Commissioner of Internal Revenue for that purpose, within a period of not more than two years after such sale or removal, upon such information as he can obtain, to estimate the amount of tax which has been omitted to be paid, and to make an assessment therefor, and certify the same to the collector. And the subsequent proceedings for collection shall be in all respects like those for the collection of taxes upon manufactures and productions.*

July 20, 1868.
June 6, 1872, § 31.

Tax on tobacco, snuff or cigars sold or removed without being properly stamped may be estimated and assessed within two years.

SEC. 92. * * * * *
And[1] *any person who shall purchase or receive for sale any such [manufactured] tobacco, snuff, or cigars, which has not been * branded, or stamped as required by law, * shall be liable to a penalty of fifty dollars for each and every offence. And any person who shall purchase or receive for sale any such tobacco, snuff, or cigars, from any manufacturer who has not paid the special tax, shall be liable for each and every offence to a penalty of one hundred dollars, and, in addition thereto, a forfeiture of all the articles, as aforesaid, so purchased or received, or the full value thereof.*

* * * * * *

June 30, 1864.
July 13, 1866.

Purchasing, &c., tobacco not branded or stamped, penalty.

Buying &c., tobacco from a manufacturer who has not paid special tax.

SEC. 72. *And be it further enacted*, That whenever any stamped box, bag, vessel, wrapper, or envelope of any kind, containing tobacco or snuff, shall be emptied, *the stamp or stamps thereon* shall be destroyed by the person in whose hands the same may be. And any person who shall wilfully neglect or refuse to do so shall, for each such offence, on conviction, be fined fifty dollars, and imprisoned not less than ten days nor more than six months. And any person who shall sell or give away, or who shall buy or accept from another, any such empty stamp[ed] box, bag, vessel, wrapper, or envelope of any kind, or *the stamp or stamps taken from any such empty box, bag, vessel, wrapper, or envelope of any kind*, shall, for each such offence, on conviction, be fined one hundred dollars and imprisoned for not less than twenty days and not more than one year. And any manufacturer or other person who shall put tobacco or snuff into any such box, bag, vessel, wrapper, or envelope, the same having been

July 20, 1868.
June 6, 1872, § 31.

Stamp on emptied package to be destroyed.

June 6, 1872, § 31.

[1] This portion of section 92 of the act of June 30, 1864, is retained, although the first sentence has been in effect modified by sections 71 and 89 of act of July 20, 1868, as amended.

June 6, 1872, § 31. Fraudulent stamping of tobacco and snuff.

either emptied or partially emptied, *or shall have in his possession, or shall affix to any box or other package any stamp or stamps which have been previously used, or who shall sell, or offer for sale, any box or other package of tobacco, snuff, or cigars, having affixed thereto any fraudulent, spurious, imitation, or counterfeit stamp or stamps, or stamp or stamps that have been previously used, or shall sell from any such fraudulently stamped box or package, or shall have in his possession any box or package as aforesaid, knowing the same to be fraudulently stamped*, shall, for each such offence, on conviction, be fined not less than one hundred nor more than five hundred dollars, and imprisoned for not less than one nor more than three years.

July 20, 1868. June 6, 1872, § 31. Exportation of manufactured tobacco, snuff, and cigars.

SEC. 73. *And be it further enacted, That manufactured tobacco, snuff, and cigars intended for immediate exportation, after being properly inspected, marked, and branded, may be removed from the manufactory in bond without having affixed thereto internal revenue stamps indicating the payment of the tax thereon. The removal from the manufactory of such tobacco, snuff, and cigars shall be made under such rules and regulations, and after making such entries and executing and filing, with the collector of the district from which the removal is to be made, such bonds and bills of lading, and giving such other additional security as may be prescribed by the Commissioner of Internal Revenue and approved by the Secretary of the Treasury. All tobacco, snuff, and cigars intended for immediate export as aforesaid, before being removed from the manufactory, shall have affixed to each package an engraved stamp, indicative of such intention, to be provided and furnished to the several collectors as in the case of other stamps, and to be charged to them and accounted for in the same manner; and for the expense attending the providing and affixing of such stamps, ten cents for each package so stamped shall be paid to the collector on making the entry for such transportation. When the manufacturer shall have made the proper entries, filed the bonds, and otherwise complied with all the requirements of the law and regulations as herein provided, the collector shall issue to him a permit for the removal, said permit accurately describing the tobacco, snuff, and cigars to be shipped, the number and kind of packages, the number of pounds, the amount of tax, the marks and brands, the State and collection-district from which the same are shipped, and the number of the manufactory and the manufacturer's name, together with the port from which the said tobacco, snuff, and cigars are to be exported, and the route or routes over which the same are to be sent to the port of shipment, and the name of the vessel or line by which they are to be conveyed to the foreign port. The bonds required to be given for the exportation of the tobacco, snuff, and cigars shall be canceled upon the presentation of the proper certificates that said tobacco, snuff, and cigars have been landed at any port without the jurisdiction of the United States, or upon satisfactory proof that after shipment the same were lost at sea.*

SEC. 74. See *Drawback*.

July 20, 1868. Tobacco manufactured by one person for another, or on shares.

SEC. 75. *And be it further enacted*, That in all cases where tobacco or snuff of any description is manufactured, in whole or in part, upon commission or shares, or where the material from which any such articles are made, or are to be made, is furnished by one person and made or manufactured by another, or where the material is furnished or sold by one person with an understanding or agreement with another that the manufactured article is to be received in payment therefor or for any part thereof, the stamps required by law shall be [af]fixed by the actual maker or manufacturer before the article passes from the place of making or manufacturing. And in case of fraud on the part of either of said persons in respect to said manufacture, or of any collusion on their part with intent to defraud the revenue, such material and manufactured articles shall be forfeited to the United States; and each party to such fraud or collusion shall be deemed guilty of a misdemeanor, and, on conviction, be fined not less than one hundred dollars nor more than five thousand dollars, and imprisoned for not less than six months nor more than three years.

Stamps, by whom affixed.

Penalties for fraud in such cases.

SEC. 76. *And be it further enacted*, That every dealer in leaf tobacco shall enter daily in a book kept for that purpose, under such regulations as the Commissioner of Internal Revenue may prescribe, the number of hogsheads, cases, and pounds of leaf tobacco purchased by him, and of whom purchased, and the number of hogsheads, cases, or pounds sold by him, with the name and residence, in each instance, of the person to whom sold, and if shipped, to whom shipped, and to what district. Such book shall be kept at his place of business, and shall be open at all hours to the inspection of any assessor, collector, or other revenue officer; and any dealer in leaf tobacco who shall neglect or refuse to keep such book shall be liable to a penalty of not less than five hundred dollars, and on conviction thereof shall be fined not less than one hundred dollars nor more than five thousand dollars, and imprisoned not less than six months nor more than two years.

July 20, 1868.

Book of dealer in leaf-tobacco.

Book to be kept open to inspection.

Penalty.

SEC. 77. *And be it further enacted*, That from and after the passage of this act, and until the first day of October, eighteen hundred and sixty-eight, all manufactured tobacco and snuff (not including cigars) imported from foreign countries shall be placed by the owner, importer, or consignee thereof in a bonded warehouse of the United States at the place of importation, in the same manner and under rules as provided for warehousing goods imported into the United States, and shall not be withdrawn from such warehouse, nor be entered for consumption or transportation in the United States prior to the said first day of October, eighteen hundred and sixty-eight. All manufactured tobacco and snuff (not including cigars) imported from foreign countries, after the passage of this act, shall, in addition to the import duties imposed on the same, pay the tax prescribed in this act for like kinds of tobacco and snuff manufactured in the United States, and have the same stamps respectively affixed. Such stamps shall be affixed and canceled on all such articles so imported by the owner or importer thereof, while such articles are in the custody of the proper custom-house officers, and such articles shall not pass out of the custody of such officers until the stamps have been affixed

July 20, 1868.

Imported tobacco and snuff.

and canceled. Such tobacco and snuff shall be put up in packages, as prescribed in this act for like articles manufactured in the United States before such stamps are affixed; and the owner or importer of such tobacco and snuff shall be liable to all the penal provisions of this act, prescribed for manufacturers of tobacco and snuff manufactured in the United States. Where it shall be necessary to take any such articles, so imported, to any place for the purpose of repacking, affixing, and canceling such stamps, other than the public stores of the United States, the collector of customs of the port where such articles shall be entered shall designate a bonded warehouse to which such articles shall be taken, under the control of such customs officer as such collector may direct. And any officer of customs who shall permit any such articles to pass out of his custody or control without compliance by the owner or importer thereof with the provisions of this section relating thereto, shall be deemed guilty of a misdemeanor, and shall, on conviction, be fined not less than one thousand dollars, nor more than five thousand dollars, and imprisoned not less than six months nor more than three years.

July 20, 1868.

Tobacco and snuff on hand July 20, 1868.

SEC. 78. *And be it further enacted*, That from and after the passage of this act it shall be the duty of every dealer in manufactured tobacco, having on hand more than twenty pounds, and every dealer in snuff having on hand more than ten pounds, to immediately make a true and correct inventory of the amount of such tobacco and snuff, respectively, under oath or affirmation, and to deposit such inventory with the assistant assessor of the proper division, who shall immediately return the same to the assessor of the district, who shall immediately thereafter make an abstract of the several inventories filed in his office, and transmit such abstract to the Commissioner of Internal Revenue, and a like inventory and return shall be made on the first day of every month thereafter, and a like abstract of inventories shall be transmitted while any such dealer has tobacco or snuff remaining on hand manufactured in the United States, or imported prior to the passage of this act, and not stamped.

Dealer to make inventory.

Monthly inventories.

Act Dec. 22, 1868.

After the *fifteenth day of February*, eighteen hundred and sixty-nine, all smoking, fine-cut chewing tobacco, or snuff, and after the first day of July, eighteen hundred and sixty-nine, all other manufactured tobacco of every description, shall be taken and deemed as having been manufactured after the passage of this act, and shall not be sold or offered for sale unless put up in packages and stamped as prescribed by this act, except at retail by retail dealers from wooden packages stamped as provided for in this act; and any person who shall sell, or offer for sale, after the *fifteenth day of February*, eighteen hundred and sixty-nine, any smoking, fine-cut chewing tobacco, or snuff, and after the first day of July, eighteen hundred and sixty-nine, any other manufactured tobacco not so put up in packages and stamped, shall, on conviction, be fined not less than five hundred dollars nor more than five thousand dollars, and imprisoned not less than six months nor more than two years.

Ibid.

SEC. 79. *And be it further enacted*, That any person who shall, after the passage of this act, sell, or offer for sale, any manufactured tobacco or snuff, representing the same to have been manufactured and the tax paid thereon prior to the passage of this act, when the same was not so manufactured, and the tax not so paid, shall be liable to a penalty of five hundred dollars for each offence, and shall be deemed guilty of a misdemeanor, and, on conviction, shall be fined not less than five hundred dollars nor more than five thousand dollars, and shall be imprisoned not less than six months nor more than two years.

July 20, 1868.

Selling tobacco as made and tax paid before 20 July, 1868, when not so made.

SEC. 80. *And be it further enacted*, That all manufactured tobacco and snuff, manufactured prior to the passage of this act, and held in bond at the time of its passage, may be sold for consumption in the original packages, with the proper stamps for the amount of the tax thereon affixed and canceled as required by law; and any person who shall, after the passage of this act, offer for sale any tobacco or snuff, in packages of a different size from those limited and prescribed by this act, representing the same to have been held in bond at the time of the passage of this act, when the same was not so held in bond, shall, on conviction, be fined fifty dollars for each package in respect to which such offence shall be committed: *Provided*, That after the first day of January, anno Domini eighteen hundred and sixty-nine, no such tobacco or snuff shall be sold or removed for sale or consumption from any bonded warehouse unless put up in packages and stamped as provided by this act.

July 20, 1868.

Tobacco and snuff in bond July 20, 1868, may be sold in original packages with proper stamps affixed until January 1, 1869, when the same must be put up in packages as provided herein.

CIGARS.

SEC. 81. *And be it further enacted*, That upon cigars which shall be manufactured and sold, or removed for consumption or use, there shall be assessed and collected the following taxes to be paid by the manufacturer thereof:

July 20, 1868.

Tax on cigars and cigarettes.

On cigars of all descriptions, made of tobacco or any substitute therefor, five dollars per thousand; on cigarettes weighing not exceeding three pounds per thousand, one dollar and fifty cents per thousand; when weighing exceeding three pounds per thousand, five dollars per thousand. And the Commissioner of Internal Revenue may prescribe such regulations for the inspection of cigars, cheroots, and cigarettes, and the collection of the tax thereon, as shall, in his judgment, be most effective for the prevention of frauds in the payment of such tax.

SEC. 82. *And be it further enacted*, That every person before commencing, or, if already commenced, before continuing, the manufacture of cigars, shall furnish, without previous demand therefor, to the assistant assessor of the

July 20, 1868.

Cigar manufacturer's statement and bond before manufacturing.

division a statement in duplicate, subscribed under oath or affirmation, accurately setting forth the place, and, if in a city, the street and number of the street, where the manufacture is to be carried on; and if the same shall be manufactured for, or to be sold and delivered to, any other person, the name and residence and business or occupation of the person for whom the cigars are to be manufactured or to whom to be delivered; and shall give a bond in conformity with the provisions of this act, in such penal sum as the assessor of the district may require, not less than five hundred dollars, with an addition of one hundred dollars for each person proposed to be employed by him in making cigars, conditioned that he will not employ any person to manufacture cigars who has not been duly registered as a cigar-maker; that he will not engage in any attempt, by himself or by collusion with others, to defraud the Government of any tax on his manufactures; that he will render truly and correctly all the returns, statements and inventories prescribed; that whenever he shall add to the number of cigar-makers employed by him, he will immediately give notice thereof to the collector of the district; that he will stamp, in accordance with law, all cigars manufactured by him before he offers the same or any part thereof for sale, and before he removes any part thereof from the place of manufacture; that he will not knowingly sell, purchase, expose, or receive for sale any cigars which have not been stamped as required by law; and that he will comply with all the requirements of law relating to the manufacture of cigars. The sum of said bond may be increased from time to time, and additional sureties required at the discretion of the assessor, or under the instructions of the Commissioner of Internal Revenue. Every cigar manufacturer shall obtain from the collector of the district, who is hereby required to issue the same, a certificate setting forth the number of cigar-makers for which the bond has been given, which certificate shall be posted in a conspicuous place within the manufactory; and any cigar manufacturer who shall neglect or refuse to obtain such certificate, or to keep the same posted as hereinbefore provided, shall, on conviction, be fined one hundred dollars. Any person manufacturing cigars of any description without first giving bond as herein required, shall, on conviction, be fined not less than one hundred dollars nor more than five thousand dollars, and imprisoned not less than three months nor more than five years. Cigarettes and cheroots shall be held to be cigars under the meaning of this act.

Collector's certificate of number of cigar-makers.

Penalties.

July 20, 1868.

Cigar manufacturer's sign.

SEC. 83. *And be it further enacted*, That within thirty days after the passage of this act every cigar manufacturer shall place and keep on the side or end of the building within which his business is carried on, so that it can be distinctly seen, a sign, with letters thereon not less than three inches in length, painted in oil colors or gilded, giving his full name and business. Any person neglecting to comply with the requirements of this section shall, on conviction, be fined not less than one hundred dollars, nor more than five hundred dollars.

Penalty.

SEC. 84. *And be it further enacted*, That it shall be the duty of every assistant assessor to keep a record, in a book to be provided for the purpose, to be open to the inspection of any person, of the name and residence of every person engaged in the manufacture of cigars in his division, the place where such manufacture is carried on, and the number of the manufactory, together with the names and residences of every cigar-maker employed in his division, and the assistant assessor shall enter in said record, under the name of each manufacturer, an abstract of his inventories and monthly returns; and each assessor shall keep a similar record for the district, and shall cause the several manufactories of cigars in the district to be numbered consecutively, which number shall not thereafter be changed.

July 20, 1868.

Assistant assessor's record of cigar manufacturers and makers.

Assessor's record for district.

SEC. 85. *And be it further enacted*, That from and after the passage of this act all cigars shall be packed in boxes, not before used for that purpose, containing, respectively, twenty-five, fifty, one hundred, two hundred and fifty, or five hundred cigars each; and any person who shall sell or offer for sale, or deliver or offer to deliver, any cigars in any other form than in new boxes as above described, or who shall pack in any box any cigars in excess of the number provided by law to be put in each box, respectively, or who shall falsely brand any box, or who shall affix a stamp on any box denoting a less amount of tax than that required by law, shall, upon conviction, for any of the above-described offences, be fined for each such offence, not less than one hundred dollars nor more than one thousand dollars, and be imprisoned not less than six months nor more than two years: *Provided*, That nothing in this section shall be construed as preventing the sale of cigars at retail by retail dealers who have paid the special tax as such from boxes packed, stamped, and branded in the manner prescribed by law.

July 20, 1868.

How cigars are to be packed.

Penalties.

Sale of cigars at retail.

SEC. 86. *And be it further enacted*, That every person now or hereafter engaged in the manufacture of cigars, shall make and deliver to the assistant assessor of the division a true inventory, in form prescribed by the Commissioner of Internal Revenue, of the quantity of leaf tobacco, cigars, stems, scraps, clippings, and waste, and the number of cigar boxes and the capacity of each box, held or owned by him on the first day of January of each year, or at the time of commencing and at the time of concluding business, if before or after the first of January, setting forth what portion of said goods, and what kinds, were manufactured or produced by him, and what were purchased from others, which inventory shall be verified by his oath or affirmation indorsed on said inventory; and the assistant assessor shall make personal examination of the stock sufficient to satisfy himself as to the correctness of the inventory, and shall verify the fact of such examination by oath or affirmation taken before the assessor, also to be indorsed on the inventory; and every such person shall enter daily in a book, the form of which shall be prescribed by the Commissioner of Internal Revenue, an accurate account of all the articles aforesaid purchased by him, the quantity of leaf tobacco, cigars, stems, or cigar

July 20, 1868.

Cigar manufacturer's annual inventory.

Book of daily entries.

boxes, of whatever description, manufactured, sold, c sumed, or removed for consumption or sale, or removed fi the place of manufacture; and shall, on or before the te day of each and every month, furnish to the assistant as sor of the division a true and accurate abstract from s book of all such purchases, sales and removals made dui the month next preceding, which abstract shall be veri by his oath or affirmation; and in case of refusal or wi neglect to deliver the inventory, or keep the account, or nish the abstract aforesaid, he shall, on conviction, be fi not less than five hundred dollars nor more than five tl sand dollars, and imprisoned not less than six months more than three years. It shall be the duty of any de in leaf tobacco or material used in manufacturing cigars demand of any officer of internal revenue authorized by to render to such officer a true and correct statement, fied by oath or affirmation, of the quantity and amoui such leaf tobacco or materials sold or delivered to any pe or persons named in such demand; and in case of refus neglect to render such statement, or if there is caus believe such statement to be incorrect or fraudulent, assessor shall make an examination of persons, books, papers, in the same manner as provided in this act in tion to frauds and evasions.

Abstract.

Penalties.

Dealer in leaf tobacco to make sworn statement when demanded.

July 20, 1868.

SEC. 87. *And be it further enacted*, That the Commissi of Internal Revenue shall cause to be prepared, for payı of the tax upon cigars, suitable stamps denoting the thereon; and all cigars shall be packed in quantiti twenty-five, fifty, one hundred, two hundred and fifty, five hundred, and all such stamps shall be furnished to lectors requiring the same, who shall, if there be any manufacturers within their respective districts, keep on at all times a supply equal in amount to two months' thereof, and shall sell the same only to the cigar man turers who have given bonds and paid the special ta required by law, in their districts respectively, and to porters of cigars who are required to affix the same t ported cigars in the custody of customs officers and to sons required by law to affix the same to cigars on hai the first day of January, anno Domini eighteen hundre sixty-nine; and every collector shall keep an account c number, amount, and denominate values of the stamps by him to each cigar manufacturer, and to other pe above described: *Provided*, That from and after the pa of this act, the duty on all cigars imported into the U States from foreign countries shall be two dollars and cents [per] pound, and twenty-five per centum ad valo

Cigar stamps, to be prepared and furnished.

How cigars are to be packed.

To whom stamp are to be sold.

Collector to keep an account of stamps sold.

Duty on imported cigars.

July 20, 1868.

SEC. 88. *And be it further enacted*, That every mai turer of cigars shall securely affix, by pasting on eacl containing cigars manufactured by or for him, a lab which shall be printed, together with the manufact name, the number of his manufactory, and the distric State in which it is situated, these words:

Label on cigars.

"NOTICE.—The manufacturer of the cigars herein tained has complied with all the requirements of Every person is cautioned, under the penalties of la to use this box for cigars again."

Any manufacturer of cigars who shall neglect to affix such label to any box containing cigars made by or for him, or sold or offered for sale by or for him, or any person who shall remove any such label, so affixed, from any such box, shall, upon conviction thereof, be fined fifty dollars for each box in respect to which such offence shall be committed. Penalty.

That section eighty-eight be amended so that either the proprietor's name or the manufacturer's name shall be printed on the label for cigars provided for in said section. April 10, 1869, § 1.

July 20, 1868.

SEC. 89. *And be it further enacted*, That all cigars which shall be removed from any manufactory or place where cigars are made without the same being packed in boxes as required by this act, or without the proper stamp thereon denoting the tax, or without burning into each box with a branding iron the number of the cigars contained therein, and the name of the manufacturer, and the number of the district and the State, or without the stamp denoting the tax thereon being properly affixed and canceled, or which shall be sold or offered for sale not properly boxed and stamped, shall be forfeited to the United States. And any person who shall commit any of the above-described offences shall, on conviction, be fined for each such offence not less than one hundred dollars nor more than one thousand dollars, and imprisoned not less than six months nor more than two years. And any person who shall pack cigars in any box bearing a false or fraudulent or counterfeit stamp, *or who shall affix to any box containing cigars a stamp in the similitude or likeness of any stamp required to be used by the laws of the United States, whether the same shall be a customs or internal-revenue stamp; or who shall buy, receive, or have in his possession any cigars on which the tax to which they are liable has not been paid*, or who shall remove or cause to be removed any stamp denoting the tax on cigars from any box, with intent to use the same, or who shall use or permit any other person to use any stamp so removed, or who shall receive, buy, sell, give away, or have in his possession any stamp so removed, or who shall make any other fraudulent use of any stamp * intended for cigars, or who shall remove from the place of manufacture any cigars not properly boxed and stamped as required by law, shall be deemed guilty of a felony, and, on conviction, shall be fined not less than one hundred dollars nor more than one thousand dollars, and imprisoned not less than six months nor more than three years.

Removal of cigars without properly boxing, stamping, or branding. Selling, &c., without properly boxing and stamping. Forfeiture. Penalties. False, fraudulent, or counterfeit stamp. June 6, 1872, § 31. Stamp in similitude or likeness of a U. S. stamp. Buying, &c., cigars on which tax has not been paid. Removing, &c., stamps. June 6, 1872, § 33. Penalties.

June 6, 1872.

SEC. 33. That whenever any stamped box containing cigars, cheroots, or cigarettes, shall be emptied, it shall be the duty of the person in whose hands the same may be to destroy utterly the stamp or stamps thereon. And any person who shall wilfully neglect or refuse so to do, shall, for each such offence, on conviction, be fined not exceeding fifty dollars and imprisoned not less than ten days nor more than six months. And any person who shall fraudulently give away or accept from another, or who shall sell, buy, or use for packing cigars, cheroots, or cigarettes, any such stamped box, shall for each such offense, on conviction, be

Stamps on emptied cigar-boxes to be destroyed. Giving away, accepting, selling, buying, or using empty stamped box.

fined not exceeding one hundred dollars and be imprison
not more than one year.

Mar. 2, 1867.

Empty cigar-box with stamp to be destroyed.

SEC. 32. *And be it further enacted*, That * * it shall be lawful for any cigar inspector or revenue offic to destroy any empty cigar box upon which a cigar stan shall be found.

July 20, 1868.

Absence of proper stamp, notice and evidence of non-payment of tax.

SEC. 90. *And be it further enacted*, That the absence of t proper revenue stamp on any box of cigars sold, or offer for sale, or kept for sale, shall be notice to all persons th the tax has not been paid thereon, and shall be prima fa evidence of the non-payment thereof; and such cigars sh be forfeited to the United States.

July 20, 1868.

Cigars manufactured on shares, commission, &c.

SEC. 91. *And be it further enacted*, That in all cases whe cigars of any description are manufactured, in whole or in pa upon commission or shares, or where the material is furnish by one party and manufactured by another, or where the m terial is furnished or sold by one party with an understan ing or agreement with another that the cigars are to be ceived in payment therefor, or for any part thereof, t

Stamps, by whom affixed.

stamps required by law shall be affixed by the actual mak before the cigars are removed from the place of manufactu ing. And in case of fraud on the part of either of sa

Fraud.

parties in respect to said manufacture, or of any collusi on their part with intent to defraud the revenue, such m terial and cigars shall be forfeited to the United States, a every person engaged in such fraud or collusion shall,

Penalties.

conviction, be fined not less than one hundred dollars n more than five thousand dollars, and imprisoned for n less than six months nor more than three years.

July 20, 1868.

Forfeiture of property for selling, &c., cigars without payment of special tax, giving bond, or affixing proper stamps; or making false entries, or affixing stamps which are false, &c.

SEC. 92. *And be it further enacted*, That any manufac rer of cigars, who shall remove or sell any cigars witho payment of the special tax as a cigar manufacturer, without having given bond as such, or without the prop stamps denoting the tax thereon, or who shall ma false or fraudulent entries of manufactures or sale any cigars, or who shall make false or fraudulent tries of the purchase or sales of leaf tobacco, toba stems, or other material used in the manufacture of ciga or who shall affix any false, forged, spurious, fraudule or counterfeit stamp, or imitation of any stamp, requi by law to any box containing any cigars, shall, in dition to the penalties elsewhere provided in this act such offences, forfeit to the United States all raw mater and manufactured or partly manufactured tobacco a cigars, and all machinery, tools, implements, apparatus, f tures, boxes, barrels, and all other materials, which shall found in the possession of such person, or in his manuf tory, and used in his business as such manufacturer, gether with his estate or interest in the building or fact and the lot or tract of ground on which such building or f tory is located, and all appurtenances thereunto belongi

July 20, 1868.

Imported cigars to pay internal revenue tax in addition to import duties.

SEC. 93. *And be it further enacted*, That all cigars import from foreign countries after the passage of this act, shall, addition to the import duties imposed on the same, pay t tax prescribed in this act for cigars manufactured in t United States, and have the same stamps affixed. S ımps shall be affixed and canceled by the owner or im- rter of cigars while they are in the custody of the proper stom-house officers; and such cigars shall not pass out of e custody of such officers until the stamps have been so ixed and canceled, but shall be put up in boxes contain- g quantities as prescribed in this act for cigars manufac- red in the United States before such stamps are affixed. ıd the owner or importer of such cigars shall be liable to . the penal provisions of this act, prescribed for manufac- rers of cigars manufactured in the United States. Where shall be necessary to take any of such cigars, so imported, any place for the purpose of affixing and canceling such ımps, other than the public stores of the United States, e collector of customs of the port where such cigars shall entered shall designate a bonded warehouse to which ey shall be taken, under the control of such customs offi- r as such collector may direct. And any officer of cus- ms who shall permit any such cigars to pass out of his stody or control without compliance by the owner or im- rter thereof with the provisions of this section relating ereto shall be deemed guilty of a misdemeanor, and shall, . conviction thereof, be fined not less than one thousand ıllars nor more than five thousand dollars, and imprisoned ıt less than six months nor more than three years.

Stamps for, when and by whom affixed.

Imported cigars to be boxed same as domestic.

Removal for stamping.

Penalty on officer of customs for permitting imported cigars to pass out of his custody, in violation of this section.

SEC. 94. *And be it further enacted*, That from and after e passage of this act it shall be the duty of every dealer cigars, either of foreign or domestic manufacture, having . hand more than five thousand thereof, imported or manu- ctured, or purporting or claimed to have been imported manufactured, prior to the passage of this act, to imme- ately make a true and correct inventory of the quantity such cigars in his possession, under oath or affirmation, ıd to deposit such inventory with the assistant assessor of .e proper division, who shall immediately return the same the assessor of the district, who shall immediately there- ter make an abstract of the several such inventories filed his office, and transmit the same to the Commissioner of ıternal Revenue; and a like inventory and return shall be ade on the first day of every month thereafter, and a like ostract of inventories shall be transmitted, while any such ealer has any such cigars remaining on hand, until the rst day of April, eighteen hundred and sixty-nine. After ıe first day of April, eighteen hundred and sixty-nine, all gars of every description shall be taken to have been either anufactured or imported after the passage of this act, and ıall be stamped accordingly; and any person who shall ıll, or offer for sale, after the first day of April, eighteen ındred and sixty-nine, any imported cigars, or cigars pur- orting or claimed to have been imported, not so put up in ıckages and stamped as provided by this act, shall, on onviction thereof, be fined not less than five hundred dol- ırs nor more than five thousand dollars, and imprisoned ot less than six months nor more than two years.

July 20, 1868.

Cigars on hand July 20, 1868.

Dealer to make inventory.

Monthly inventories.

After 1st April, 1869, all cigars taken to be manufactured or imported after the passage of this act, and to be stamped.

Selling imported cigars not packed and stamped as required by law.

July 20, 1868.

Falsely representing cigars to have been made and tax paid prior to July 20, 1868.

SEC. 95. *And be it further enacted*, That any person who shall, after the passage of this act, sell or offer for sale any cigars, representing the same to have been manufactured and the tax paid thereon prior to the passage of this act, when the same were not so manufactured and the tax not so paid, shall be liable to a penalty of five hundred dollars for each offence, and shall be deemed guilty of a misdemeanor, and, on conviction, shall be fined not less than five hundred dollars nor more than five thousand dollars, and imprisoned not less than six months nor more than three years.

The remaining sections of the act of July 20, 1868, *are accounted for as follows :*

SEC. 96. See *Miscellaneous provisions.*
SEC. 97. See *General duties, &c., of Officers.*
SEC. 98. See *General duties, &c., of Officers.*
SEC. 99. See *Miscellaneous provisions.*
SEC. 100. See *Collectors' accounts.*
SEC. 101. See *Miscellaneous provisions.*
SEC. 102. See *Seizures, suits, and prosecutions.*
SEC. 103. See *Miscellaneous provisions.*
SEC. 104. See *Miscellaneous provisions.*
SEC. 105. See *Repealing and saving sections.*
SEC. 106. See *Collection of taxes.*
SEC. 107. See *Miscellaneous provisions.*
SEC. 108. See *Miscellaneous provisions.*
SEC. 109. *Repealed by subsequent legislation.*

FERMENTED LIQUORS.

June 6, 1872.

Brewer to file notice in writing with the assistant assessor.

SEC. 16. That every brewer shall, before commencing or continuing business, file with the assistant assessor of the assessment district in which he shall design to carry on his business, a notice in writing, stating therein the name of the person, company, corporation, or firm, and the names of the members of any such company or firm, together with the place or places of residence of such person or persons, and a description of the premises on which the brewery is situated, and of his or their title thereto, and the name or names of the owner or owners thereof.

June 6, 1872.

Brewer to execute bond, to be renewed May 1st each year.

Conditions of bond.

SEC. 17. That every brewer shall execute a bond to the United States, to be approved by the collector of the district, in a sum equal to twice the amount of tax which, in the opinion of the assessor, said brewer will be liable to pay during any one month, which bond shall be renewed on the first day of May in each year, and shall be conditioned that he will pay, or cause to be paid, as herein provided, the tax quired by law on all beer, lager-beer, ale, porter, and other mented liquors aforesaid made by him, or for him, before e same is sold or removed for consumption or sale, except hereinafter provided; and that he will keep, or cause to be pt, a book in the manner and for the purposes hereinafter ecified, which shall be open to inspection by the proper ficers, as by law required; and that he will in all respects ithfully comply, without fraud or evasion, with all requirements of law relating to the manufacture and sale of any alt-liquors before mentioned: *Provided*, That no brewer hall be required to pay a special tax as a wholesale dealer, y reason of selling at wholesale, at a place other than his rewery, malt-liquors manufactured by him.

Brewer not required to pay special tax as wholesale dealer in certain cases.

June 6, 1872.

Rate of tax on fermented liquors.

SEC. 18. That there shall be paid on all beer, lager-beer, e, porter, and other similar fermented liquors, by whatever name such liquors may be called, a tax of one dollar r every barrel containing not more than thirty-one gallons; nd at a like rate for any other quantity, or for any fractional part of a barrel, which shall be brewed or manufactured and sold, or removed for consumption or sale, ithin the United States; which tax shall be paid by the wner, agent, or superintendent of the brewery or premises which such fermented liquors shall be made, in the manner and at the time hereinafter specified: *Provided*, That actional parts of a barrel shall be halves, quarters, sixths, nd eighths; and any fractional part of a barrel containing ss than one-eighth shall be accounted one-eighth; more an one-eighth and not more than one-sixth, shall be ccounted one-sixth; more than one-sixth and not more than ne-quarter, shall be accounted one quarter; more than one-quarter and not more than one-half, shall be accounted one-half; more than one-half and not more than one barrel, shall e accounted one barrel; and more than one barrel and ot more than sixty-three gallons, shall be accounted two arrels, or a hogshead.

By whom to be paid.

Fractional parts of a barrel, how accounted.

June 6, 1872.

Brewer to keep books.

SEC. 19. That every person owning or occupying any rewery, or premises used or intended to be used for the urpose of brewing or making such fermented liquors, or who shall have such premises under his control or superintendence, as agent for the owner or occupant, or shall ave in his possession or custody any brewing materials, tensils, or apparatus, used or intended to be used on said remises in the manufacture of beer, lager-beer, ale, porter, r other similar fermented liquors, either as owner, agent, r superintendent, shall, from day to day, enter, or cause to e entered, in a book to be kept by him for that purpose, he kind of such malt liquors, the estimated quantity produced in barrels, and the actual quantity sold or removed or consumption or sale in barrels or fractional parts of arrels, and shall also, from day to day, enter, or cause to e entered, in a separate book to be kept by him for that urpose, an account of all materials by him purchased for he purpose of producing such fermented liquors, including grain and malt; and shall render to said assessor or assist-

Brewer to render monthly statement to the assessor.

ant assessor, on or before the tenth day of each month, a true statement, in writing, taken from his books, of the estimated quantity in barrels of such malt-liquors brewed, and the actual quantity sold or removed for consumption or sale during the preceding month; and shall verify, or cause to be verified, the said statement, and the facts therein set forth, by oath or affirmation, to be taken before the assessor or assistant assessor of the district, according to the form required by law, and shall immediately forward to the collector of the district a duplicate of said statement duly certified by the assessor or assistant assessor; and said books shall be open at all times for the inspection of any assessor or assistant assessor, collector, deputy-collector, inspector, or revenue-agent, who may take memorandums and transcripts therefrom.

Duplicate statement to be forwarded to the collector.

Books to be open at all times to inspection of revenue officers.

June 6, 1872.

Entries in brewery-books to be verified by oath.

SEC. 20. That the entries made in such books shall, on or before the tenth day of each month, be verified by the oath or affirmation of the person or persons by whom such entries shall have been made; which oath or affirmation shall be written in the book at the end of such entries, and be certified by the officer administering the same, and shall be in form as follows: "I do swear (or affirm) that the foregoing entries were made by me; and that they state truly, according to the best of my knowledge and belief, the estimated quantity of the whole amount of such malt-liquors brewed, and the actual quantity sold, and the actual quantity removed from the brewery owned by ———, in the county of ———; and, further, that I have no knowledge of any matter or thing required by law to be stated in said entries which has been omitted therefrom." And the owner, agent, or superintendent aforesaid shall also, in case the original entries made in his book shall not have been made by himself, subjoin thereto the following oath or affirmation, to be taken in manner as aforesaid: "I do swear (or affirm) that, to the best of my knowledge and belief, the foregoing entries fully set forth all the matters therein required by law; and that the same are just and true; and that I have taken all the means in my power to make them so."

Form of oath.

Oath of owner &c.

June 6, 1872.

Evasion of tax on fermented liquors.

Fraudulently failing to make entry and report, or to do anything required by law, or making false entry.

SEC. 21. That the owner, agent, or superintendent of any brewery, vessels, or utensils used in making fermented liquors, who shall evade, or attempt to evade, the payment of the tax thereon, or fraudulently neglect or refuse to make true and exact entry and report of the same in the manner required by law, or to do, or cause to be done, any of the things by law required to be done by him as aforesaid, or who shall intentionally make false entry in said book or in said statement, or knowingly allow or procure the same to be done, shall forfeit, for every such offence, all the liquors made by him or for him, and all the vessels, utensils, and apparatus used in making the same, and be liable to a penalty of not less than five hundred nor more than one thousand dollars, to be recovered with costs of suit, and shall be deemed guilty of a misdemeanor, and shall be imprisoned for a term not exceeding one year. And any brewer who shall neglect to keep books, or refuse to furnish the account and duplicate thereof as provided by law, or shall

Penalty.

Brewer neglecting to keep books or refusing to furnish account, &c.

refuse to permit the proper officer to examine the books in the manner provided, shall, for every such refusal or neglect, forfeit and pay the sum of three hundred dollars.

Penalty.

June 6, 1872.

Stamps for fermented liquors to be prepared by Commissioner and furnished to collectors.

Also suitable permits.

SEC. 22. That the Commissioner of Internal Revenue shall cause to be prepared, for the payment of the tax aforesaid, suitable stamps denoting the amount of tax required to be paid on the hogsheads, barrels, and halves, quarters, sixths, and eighths of a barrel of such fermented liquors (and shall also cause to be prepared suitable permits for the purpose hereinafter mentioned), and shall furnish the same to the collectors of internal revenue, who shall each be required to keep on hand at all times a sufficient supply of permits, and a supply of stamps equal in amount to two months' sale thereof, if there shall be any brewery or brewery warehouse in his district, and the said stamps shall be sold, and the said permits granted and delivered by such collectors, only to the brewers of their district respectively; and such collectors shall keep an account of the number of permits delivered and also the number and value of the stamps sold by them to each of such brewers respectively; and the Commissioner of Internal Revenue shall allow upon all sales of such stamps to any brewer, and by him used in his business, a deduction of seven and a half per centum. And the amount paid into the Treasury by any collector on account of the sale of such stamps to brewers shall be included in estimating the commissions of such collector and of the assessor of the same district.

Collectors to keep on hand two months' supply.

Collectors to keep an account of stamps and permits.

Deduction of 7½ per cent. on sales of stamps to brewers.

Amount of stamps sold to brewers to be included in estimating commissions.

June 6, 1872.

Brewer to obtain stamps from the collector of his district.

Mode of affixing the same.

SEC. 23. That every brewer shall obtain, from the collector of the district in which his brewery or brewery warehouse may be situated, and not otherwise, unless such collector shall fail to furnish the same upon application to him, the proper stamp or stamps, and shall affix upon the spigot-hole, or tap, (of which there shall be but one one) of each and every hogshead, barrel, keg, or other receptacle, in which any fermented liquor shall be contained, when sold or removed from such brewery or warehouse (except in case of removal under permit as hereinafter provided), a stamp denoting the amount of the tax required upon such fermented liquor, in such a way that the said stamp or stamps will be destroyed upon the withdrawal of the liquor from such hogshead, barrel, keg, or other vessel, or upon the introduction of a faucet or other instrument for that purpose; and shall also, at the time of affixing such stamp or stamps, as aforesaid, cancel the same by writing or imprinting thereon the name of the person, firm, or corporation by whom such liquor may have been made, or the initial letters thereof, and the date when canceled. Every brewer who shall refuse or neglect to affix and cancel the stamp or stamps required by law in the manner aforesaid, or who shall affix a false or fraudulent stamp thereto, or knowingly permit the same to be done, shall be liable to pay a penalty of one hundred dollars for each barrel or package on which such omission or fraud occurs, and shall be liable to imprisonment for not more than one year.

Mode of canceling stamps.

Brewer neglecting or refusing to affix and cancel, or affixing fraudulent stamps.

Penalties.

June 6, 1872.

Selling, removing, buying, &c., fermented liquors in packages without stamp or permit, or with false stamps, &c., or twice-used stamps, &c.

SEC. 24. That any brewer, cartman, agent for transportation, or other person who shall sell, remove, receive, or purchase, or in any way aid in the sale, removal, receipt, or purchase, of any fermented liquor contained in any hogshead, barrel, keg, or other vessel from any brewery or brewery warehouse, upon which the stamp or permit in case of removal required by law shall not have been affixed, or on which a false or fraudulent stamp or permit, in case of removal is affixed, with knowledge that it is such, or on which a stamp or permit, in case of removal, once canceled, is used a second time; and any retail dealer or other person who shall withdraw or aid in the withdrawal of any fermented liquor from any hogshead, barrel, keg, or other vessel containing the same, without destroying or defacing the stamp affixed upon the same, or shall withdraw or aid in the withdrawal of any fermented liquor from any hogshead, barrel, keg, or other vessel, upon which the proper stamp shall not have been affixed, or on which a false or fraudulent stamp is affixed, shall be liable to a fine of one hundred dollars, and to imprisonment for not more than one year. Every person who shall make, sell, or use any false or counterfeit stamp, or permit, or die for printing or making stamps or permits which shall be in imitation of, or purport to be a lawful stamp, permit, or die of the kind before mentioned, or who shall procure the same to be done, shall be imprisoned for not less than one nor more than five years: *Provided*, That every brewer who sells fermented liquor at retail at the brewery, or other place where the same is made, shall affix and cancel the proper stamp or stamps upon the hogsheads, barrels, kegs, or other vessels in which the same is contained, and shall keep an account of the quantity so sold by him, and of the number and size of the hogsheads, barrels, kegs, or other vessels in which the same has been contained, and shall make a report thereof, verified by oath, monthly, to the assessor, and forward a duplicate of the same to the collector of the district: *And provided further*, That brewers may remove or transport, or cause to be removed or transported, malt liquor of their own manufacture, known as lager-beer, in quantities of not less than six barrels in one vessel, and may also remove or transport, or cause to be removed or transported, malt liquors known as ale or porter, or any other malt liquor not heretofore mentioned, in quantities not less than fifty barrels at a time, from their breweries or other places of manufacture, to a depot, warehouse, or other place used exclusively for storage or sale in bulk, and occupied by them, from one part of one collection-district to another part of the same collection-district, or from one collection-district to another collection-district, without affixing the proper stamp on said vessels of lager-beer, ale, porter, and other malt liquor at the brewery or place of manufacture, under a permit to be obtained from the collector of the district (who is to grant the same upon application) wherein said malt liquor is manufactured, to said depot or warehouse, but to no other place, under such rules and regulations as the Commissioner

Drawing fermented liquor from packages without stamp, or with false stamp, or without defacing stamp.

Penalty.

Brewers selling at retail at brewery.

Removal or transportation of fermented liquors under permit.

of Internal Revenue may prescribe, and thereafter the manufacturer of the malt liquor so removed shall stamp the same when it leaves such depot or warehouse, in the same manner and under the same penalties and liabilities as when stamped at the brewery as herein provided; and the collector of the district in which such depot or warehouse is situated shall furnish the manufacturer with the stamps for stamping the same, as if the said malt liquor had been manufactured in his district: *And provided further*, That said permit must be affixed to each and every such vessel or cask, and canceled or destroyed in such manner as the Commissioner of Internal Revenue shall prescribe, and under the same penalties and liabilities as herein provided as to stamps: *And provided further*, That when fermented liquor has become sour or damaged, so as to be incapable of use as such, brewers may sell the same for manufacturing purposes, and may remove the same to places where it may be used for such purposes, in casks or other vessels, unlike those ordinarily used for fermented liquors, containing, respectively, not less than one barrel each, and having the nature of their contents marked upon them, without affixing thereon the permit, stamp, or stamps required.

Fermented liquor becoming sour or damaged.

SEC. 25. That every brewer shall by branding mark, or cause to be marked, upon every hogshead, barrel, keg, or other vessel containing the fermented liquor made by him, before it is sold or removed from the brewery, or brewery warehouse, or other place of manufacture, the name of the person, firm, or corporation by whom such liquor was manufactured, and the place where the same shall have been made. And any person, other than the owner thereof, or his agent, authorized so to do, who shall intentionally remove or deface such marks therefrom, shall be liable to a penalty of fifty dollars for each cask or vessel from which the mark is so removed or defaced: *Provided, however*, That when a brewer shall purchase fermented liquor finished and ready for sale from another brewer, in order to supply the customers of such purchaser, such purchaser may, upon written notice to the collector of his intention so to do, and under such regulations as the Commissioner of Internal Revenue may prescribe, furnish his own vessels, branded with his name and the place where his brewery is located, to be filled with the fermented liquor so purchased, and to be so removed; the proper stamp or stamps to be affixed and canceled as aforesaid, by the manufacturer, before removal.

June 6, 1872.

Name of manufacturer and place of manufacture to be marked on packages of fermented liquor.

Penalty for removing such marks.

Brewer purchasing fermented liquor from another brewer.

SEC. 26. That where *a brewer shall*, by reason of an accident by fire or flood, or by reason of his brewery undergoing repairs, or other circumstances which may, in the opinion of the collector of the proper district, require or render it proper that *such* [a] brewer shall be permitted to conduct his business wholly or partially at some other place within the same or adjoining district for a temporary period, it shall be lawful for such collector, under such regulations and subject to such limitation of time as the Com-

June 6, 1872.

Permit to brewer to conduct his business at another place on account of accident, &c.

missioner of Internal Revenue may prescribe, to issue a permit to such brewer authorizing him to conduct his business wholly or partially, according to the circumstances, at such other place for a period in such permit to be stated, and such brewer shall not be required to pay another special tax for the purpose.

June 6, 1872.

Unfermented worts sold to other brewers for certain purposes, how taxed.

SEC. 27. That where malt liquor or tun liquor, in the first stages of fermentation, known as unfermented worts, of whatever kind, is sold by one brewer to another for the purpose of producing fermentation or enlivening old or stale ale, porter, lager-beer, or other fermented liquors, it shall not be liable to a tax to be paid by the seller thereof, but the tax on the same shall be paid by the purchaser thereof, when the same, having been mixed with the old or stale beer, is sold by him as provided by law, and such sale or transfer shall be subject to such restrictions and regulations as the Commissioner of Internal Revenue may prescribe.

June 6, 1872.

Possession of fermented liquor after sale or removal from brewery, &c., on which tax was not paid, cause of forfeiture.

Absence of stamp to be notice and evidence that tax is not paid.

SEC. 28. That the ownership or possession by any person of any fermented liquor after its sale or removal from brewery or warehouse, or other place where it was made, upon which the tax required shall not have been paid, shall render the same liable to seizure wherever found, and to forfeiture, removal under said permits excepted, and that the want of a proper stamp or stamps upon any hogshead, barrel, keg, or other vessel in which fermented liquor may be contained after its sale or removal from the brewery where the same was made, or warehouse, as aforesaid, shall be notice to all persons that the tax has not been paid thereon, and shall be prima-facie evidence of the non-payment thereof.

June 6, 1872.

Removal or defacement of stamp or permit by other than the owner.

Penalty.

SEC. 29. That any person, other than the purchaser or owner of any fermented liquor, or person acting on his behalf, or as his agent, who shall intentionally remove or deface the stamp or permit affixed upon the hogshead, barrel, keg, or other vessel in which the same may be contained, shall be liable to a fine of fifty dollars for each such vessel from which the stamp or permit is so removed or defaced, and to render compensation to such purchaser or owner for all damage sustained by him therefrom.

June 6, 1872.

Withdrawing fermented liquor, for bottling, from unstamped packages, or bottling on brewery premises.

Penalty.

SEC. 30. That any person who shall withdraw any fermented liquor from any hogshead, barrel, keg, or other vessel upon which the proper stamp or stamps shall not have been affixed, for the purpose of bottling the same, or who shall carry on, or attempt to carry on, the business of bottling fermented liquor in any brewery or other place in which fermented liquor is made, or upon any premises having communication with such brewery or any warehouse, shall be liable to a fine of five hundred dollars, and the property used in such bottling or business shall be liable to forfeiture.

SEC. 79. * * * * *Every incorporated or other bank, and every person, firm, or company having a place of business where credits are opened by the deposit or collection of money or currency, subject to be paid or remitted upon draft, check, or order, or where money is advanced or loaned on stocks, bonds, bullion, bills of exchange, or promissory notes, or where stocks, bonds, bullion, bills of exchange, or promissory notes are received for discount or for sale, shall be regarded as a bank or as a banker.* * * * * * *

June 30, 1864.
July 13, 1866, § 9.
Definition of a bank or banker.

SEC. 110. *And be it further enacted, That there shall be levied, collected, and paid a tax of one twenty-fourth of one per centum each month upon the average amount of the deposits of money, subject to payment by check or draft, or represented by certificates of deposit or otherwise, whether payable on demand or at some future day, with any person, bank, association, company, or corporation engaged in the business of banking; and a tax of one twenty-fourth of one per centum each month, as aforesaid, upon the capital of any bank, association, company, or corporation, and on the capital employed by any person in the business of banking beyond the average amount invested in United States bonds; and a tax of one twelfth of one per centum each month upon the average amount of circulation issued by any bank, association, corporation, company, or person, including as circulation all certified checks and all notes and other obligations calculated or intended to circulate or to be used as money, but not including that in the vault of the bank, or redeemed and on deposit for said bank; and an additional tax of one sixth of one per centum, each month, upon the average amount of such circulation, issued as aforesaid, beyond the amount of ninety per centum of the capital of any such bank, association, corporation, company, or person. And a true and accurate return of the amount of circulation, of deposit and of capital, as aforesaid, and of the amount of notes of persons, State banks or State banking associations, paid out by them for the previous month, shall be made and rendered monthly,*[1] *by each of such banks, associations, corporations, companies, or persons to the assessor of the district in which any such bank, association, corporation, or company may be located, or in which such person has his place of business, with a declaration annexed thereto, and the oath or affirmation of such person, or of the president or cashier of such bank, association, corporation, or company, in such form and manner as may be prescribed by the Commissioner of Internal Revenue, that the same contains a true and faithful statement of the amounts subject to tax as aforesaid; and for any refusal or neglect to make or to render return and payment, any such bank, association, corporation, company, or person so in default, shall be subject to and pay a penalty of two hundred dollars, besides the additional penalty and forfeitures in other cases provided by law; and the amount*

June 30, 1864.
July 13, 1866, § 9.
Tax of one twenty-fourth of one per cent. per month upon deposits in banks or with any person engaged in banking.
Tax of one twenty-fourth of one per cent. per month upon the capital of banks and persons engaged in banking.
Amount invested in United States bonds exempted.
Tax of one-twelfth of one per cent. per month upon average amount of circulation issued by any bank, &c.
Additional tax of one sixth of one per cent. per month upon average amount of circulation beyond ninety per cent. of capital.
Return to be verified by the oath of the president or cashier in the form prescribed by the Commissioner.
Penalty for neglect.
Proceedings in case of neglect.

[1] The act of December 24, 1872, sec. 5, (see APPENDIX,) provides that the returns required by this section shall be made and rendered semi-annually on the first day of December and the first day of June, in duplicate; one copy of which shall be transmitted to the collector of the proper district, and one copy to the Commissioner of Internal Revenue.

of circulation, deposit, capital, and notes of persons, State banks and banking associations paid out, as aforesaid, in default of the proper return, shall be estimated by the assessor or assistant assessor of the district as aforesaid, upon the best information he can obtain; and every such penalty may be recovered for the use of the United States in any court of competent jurisdiction.

Banks with branches.

And in the case of banks with branches, the tax herein provided for shall be assessed upon the circulation of each branch, severally, and the amount of capital of each branch shall be considered to be the amount allotted to such branch; and so much of an act entitled "An act to provide ways and means for the support of the government," approved March three, eighteen hundred and sixty-three, as imposes any tax on banks, their circulation, capital, or deposits, other than is herein provided, is hereby repealed:

This section not to apply to national banks.

Provided, That this section shall not apply to associations which are taxed under and by virtue of the act "to provide a national currency secured by a pledge of United States bonds, and to provide for the circulation and redemption thereof."

Deposits in savings institutions having no capital stock, &c., exempt where invested in securities of the United States.

And the deposits in associations or companies known as Provident Institutions, Savings Banks, Savings Funds, or Savings Institutions, having no capital stock and doing no other business than receiving deposits to be loaned or invested for the sole benefit of the parties making such deposits, without profit or compensation to the association or company, shall be exempt from tax on so much of their deposits as they have invested in securities of the United States,

June 6, 1872, § 37. Deposits not exceeding $2000 in the name of any one person, exempt.

and on all deposits NOT EXCEEDING TWO THOUSAND DOLLARS,[1] *made in the name of any one person;*

Returns to be made semi-annually.

and the returns required to be made by such Provident Institutions and Savings Banks after July, eighteen hundred and sixty six, shall be made on[2] *the first Monday of January and July of each year, in such form and manner as may be prescribed by the Commissioner of Internal Revenue.*

June 6, 1872.

Tax on banks and bankers to be paid hereafter semi-annually.

SEC. 37. That the taxes imposed by section one hundred and ten of the act entitled "An act to provide internal revenue to support the government, to pay interest on the public debt, and for other purposes," approved June thirtieth, eighteen hundred and sixty-four, as amended by section nine of the act of July thirteenth, eighteen hundred and sixty-six, to reduce internal taxation and to amend the act aforesaid and acts amendatory thereof, upon the deposits, capital, and circulation of banks, or persons, associations, companies, or corporations engaged in the business of banking, shall hereafter be paid semi-annually, on the first day of January and the first day of July; but the same shall be calculated at the rate per month as prescribed by said section, so that the tax for six months shall not be less than the aggregate would be if the said taxes were collected monthly, as prescribed by said section.

Words "capital employed" shall not include money borrowed from day to day, in certain cases.

And the words "capital employed," in said section, shall not include money borrowed or received from day to day, in the usual course of business, from any person not a partner of or in-

[1] This exemption was of deposits of less than five hundred dollars, but was extended to deposits of two thousand dollars by act of June 6, 1872, § 37, following, which took effect August 1, 1872.

[2] This is changed by sec. 5, act of December 24, 1872. See note on preceding page.

terested in the said bank, association, or firm. And the exemption from tax, authorized by said section, of deposits of less than five hundred dollars, made in the name of one person, in associations or companies known as provident institutions, savings-banks, savings-funds, or savings-institutions, is hereby extended to deposits so made of not exceeding two thousand dollars.

Exemption of deposits in savings-banks extended to $2,000.

SEC. 6. *And be it further enacted, That every national banking association, State bank, or State banking association, shall pay a tax of ten per centum on the amount of notes of any person, State bank, or State banking association, used for circulation and paid out by them after the first day of August, eighteen hundred and sixty-six, and such tax shall be assessed and paid in such a manner as shall be prescribed by the Commissioner of Internal Revenue.*

March 3, 1865.

July 13, 1866, § 9 bis.

Tax of 10 per cent. upon circulation of State banks, &c., after Aug. 1, 1866.

SEC. 2. *And be it further enacted,* That every national banking association, State bank or banker, or association, shall pay a tax of ten per centum on the amount of notes of any town, city, or municipal corporation paid out by them after the first day of May, anno Domini eighteen hundred and sixty-seven, to be collected in the mode and manner in which the tax on the notes of State banks is collected.

March 26, 1867.

All banks, &c., to pay 10 per cent. on notes of any town, &c., paid out by them.

SEC. 14. *And be it further enacted, That the capital of any State bank or banking association which has ceased or shall cease to exist, or which has been or shall be converted into a national bank, shall be assumed to be the capital as it existed immediately before such bank ceased to exist or was converted as aforesaid; and whenever the outstanding circulation of any bank, association, corporation, company, or person shall be reduced to an amount not exceeding five per centum of the chartered or declared capital existing at the time the same was issued, said circulation shall be free from taxation; and whenever any bank which has ceased to issue notes for circulation shall deposit in the Treasury of the United States, in lawful money, the amount of its outstanding circulation, to be redeemed at par, under such regulations as the Secretary of the Treasury shall prescribe, it shall be exempt from any tax upon such circulation; and whenever any State bank or banking association has been converted into a national banking association, and such national banking association has assumed the liabilities of such State bank or banking association, including the redemption of its bills, by any agreement or understanding whatever with the representatives of such State bank or banking association, such national banking association shall be held to make the required return and payment on the circulation outstanding, so long as such circulation shall exceed five per centum of the capital before such conversion of such State bank or banking association.*

March 3, 1865.

July 13, 1866, § 9 bis.

Capital of State banks converted into national banks to be considered the same as before conversion.

When circulation does not exceed 5 per cent. of capital, to be exempt from tax.

National banks to be held for the tax due on outstanding circulation of the State bank, in certain cases.

STAMP TAXES.—SCHEDULES B AND C.

SEC. 151. *And be it further enacted,* That * * * on and after the first day of August, eighteen hundred and sixty-four, there shall be levied, collected, and paid, for and in respect of the several instruments, matters, and things mentioned and described in the schedule (marked B) here-

June 30, 1864.

Imposing stamp taxes in Schedule B.

unto annexed,[1] or for or in respect of the vellum, parchment, or paper upon which such instruments, matters, or things, or any of them shall be written or printed, by any person or persons, or party who shall make, sign, or issue the same, or for whose use or benefit the same shall be made, signed, or issued, the several duties or sums of money set down in figures against the same, respectively, or otherwise specified or set forth in the said schedule.

SCHEDULE B.[1]

STAMP DUTIES.

June 6, 1872, § 36. * * * * * * *

		Duty.
Ibid.	BANK CHECK, draft, or order for the payment of any sum of money whatsoever, drawn upon any bank, banker, or trust company,* at sight or on demand, two cents	*Cts.* 2

Ibid. * * * * * * *

June 6, 1872.

Repealing stamp duties in Schedule B, excepting bank checks, drafts, or orders.

SEC. 36. That on and after the first day of October, eighteen hundred and seventy-two, all the taxes imposed by stamps under and by virtue of Schedule B of section one hundred and seventy of the act approved June thirtieth, eighteen hundred and sixty-four, and the several acts amendatory thereof, be, and the same are hereby repealed, excepting only the tax of two cents on bank checks, drafts, or orders: *Provided*, That where any mortgage has been executed and recorded, or may be executed and recorded, before the first day of October, anno Domini eighteen hundred and seventy-two, to secure the payment of bonds or obligations that may be made and issued from time to time, and such mortgage not being stamped, all such bonds or obligations so made and issued on or after the said first day of October, anno Domini eighteen hundred and seventy-two, shall not be subject to any stamp duty, but only such of their bonds or obligations as may have been made and issued before the day last aforesaid: *And provided further*, That in the mean time the holder of any instrument of writing of whatever kind and description which has been made or issued without being duly stamped, or with a *defunct* [deficient] stamp, may make application to any collector of internal revenue, and that upon such application such collector shall thereupon affix the stamp provided by such holder upon such instrument of writing as [is] required by law to be put upon the same, and subject to the provisions of section one hundred and fifty-eight of the internal revenue laws.

Unstamped mortgage to secure payment of bonds, only certain bonds to be stamped.

June 30, 1864.

July 13, 1866, § 9.

Instrument not to be recorded unless properly stamped.

SEC. 152. *And be it further enacted, That it shall not be lawful to record any instrument, document, or paper required by law to be stamped, unless a stamp or stamps of the proper amount shall have been affixed, and canceled in the manner required by law; and the record of any such instrument, upon which the proper stamp or stamps aforesaid shall not have been affixed and canceled as aforesaid, shall be utterly void, and shall not be used in evidence.*

[1] Schedule B is printed in the Statutes at Large, (vol. 13, p. 298,) immediately following sec. 170 of the act of June 30, 1864; but in sec. 151 of said act it is described as "hereunto annexed," for which reason it is so printed above.

SEC. 153. *And be it further enacted*, That no instrument, document, writing, or paper of any description, required by law to be stamped, shall be deemed or held invalid and of no effect for the want of the particular kind or description of stamp designated for and denoting the duty charged on any such instrument, document, writing, or paper, provided a legal stamp, or stamps, denoting a duty of equal amount, shall have been duly affixed and used thereon: *Provided*, That the provisions of this section shall not apply to any stamp appropriated to denote the duty charged on proprietary articles, or articles enumerated in schedule C.

June 30, 1864.

No instrument to be invalid fo want of particular stamp, if stamps of proper amount are affixed.

Provisions of this section not to apply to proprietary stamps, &c.

SEC. 154. *And be it further enacted, That all official instruments, documents, and papers issued by the officers of the United States Government, or by the officers of any State, county, town, or other municipal corporation, shall be, and hereby are, exempt from taxation: Provided, That it is the intent hereby to exempt from liability to taxation such State, county, town, or other municipal corporation, in the exercise only of functions strictly belonging to them in their ordinary governmental and municipal capacity.*

June 30, 1864.

July 13, 1866, § 9.

Exemptions.

Limited.

SEC. 155. *And be it further enacted, That if any person shall forge or counterfeit, or cause or procure to be forged or counterfeited, any stamp, die, plate, or other instrument, or any part of any stamp, die, plate, or other instrument, which shall have be[en] provided, or may hereafter be provided, made, or used in pursuance of this act, or shall forge, counterfeit, or resemble, or cause or procure to be forged, counterfeited, or resembled, the impression, or any part of the impression, of any such stamp, die, plate, or other instrument as aforesaid, upon any vellum, parchment, or paper, or shall stamp or mark, or cause or procure to be stamped or marked, any vellum, parchment, or paper, with any such forged or counterfeited stamp, die, plate, or other instrument, or part of any stamp, die, plate, or other instrument, as aforesaid, with intent to defraud the United States of any of the taxes hereby imposed, or any part thereof; or if any person shall utter, or sell, or expose to sale, any vellum, parchment, paper, article, or thing, having thereupon the impression of any such counterfeited stamp, die, plate, or other instrument, or any part of any stamp, die, plate, or other instrument, or any such forged, counterfeited, or resembled impression, or part of impression, as aforesaid, knowing the same to be forged, counterfeited, or resembled; or if any person shall knowingly use or permit the use of any stamp, die, plate, or other instrument, which shall have been so provided, made, or used, as aforesaid, with intent to defraud the United States; or if any person shall fraudulently cut, tear, or remove, or cause or procure to be cut, torn, or removed, the impression of any stamp, die, plate, or other instrument, which shall have been provided, made, or used, in pursuance of this act, from any vellum, parchment, or paper, or any instrument or writing charged or chargeable with any of the taxes imposed by law; or if any person shall fraudulently use, join, fix, or place, or cause to be used, joined, fixed, or placed, to, with, or upon any vellum, parchment, paper, or any instrument or writing charged or chargeable with any of the taxes hereby imposed, any adhesive stamp, or the impression of any stamp, die, plate, or other instrument, which shall*

June 30, 1864.

July 13, 1866, § 9.

Forging, counterfeiting, or misusing stamp or dies, &c.

Fraudulently removing stamp, &c.

have been provided, made, or used in pursuance of law, and which shall have been cut, torn, or removed from any other vellum, parchment, or paper, or any instrument or writing charged or chargeable with any of the taxes imposed by law; or if any person shall wilfully remove or cause to be removed, alter or cause to be altered, the canceling or defacing marks on any adhesive stamp, with intent to use the same, or to cause the use of the same after it shall have been once used, or shall knowingly or wilfully sell or buy such washed or restored stamps, or offer the same for sale, or give or expose the same to any person for use, or knowingly use the same, or prepare the same with intent for the further use thereof; or if any person shall knowingly and without lawful excuse (the proof whereof shall lie on the person accused) have in his possession any washed, restored, or altered stamps, which have been removed from any vellum, parchment, paper, instrument, or writing, then, and in every such case, every person so offending, and every person knowingly and wilfully aiding, abetting, or assisting in committing any such offence as aforesaid, shall, on conviction thereof, forfeit the said counterfeit stamps and the articles upon which they are placed, and be punished by fine not exceeding one thousand dollars, or by imprisonment and confinement to hard labor not exceeding five years, or both, at the discretion of the court. And the fact that any adhesive stamp so bought, sold, offered for sale, used, or had in possession as aforesaid, has been washed or restored by removing or altering the canceling or defacing marks thereon, shall be prima facie proof that such stamp has been once used and removed by the possessor thereof from some vellum, parchment, paper, instrument, or writing, charged with taxes imposed by law, in violation of the provisions of this section.

Removing canceling marks, &c.

Having in possession any stamps which have been washed.

Penalties.

The last eight lines added to this section by sec. 2, April 10, 1869.

June 30, 1864.

Mode of canceling adhesive stamps.

SEC. 156. *And be it further enacted*, That in any and all cases where an adhesive stamp shall be used for denoting any duty imposed by this act, except as hereinafter provided, the person using or affixing the same shall write thereupon the initials of his name and the date upon which the same shall be attached or used, so that the same may not again be used. And if any person shall fraudulently make use of an adhesive stamp to denote any duty imposed by this act without so effectually canceling and obliterating such stamp, except as before mentioned, he, she, or they shall forfeit the sum of fifty dollars: *Provided*, That any proprietor or proprietors of proprietary articles, or articles subject to stamp duty under schedule C of this act, shall have the privilege of furnishing, without expense to the United States, in suitable form, to be approved by the Commissioner of Internal Revenue, his or their own dies or designs for stamps to be used thereon, to be made under the direction, and to be retained in the possession of, the Commissioner of Internal Revenue for his or their separate use, which shall not be duplicated to any other person. That in all cases where such stamp is used, instead of his or their writing the date thereon, the said stamp shall be so affixed on the box, bottle, or package, that in opening the same, or using the contents thereof, the said stamp shall be effectually destroyed; and in default thereof, shall be liable

Penalty for failure to cancel.

Proprietors of articles in Schedule C may furnish private dies.

Mode of canceling stamps from private dies.

to the same penalty imposed for neglect to affix said stamp as hereinbefore prescribed in this act. Any person who shall fraudulently obtain or use any of the aforesaid stamps or designs therefor, and any person forging, or counterfeiting, or causing or procuring the forging or counterfeiting any representation, likeness, similitude, or colorable imitation of the said last-mentioned stamp, or any engraver or printer who shall sell or give away said stamps, or selling the same, or, being a merchant, broker, peddler, or person dealing, in whole or in part, in similar goods, wares, merchandise, manufactures, preparations, or articles, or those designed for similar objects or purposes, shall have knowingly or fraudulently in his, her, or their possession, any such forged, counterfeited likeness, similitude, or colorable imitation of the said last-mentioned stamp, shall be deemed guilty of a felony, and, upon conviction thereof, shall be subject to all the penalties, fines, and forfeitures prescribed in the preceding section of this act.

Penalty for forging, counterfeiting or fraudulently obtaining stamps from private dies.

SEC. 157. *And be it further enacted*, That the Commissioner of Internal Revenue be, and he is hereby, authorized to prescribe such method for the cancellation of stamps, as substitute for, or in addition to, the method now prescribed by law, as he may deem expedient and effectual. And he is further authorized in his discretion to make the application of such method imperative upon the manufacturers of proprietary articles, or articles included in schedule C, and upon stamps of a nominal value exceeding twenty-five cents each.

June 30, 1864.

Commissioner may prescribe method of cancellation.

SEC. 158. *And be it further enacted, That any person or persons who shall make, sign, or issue, or who shall cause to be made, signed, or issued, any instrument, document, or paper of any kind or description whatsoever, or shall accept, negotiate, or pay, or cause to be accepted, negotiated, or paid, any * * * draft, or order, * * * for the payment of money, without the same being duly stamped, or having thereupon an adhesive stamp for denoting the tax chargeable thereon, and canceled in the manner required by law, with intent to evade the provisions of this act, shall, for every such offence, forfeit the sum of fifty dollars, and such instrument, document, or paper, * draft, order, * not being stamped according to law, shall be deemed invalid and of no effect: Provided, That the title of a purchaser of land by deed duly stamped shall not be defeated or affected by the want of a proper stamp on any deed conveying said land by any person from, through, or under whom his grantor claims or holds title: And provided further, That hereafter, in all cases where the party has not affixed to any instrument the stamp required by law thereon, at the time of making or issuing the said instrument, and he or they, or any party having an interest therein, shall be subsequently desirous of affixing such stamp to said instrument, or if said instrument be lost, to a copy thereof, he or they shall appear before the collector of the revenue of the proper district, who shall, upon the payment of the price of the proper stamp required by law, and of a penalty of* DOUBLE THE AMOUNT OF TAX REMAINING UNPAID, BUT IN NO CASE LESS THAN FIVE DOLLARS, *and where the whole amount of the tax denoted by the stamp required shall exceed the sum of fifty dollars, on payment*

June 30, 1864.

July 13, 1866, § 9.

Issuing, &c., instruments without proper stamps.

June 6, 1872, § 36.

Ibid.

Instruments unstamped invalid.

Title of second purchaser not affected.

Instruments issued without stamps may be subsequently stamped as here prescribed.

July 14, 1870.

Where stamp-duty exceeds $50, interest to be paid.

also of interest, at the rate of six per centum on said tax from the day on which such stamp ought to have been affixed, affix the proper stamp to such instrument or copy, and note upon the margin thereof the date of his so doing, and the fact that such penalty has been paid; and the same shall thereupon be deemed and held to be as valid, to all intents and purposes, as if stamped when made or issued: And provided further, That where it shall appear to said collector, upon oath or otherwise, to his satisfaction that any such instrument has not been duly stamped at the time of making or issuing the same, by reason of accident, mistake, inadvertence, or urgent necessity, and without any wilful design to defraud the United States of the stamp, or to evade or delay the payment thereof, then and in such case, if such instrument, or, if the original be lost, a copy thereof, duly certified by the officer having charge of any records in which such original is required to be recorded, or otherwise duly proven to the satisfaction of the collector, shall, within twelve calendar months after the first day of August, eighteen hundred and SEVENTY-ONE, *or within twelve calendar months after the making or issuing thereof, be brought to the said collector of revenue to be stamped, and the stamp tax chargeable thereon shall be paid, it shall be lawful for the said collector to remit the penalty aforesaid, and to cause such instrument to be duly stamped. And when the original instrument, or a certified or duly proved copy thereof, as aforesaid, duly stamped so as to entitle the same to be recorded, shall be presented to the clerk, register, recorder, or other officer having charge of the original record, it shall be lawful for such officer, upon the payment of the fee legally chargeable for the recording thereof, to make a new record thereof, or to note upon the original record the fact that the error or omission in the stamping of said original instrument has been corrected pursuant to law; and the original instrument or such certified copy or the record thereof may be used in all courts and places in the same manner and with like effect as if the instrument had been originally stamped: And provided further, That in all cases where the party has not affixed the stamp required by law upon any instrument made, signed, or issued, at a time when and at a place where no collection district was established, it shall be lawful for him or them, or any party having an interest therein, to affix the proper stamp thereto, or, if the original be lost, to a copy thereof; and the instrument or copy to which the proper stamp has been thus affixed prior to the first day of January, one thousand eight hundred and* SEVENTY-TWO, *and the record thereof, shall be as valid, to all intents and purposes, as if stamped by the collector in the manner hereinbefore provided. But no right acquired in good faith before the stamping of such instrument or copy thereof, and the recording thereof, as herein provided, if such record be required by law, shall in any manner be affected by such stamping as aforesaid.*

Collector may remit penalty in certain cases.

July 14, 1870, § 5.

Subsequent stamping may be noted on record, or instrument be newly recorded.

Proviso as to where no collection district was established.

July 14, 1870, § 5.

Rights acquired before stamping not affected.

June 30, 1864.

Commissioner authorized to sell stamps and allow a commission.

SEC. 161. *And be it further enacted*, That the Commissioner of Internal Revenue be, and he is hereby, authorized to sell to and supply collectors, deputy collectors, postmasters, stationers, or any other persons, at his discretion, with adhesive stamps, or stamped paper, vellum, or parchment, as herein provided for, in amounts of not less than fifty dollars, upon the payment, at the time of delivery, of the amount of duties said stamps, stamped paper, vellum, or parchment, so sold or supplied, represent, and may allow, upon the aggregate amount of such stamps, as aforesaid, the sum of not exceeding five per centum as commission to the collectors, postmasters, stationers, or other purchasers; but the cost of any paper, vellum, or parchment shall be paid by the purchaser of such stamped paper, vellum, or parchment, as aforesaid: *Provided*, That *the* proprietor or proprietors of articles named in schedule C, who shall furnish his or heir own die or design for stamps to be used especially for his or their own proprietary articles, shall be allowed the following commissions, namely: On amounts purchased at one time of not less than fifty *dollars* nor more than five hundred dollars, five per centum; *and* on amounts over five hundred dollars, ten per centum *on the whole amount purchased.* The Commissioner of Internal Revenue may, from time to time, make regulations, upon proper evidence of the facts, for the allowance of such of the stamps issued under the provisions of *any internal revenue act* as may have been spoiled, destroyed, or rendered useless or unfit for the purpose intended, or for which the owner may have no use, or which through mistake may have been improperly or unnecessarily used, or where the rates or duties represented thereby have been paid in error or remitted; and such allowance shall be made either by giving other stamps in lieu of the stamps so allowed for, or by repaying the amount or value, after deducting therefrom, in case of repayment, the sum of five per centum to the owner thereof; but no allowance shall be made in any case until the stamps so spoiled or rendered useless shall have been returned to the Commissioner of Internal Revenue, or until satisfactory proof has been made, showing the reason why said stamps cannot be so returned: *Provided*, That the Commissioner of Internal Revenue may, from time to time, furnish, supply, and deliver to any manufacturer of friction or other matches, cigar-lights, or wax tapers, a suitable quantity of adhesive or other stamps, such as may be prescribed for use in such cases, without prepayment therefor, on a credit not exceeding sixty days, requiring, in advance, such security as he may judge necessary to secure payment therefor to the Treasurer of the United States, within the time prescribed for such payment. And upon all bonds or other securities taken by said Commissioner, under the provisions of this act, suits may be maintained by said Treasurer in the circuit or district court of the United States, in the several districts where any of the persons giving said bonds or other securities reside, or may be found, in any appropriate form of action.

Commission on stamps from private dies.

July 14, 1870, § 4.

Commissioner may make allowance for stamps spoiled, &c.

June 6, 1872, § 41.

Manufacturers of matches, &c., may be supplied on credit.

SEC. 162. *And be it further enacted*, That it shall be lawful for any person to present to the collector of the district, subject to the rules and regulations of the Commissioner of Internal Revenue, any instrument not previously issued or used, and require his opinion whether or not the same is chargeable with any stamp duty; and if the said collector

June 30, 1864.

Collectors to stamp instruments as exempt from duty or subject to certain duty.

shall be of opinion that such instrument is chargeable with any stamp duty, he shall, upon the payment therefor, affix and cancel the proper stamp; and if of the opinion that such instrument is not chargeable with any stamp duty, or is chargeable only with the duty by him designated, he is hereby required to impress thereon a particular stamp, to be provided for that purpose, with such words or device thereon as he shall judge proper, which shall denote that such instrument is not chargeable with any stamp duty, or is chargeable only with the duty denoted by the stamp affixed; and every such instrument, upon which the said stamp shall be impressed shall be deemed to be not chargeable, or to be chargeable only with the duty denoted by the stamp so affixed, and shall be received in evidence in all courts of law or equity, notwithstanding any objections made to the same by reason of it being unstamped, or of it being insufficiently stamped.

June 30, 1864.

July 13, 1866, § 9.

Instruments issued without stamps not to be used as evidence or recorded until stamps are affixed.

SEC. 163. *And be it further enacted, That hereafter no deed, instrument, document, writing, or paper, required by law to be stamped, which has been signed or issued without being duly stamped, or with a deficient stamp, nor any copy thereof, shall be recorded, or admitted, or used as evidence in any court until a legal stamp or stamps, denoting the amount of tax, shall have been affixed thereto, as prescribed by law: Provided, That any power of attorney, conveyance, or document of any kind, made or purporting to be made in any foreign country to be used in the United States, shall pay the same tax as is required by law on similar instruments or documents when made or issued in the United States; and the party to whom the same is issued, or by whom it is to be used, shall, before using the same, affix thereon the stamp or stamps indicating the tax required.*

June 30, 1864.

Certain provisions of law applied to articles in Schedule C.

SEC. 164. *And be it further enacted*, That all the provisions of this act relating to dies, stamps, adhesive stamps, and stamp duties shall extend to and include (except where manifestly impracticable) all the articles or objects enumerated in schedule marked C, subject to stamp duties, and apply to the provisions in relation thereto.

SCHEDULE C.[1]

MEDICINES OR PREPARATIONS.

Medicines or preparations.

	Duty. Cts.
For and upon every packet, box, bottle, pot, phial, or other enclosure, containing any pills, powders, tinctures, troches, lozenges, sirups, cordials, bitters, anodynes, tonics, plasters, liniments, salves, ointments, pastes, drops, waters, essences, spirits, oils, or other medicinal preparations or compositions whatsoever, made and sold, or removed for consumption and sale, by any person or persons whatever, wherein the person making or preparing the same has, or claims to have, any private formula or occult secret or art for the making or preparing the same, or has, or claims to have, any exclusive right or title to the making or preparing the same, or which are prepared, uttered, vended, or exposed for sale under any letters-patent, or held out or recommended to the public by the makers, venders, or proprietors thereof as proprietary medicines, or as remedies or specifics for any disease, diseases, or affections whatever affecting the human or animal body, as follows: Where such packet, box, bottle, pot, phial, or other enclosure, with its contents, shall not exceed, at retail price, or value, the sum of twenty-five cents, one cent	1

[1] Schedule C is here printed following sec. 164 act of June 30, 1864, instead of sec. 17 same act (as in Statutes at Large,) as being a more appropriate and convenient arrangement for reference.

	Duty. Cts.	
Where such packet, box, bottle, pot, phial, or other enclosure, with its contents, shall exceed the retail price or value of twenty-five cents, and not exceed the retail price or value of fifty cents, two cents	2	
Where such packet, box, bottle, pot, phial, or other enclosure, with its contents, shall exceed the retail price or value of fifty cents, and shall not exceed the retail price or value of seventy-five cents, three cents	3	
Where such packet, box, bottle, pot, phial, or other inclosure, with its contents, shall exceed the retail price or value of seventy-five cents, and shall not exceed the retail price or value of one dollar, four cents	4	
Where such packet, box, bottle, pot, phial, or other enclosure, with its contents, shall exceed the retail price or value of one dollar, for each and every fifty cents or fractional part thereof over and above the one dollar, as before mentioned, an additional two cents	2	

PERFUMERY, COSMETICS, * MATCHES AND CARDS. — July 13, 1866, § 9.

For and upon every packet, box, bottle, pot, phial, or other enclosure, containing any essence, extract, toilet water, cosmetic, hair oil, pomade, hair-dressing, hair restorative, hair dye, tooth-wash, dentifrice, tooth-paste, aromatic cachous, or any similar articles, by whatsoever name the same heretofore have been, now are, or may hereafter be called, known, or distinguished, used or applied, or to be used or applied as perfumes or applications to the hair, mouth, or skin, made, prepared, and sold or removed for consumption and sale in the United States, where such packet, box, bottle, pot, phial, or other enclosure, with its contents, shall not exceed, at the retail price or value, the sum of twenty-five cents, one cent	1	Perfumery and cosmetics.
Where such packet, box, bottle, pot, phial, or other enclosure, with its contents, shall exceed the retail price or value of twenty-five cents, and shall not exceed the retail price or value of fifty cents, two cents	2	
Where such packet, box, bottle, pot, phial, or other enclosure, with its contents, shall exceed the retail price or value of fifty cents, and shall not exceed the retail price or value of seventy-five cents, three cents	3	
Where such packet, box, bottle, pot, phial, or other enclosure, with its contents, shall exceed the retail price or value of seventy-five cents, and shall not exceed the retail price or value of one dollar, four cents	4	
Where such packet, box, bottle, pot, phial, or other enclosure, with its contents, shall exceed the retail price or value of one dollar, for each and every fifty cents or fractional part thereof over and above the one dollar, as before mentioned, an additional two cents	2	
FRICTION MATCHES, or lucifer matches, or other articles made in part of wood, and used for like purposes, in parcels or packages containing one hundred matches or less, for each parcel or package, one cent	1	Friction matches.
When in parcels or packages containing more than one hundred and not more than two hundred matches, for each parcel or package, two cents	2	
And for every additional one hundred matches or fractional part thereof, one cent	1	
For wax tapers, double the rates herein imposed upon friction or lucifer matches; on cigar lights, made in part of wood, wax, glass, paper, or other materials, in parcels or packages containing twenty-five lights or less in each parcel or package, one cent	1	July 13, 1866, § 9. Wax tapers and cigar lights.
When in parcels or packages containing more than twenty-five and not more than fifty lights, two cents	2	
For every additional twenty-five lights or fractional part of that number, one cent additional	1	
PLAYING CARDS.—*For and upon every pack, not exceeding fifty-two cards in number, irrespective of price or value, five cents*	5	Playing cards.

*   *   *   *   *   *   *

Act March 5, 1872.

June 30, 1864.

July 13, 1866, § 9.

Penalty for selling, &c., articles in Schedule C without proper stamps.

Act March 5, 1872.

SEC. 165. *And be it further enacted, That if any person, firm, company, or corporation shall make, prepare, and sell, or remove for consumption or sale, drugs, medicines, preparations, compositions, articles, or things, including perfumery, cosmetics, lucifer or friction matches, cigar lights, or wax tapers, and playing cards, * * * * whether of domestic manufacture or imported, upon which a duty or tax is imposed by law, as enumerated and mentioned in schedule C, without affixing thereto an adhesive stamp or label denoting the tax before mentioned, he or they shall incur a penalty of fifty dollars for every omission to affix such stamp.*

June 30, 1864.

Penalty for removing or misusing stamps on articles in Schedule C.

SEC. 166. *And be it further enacted*, That every manufacturer or maker of any of the articles for sale mentioned in schedule C, after the same shall have been so made, and the particulars hereinbefore required as to stamps have been complied with, who shall take off, remove, or detach, or cause, or permit, or suffer to be taken off, or removed, or detached, any stamp, or who shall use any stamp, or any wrapper or cover to which any stamp is affixed, to cover any other article or commodity than that originally contained in such wrapper or cover, with such stamp when first used, with the intent to evade the stamp duties, shall for every such article, respectively, in respect of which any such offence shall be committed, be subject to a penalty of fifty dollars, to be recovered together with the costs thereupon accruing; and every such article or commodity as aforesaid shall also be forfeited.

June 30, 1864.

March 3, 1865, § 1.

Penalty for selling articles in Schedule C without stamping.

SEC. 167. *And be it further enacted*, That on and after the passage of this act every maker or manufacturer of any of the articles or commodities mentioned in schedule C, as aforesaid, who shall sell, *expose for sale*, send out, remove, or deliver any article or commodity, manufactured as aforesaid, before the duty thereon shall have been fully paid, by affixing thereon the proper stamp, as provided by law, or who shall hide or conceal, or cause to be hidden or concealed, or who shall remove or convey away, or deposit, or cause to be removed or conveyed away from or deposited in any place, any such article or commodity, to evade the duty chargeable thereon, or any part thereof, shall be subject to a penalty of one hundred dollars, together with the forfeiture of any such article or commodity.

June 30, 1864.

March 3, 1865, § 1.

Certain articles intended for exportation may be manufactured in bonded warehouse.

SEC. 168. *And be it further enacted*, That all medicines, preparations, compositions, perfumery, cosmetics, * cordials, and other liquors manufactured wholly or in part of domestic spirits, intended for exportation, as provided for by law, in order to be manufactured and sold or removed, without being charged with duty, and without having a stamp affixed thereto, shall, under such rules and regulations as the Secretary of the Treasury may prescribe, be made and manufactured in warehouses similarly constructed to those known and designated in Treasury regulations as bonded warehouses, class two: *Provided*, That such manufacturer shall

Bonds to be given.

first give satisfactory bonds to the collector of internal revenue for the faithful observance of all the provisions of law and the rules and regulations as aforesaid, in amount not less than half of that required by the regulations of the

Secretary of the Treasury from persons allowed bonded warehouses. Such goods, when manufactured in such warehouses, may be removed for exportation, under the direction of the proper officer having charge thereof, who shall be designated by the Secretary of the Treasury, without being charged with duty, and without having a stamp affixed thereto. Any manufacturer of the articles aforesaid, or of any of them, having such bonded warehouse, as aforesaid, shall be at liberty, under such rules and regulations as the Secretary of the Treasury may prescribe, to convey therein any materials to be used in such manufacture which are allowed by the provisions of law to be exported free from tax or duty, as well as the necessary materials, implements, packages, vessels, brands, and labels for the preparation, putting up, and export of the said manufactured articles; and every article so used shall be exempt from the payment of stamp and excise duty by such manufacturer. Articles and materials so to be used may be transferred from any bonded warehouse in which the same may be, under such regulations as the Secretary of the Treasury may prescribe, into any bonded warehouse in which such manufacture may be conducted, and may be used in such manufacture, and, when so used, shall be exempt from stamp and excise duty; and the receipt of the officer in charge, as aforesaid, shall be received as a voucher for the manufacture of such articles. Any materials imported into the United States may, under such rules as the Secretary of the Treasury may prescribe, and under the direction of the proper officer, be removed in original packages from on shipboard, or from the bonded warehouse in which the same may be, into the bonded warehouse in which such manufacture may be carried on, for the purpose of being used in such manufacture, without payment of duties thereon, and may there be used in such manufacture. No article so removed, nor any article manufactured in said bonded warehouse, shall be taken therefrom, except for exportation, under the direction of the proper officer having charge thereof, as aforesaid, whose certificate, describing the articles by their marks, or otherwise, the quantity, the date of importation, and name of vessel, with such additional particulars as may from time to time be required, shall be received by the collector of customs in cancellation of the bonds, or return of the amount of foreign import duties. All labor performed and services rendered under these regulations shall be under the supervision of an officer of the customs, and at the expense of the manufacturer.

Goods may be removed without stamps.

As to material to be used in manufacture.

Articles &c. used in such manufacture may be transferred from any bonded warehouse and when used exempt from stamp-duty.

May be removed from ships or bonded warehouse into warehouse where the same are to be used.

Articles not to be removed from bonded warehouse except, &c.

Bonds to be cancelled &c. on officer's certificate of removal.

Labor and services to be under supervision of customs officer, and at manufacturer's expense.

July 13, 1866.

July 20, 1868.

SEC. 28. * *Provided*, That any article manufactured in a bonded warehouse established under the one hundred and sixty-eighth section of the internal revenue act of June thirtieth, eighteen hundred and sixty-four, and located in any of the Atlantic States, may be removed therefrom for transportation to a customs bonded warehouse at any port on the Pacific coast of the United States, for the purpose only of being exported therefrom, under such rules and

Removal to Pacific coast from bonded warehouse established under § 168, June 30, 1864.

regulations and upon the execution of such bonds or other security as the Secretary of the Treasury may prescribe.

July 14, 1870.

Matches, &c., may be removed from manufactory for export.

SEC. 4. * * * *Provided*, That lucifer or friction matches, and cigar lights, and wax tapers, may be removed from the place of manufacture for export to a foreign country without payment of tax, or affixing stamps thereto, under such rules and regulations as the Commissioner of Internal Revenue may prescribe; and all provisions of existing laws inconsistent herewith are hereby repealed.

June 30, 1864.

July 13, 1866, § 9.

Persons offering for sale articles in schedule C to be deemed the manufacturers.

SEC. 169. *And be it further enacted, That any person who shall offer or expose for sale any of the articles named in schedule C, or in any amendments thereto, whether the articles so offered or exposed are imported or are of foreign or domestic manufacture, shall be deemed the manufacturer thereof, and subject to all the duties, liabilities, and penalties imposed by law in regard to the sale of domestic articles without the use of the proper stamp or stamps denoting the tax paid thereon, and all such articles imported, or of foreign manufacture, shall, in addition to the import duties imposed on the same, be subject to the stamp tax, respectively, prescribed in schedule C, as aforesaid.* * * * * * * * *

June 6, 1872, § 34.

July 13, 1866.

No tax upon certain medicines, drugs, or chemicals.

SEC. 13. *And be it further enacted*, That no stamp tax shall be imposed upon any uncompounded medicinal drug or chemical, nor upon any medicine compounded according to the United States or other national pharmacopœia, or of which the full and proper formula is published in any of the dispensatories now or hitherto in common use among physicians or apothecaries, or in any pharmaceutical journal now issued by any incorporated college of pharmacy, when not sold or offered for sale, or advertised under any other name, form, or guise than that under which they may be severally denominated and laid down in said pharmacopœias, dispensatories, or journals as aforesaid; nor upon medicines sold to or for the use of any person, which may be mixed and compounded for said person according to the written receipt or prescription of any physician or surgeon. But nothing in this section shall be construed to exempt from stamp tax any medicinal articles, whether simple or compounded by any rule, authority, or formula, published or unpublished, which are put up in a style or manner similar to that of patent or proprietary medicines in general, or advertised in newspapers or by public handbills for popular sale and use, as having any special proprietary claim to merit, or to any peculiar advantage in mode of preparation, quality, use, or effect, whether such claim be real or pretended.

No patent or proprietary medicine exempt.

June 30, 1864.

Commiss'r may furnish stamps to certain officers for sale.

SEC. 170. *And be it further enacted*, That in any collection district where, in the judgment of the Commissioner of Internal Revenue, the facilities for the procurement and distribution of stamped vellum, parchment, or paper, and adhesive stamps, are or shall be insufficient, the Commissioner, as aforesaid, is authorized to furnish, supply, and deliver to the collector and to the assessor of any such district, and to any assistant treasurer of the United States, or designated depositary thereof, or any postmaster, a suitable quantity or amount of stamped vellum, parchment or paper, and adhesive stamps, without prepayment therefor, and shall allow the highest rate of commissions allowed by law to any other parties purchasing the same, and may in advance require of any such collector, assessor, assistant treasurer of the United States, or postmaster, a bond, with sufficient sureties, to an amount equal to the value of any stamped vellum, parchment, or paper, and adhesive stamps which may be placed in his hands and remain unaccounted for, conditioned for the faithful return, whenever so required, of all quantities or amounts undisposed of, and for the payment, monthly, of all quantities or amounts, sold or not, remaining on hand. And it shall be the duty of such collector to supply his deputies with, or sell to other parties within his district who may make application therefor, stamped vellum, parchment, or paper, and adhesive stamps, upon the same terms allowed by law, or under the regulations of the Commissioner of Internal Revenue, who is hereby authorized to make such other regulations, not inconsistent herewith, for the security of the United States and the better accommodation of the public, in relation to the matters hereinbefore mentioned, as he may judge necessary and expedient. And the Secretary of the Treasury may, from time to time, make such regulations as he may find necessary to insure the safe-keeping or prevent the illegal use of all such stamped vellum, parchment, paper, and adhesive stamps.

May require bond.

Commissioner may make regulations in relation to matters in this section.

Secretary may make regulations for safe keeping, &c., of stamps, &c.

SEIZURES, SUITS, AND PROSECUTIONS, INCLUDING COMPROMISES, REWARDS TO INFORMERS, ETC.

June 30, 1864.

July 13, 1866, § 9.

SEC. 41. *And be it further enacted, That it shall be the duty of the collectors aforesaid, or their deputies, in their respective districts, and they are hereby authorized, to collect all the taxes imposed by law, however the same may be designated, and to prosecute for the recovery of any sum or sums which may be forfeited by law; and all fines, penalties, and forfeitures which may be incurred or imposed by law, shall be sued for and recovered, in the name of the United States, in any proper form of action, or by any appropriate form of proceeding, qui tam or otherwise, before any circuit or district court of the United States for the district within which said fine, penalty, or forfeiture may have been incurred, or before any other court of competent jurisdiction. And taxes may be sued for and recovered, in the name of the United States, in any proper form of action before any circuit or district court of the United States for the district within which the liability to such tax may have been or shall be incurred, or where the party from whom such tax is due may reside at the time of the commencement of said action. But no such suit shall be commenced unless the Commissioner of Internal Revenue shall authorize or sanction the proceedings: Provided, That in case of any suit for penalties or forfeitures brought upon information received from any person, other than a collector, deputy collector, assessor,* [or] *assistant assessor,* * * * * * * * *the United States shall not be subject to any costs of suit, nor shall the fees of any attorney or counsel employed by any such*

Collectors to collect taxes, and sue for fines and penalties.

Suits to be in name of the United States.

Taxes may be sued for.

But not without sanction of the Commissioner.

July 20, 1868, § 50.

United States not subject to costs in certain cases.

Counsel fees not to be paid unless employment authorized.

officer be allowed in the settlement of his account unless the employment of such attorney or counsel shall be authorized by the Commissioner of Internal Revenue, either expressly or by general regulations.

June 30, 1864.

July 13, 1866, § 9.

Collectors to prosecute for fines, penalties, and forfeitures.

Form of proceeding.

SEC. 179. *And be it further enacted, That, where it is not otherwise provided for, it shall be the duty of the collectors, in their respective districts, and they are hereby authorized, to prosecute for the recovery of any sum or sums that may be forfeited; and all fines, penalties, and forfeitures which may be imposed or incurred shall and may be sued for and recovered, where not otherwise provided, in the name of the United States, in any proper form of action, or by any appropriate form of proceeding, before any circuit or district court of the United States for the district within which said fine, penalty, or forfeiture may have been incurred, or before any court of competent jurisdiction.* * * * * * * * *

June 6, 1872, § 39.

When informer's right accrues.

Existing power to remit not affected.

It is hereby declared to be the true intent and meaning of the present[1] *and all previous provisions of internal revenue acts granting shares to informers, that no right accrues to or is vested in any informer in any case until the fine, penalty, or forfeiture in such case is fixed by judgment or compromise and the amount or proceeds shall have been paid, when the informer shall become entitled to his legal share of the sum adjudged or agreed upon and received: Provided, That nothing herein contained shall be construed to limit or affect the power of remitting the whole or any portion of a fine, penalty, or forfeiture conferred on the Secretary of the Treasury by existing laws.* *

July 20, 1868, § 102.

Jurisdiction of circuit and district courts.

When informer is witness in certain cases, the other party may be.

Penalty for receiving money, &c., under threat of informing or for not informing.

The several circuit and district courts of the United States shall have jurisdiction of all offences against any of the provisions of this act committed within their several districts: Provided, That whenever in any civil action for a penalty the informer may be a witness for the prosecution, the party against whom such penalty is claimed may be and shall be admitted as a witness on his own behalf. Every person who shall receive any money or other valuable thing under a threat of informing or as a consideration for not informing against any violation of this act, shall, on conviction thereof, be punished by a fine not exceeding two thousand dollars, or by imprisonment not exceeding one year, or both, at the discretion of the court, with costs of prosecution.

June 6, 1872.

Repeal of so much of § 179 as related to informers' moieties.

Appropriation for detection, &c., of persons guilty of violating internal revenue laws.

SEC. 39. That so much of section *one hundred and seventy*-nine[2] of the act of July thirteenth, eighteen hundred and sixty-six, as provides for moieties to informers be, and the same is hereby, repealed; and the Commissioner of Internal Revenue, with the approval of the Secretary of the Treasury, is hereby authorized to pay such sums, not exceeding in the aggregate the amount appropriated therefor, as may, in his judgment, be deemed necessary for detecting and bringing to trial and punishment persons guilty of violating the internal-revenue laws, or conniving at the same, in cases where such expenses are not otherwise provided for by law; and for this purpose there is hereby appropriated one hundred thousand dollars, or so much thereof

[1] The clause omitted above provided for shares to informers.

[2] The reference here intended is to section 179, act of June 30, 1864, as amended by section 9, act of July 13, 1866.

as may be necessary, out of any money in the Treasury not otherwise appropriated.

March 2, 1867.

Authority to pay for detecting and punishing frauds.

SEC. 7. *And be it further enacted*, That the Commissioner of Internal Revenue, with the approval of the Secretary of the Treasury, is hereby authorized to pay such sums, not exceeding in the aggregate the amount appropriated therefor, as may in his judgment be deemed necessary for detecting and bringing to trial and punishment persons guilty of violating the internal revenue laws, or conniving at the same, in cases where such expenses are not otherwise provided for by law. * * * * * * *

July 13, 1866.

June 6, 1872, § 40.

Proceedings on seizure of goods valued at $500 or less.

SEC. 63. *And be it further enacted*, That hereafter in all cases of seizure of any goods, wares, or merchandise which shall, in the opinion of the collector or deputy collector making such seizure, be of the appraised value of *five hundred* dollars or less, and which shall have been so seized as being subject to forfeiture *under any of the provisions of any internal-revenue act*, excepting in cases otherwise provided, the said collector or deputy collector shall proceed as follows, that is to say: He shall cause a list containing a particular description of the goods, wares, or merchandise seized to be prepared in duplicate, and an appraisement of the same to be made by three sworn appraisers, to be selected by him for said purpose, who shall be respectable and disinterest[ed] citizens of the United States residing within the collection district wherein the seizure was made. The aforesaid list and appraisement shall be properly attested by such collector or deputy collector and the persons making the appraisement, for which service said appraisers shall be allowed the sum of one dollar and fifty cents per day each, to be paid as other necessary charges of collectors according to law. If the said goods shall be found by such appraisers to be of the value of *five hundred* dollars or less, the said collector or deputy collector shall publish a notice, for the space of three weeks, in some newspaper of the district where the seizure was made, describing the articles and stating the time, place, and cause of their seizure, and requiring any person or persons claiming them to appear and make such claim within thirty days from the date of the first publication of such notice: *Provided*, That any person or persons claiming the goods, wares, or merchandise, so seized, within the time specified in the notice, may file with such collector or deputy collector a claim, stating his or their interest in the articles seized, and may execute a bond to the United States in the penal sum of two hundred and fifty dollars, with sureties, to be approved by said collector or deputy collector, conditioned that, in case of condemnation of the articles so seized, the obligors will pay all the costs and expenses of the proceedings, to obtain such condemnation; and upon the delivery of such bond to the collector or deputy collector, he shall transmit the same, with the duplicate list or description of the goods seized, to the United States district attorney for the district, who shall proceed thereon in the ordinary manner prescribed by law: *And provided also*, That if there shall be no claim interposed, and no bond given within the time above specified, the collector or deputy collector, as the case may be,

Appraisement.

Appraisers' fees.

Notice of sale.

Claimant may give bond.

Proceedings thereon.

Sale in default of claim or bond.

shall give ten days' notice of the sale of the goods, wares, or merchandise, by publication; and at the time and place specified in said notice, shall sell the article so seized at public auction, and after deducting the expense of appraisement and sale he shall deposit the proceeds to the credit of the Secretary of the Treasury. And within one year after the sale of any goods, wares, or merchandise, as aforesaid, any person or persons claiming to be interested in the goods, wares, or merchandise so sold may apply to the Secretary of the Treasury for a remission of the forfeiture thereof, or any of them, and a restoration of the proceeds of the said sale, which may be granted by the said Secretary upon satisfactory proof, to be furnished in such manner as he shall prescribe: *Provided*, That it shall be satisfactorily shown that the applicant, at the time of the seizure and sale of the goods in question, and during the intervening time, was absent out of the United States, or in such circumstances as prevented him from knowing of such seizure, and that he did not know of the same; and also that the said forfeiture was incurred without wilful negligence or any intention of fraud on the part of the owner or owners of such goods. If no application for such restoration be made within one year, as hereinbefore prescribed, then, at the expiration of the said time, the Secretary of the Treasury shall cause the proceeds of the sale of the said goods, wares, or merchandise to be distributed according to law, as in the case of goods, wares, or merchandise condemned and sold pursuant to the decree of a competent court.

Application for remission.

When proceeds to be distributed.

March 31, 1868.

July 20, 1868, § 102.

Discontinuance or nolle prosequi.

SEC. 7. *And be it further enacted*, That no * discontinuance or nolle prosequi of any prosecution under this act [approved March 31, 1868] shall be allowed without the permission in writing of the Secretary of the Treasury and the Attorney-General.

July 20, 1868.

Commissioner authorized to compromise, with advice and consent of the Secretary.

SEC. 102. *And be it further enacted*, That in all cases arising under the internal revenue laws where, instead of commencing or proceeding with a suit in court, it may appear to the Commissioner of Internal Revenue to be for the interest of the United States to compromise the same, he is empowered and authorized to make such compromise with the advice and consent of the Secretary of the Treasury; and in every case where a compromise is made there shall be placed on file in the office of the Commissioner the opinion of the solicitor of internal revenue, or officer acting as such, with his reasons therefor, together with a statement of the amount of tax assessed, the amount of additional tax or penalty imposed by law in consequence of the neglect or delinquency of the person against whom the tax is assessed, and the amount actually paid in accordance with the terms of the compromise; but no such compromise shall be made of any case after a suit or proceeding in court has been commenced, without the recommendation also of the Attorney-General: *Provided*, That it shall be lawful for the court at any stage of such suit or criminal proceedings to continue the same for good cause shown on motion of the district attorney.

Recommendation of Attorney-General necessary in certain cases.

Continuance.

March 2, 1867.

SEC. 3. *And be it further enacted*, That in all suits or proceedings arising under the internal revenue laws, to which the United States is party, and in all suits or proceedings against a collector or other officer of the internal revenue, wherein a district attorney shall appear for the purpose of prosecuting or defending, it shall be the duty of said attorney, instead of reporting to the solicitor of the treasury, immediately at the end of every term of the court in which said suit or proceeding is or shall be instituted, to forward to the Commissioner of Internal Revenue a full and particular statement of the condition of all such suits or proceedings appearing upon the docket of said court: *Provided*, That upon the institution of any such suit or proceeding it shall be the duty of said attorney to report to said Commissioner the full particulars relating to such suit or proceeding; and it shall be the duty of the Commissioner of Internal Revenue, (with the approval of the Secretary of the Treasury) to establish such rules and regulations, not inconsistent with law, for the observance of revenue officers, district attorneys and marshals, respecting suits arising under the internal revenue laws, in which the United States is a party, as may be deemed necessary for the just responsibility of those officers and the prompt collection of all revenues and debts due and accruing to the United States under such laws.

District attorneys to report concerning suits, &c., to Commissioner.

Commissioner authorized to establish rules and regulations relative to suits for observance of revenue officers, district attorneys, and marshals.

SEC. 67. *And be it further enacted*, That in any case, civil or criminal, *at law or in equity*, where suit or prosecution shall be commenced in any court of any State against any officer of the United States, appointed under or acting by authority of the act entitled "An act to provide internal revenue to support the Government, to pay interest on the public debt, and for other purposes," passed June thirtieth, eighteen hundred and sixty-four, or of any act in addition thereto or in amendment thereof, or against any person acting under or by authority of any such officer on account of any act done under color of his office, or against any person holding property or estate by title derived from any such officer, concerning such property or estate, and affecting the validity of this act or acts of which it is amendatory, it shall be lawful for the defendant, in such suit or prosecution, at any time before trial,[1] upon a petition to the circuit court of the United States in and for the district in which the defendant shall have been served with process, setting forth the nature of said suit or prosecution, and verifying the said petition by affidavit, together with a certificate, signed by an attorney or counsellor at law of some court of record of the State in which such suit shall have been commenced, or of the United States, setting forth that, as counsel for the petitioner, he has examined the proceedings against him, and carefully inquired into all the matters set forth in the petition, and that he believes the same to be true; which petition, affidavit, and certificate shall be presented to the said circuit court if in session, and if not, to the clerk thereof, at his office, and shall be filed in said office, and the cause shall thereupon be entered on the docket of said court, and shall be thereafter proceeded in as a cause, originally commenced in that court; and it shall

July 13, 1866.

July 14, 1870, § 20.

Suit or prosecution against internal revenue officer, &c., in State court.

May be removed to United States circuit court.

Proceedings therefor.

[1] The defect in the language of this section is not clerical, and cannot be indicated in the usual manner.

be the duty of the clerk of said court, if the suit were com-
July 14, 1870, § 20. menced in the court below by summons, *subpœna*, *petition*, *or by any other form of action except as hereinafter provided*, to issue a writ of certiorari to the State court, requiring said court to send to the said circuit court the record and proceedings in said cause; or if it were commenced by
July 14, 1870, § 20. capias, *or by any similar form of proceeding by which a personal arrest is ordered*, he shall issue a writ of habeas corpus cum causa, a duplicate of which said writ shall be delivered to the clerk of the State court, or left at his office, by the marshal of the district, or his deputy, or some person duly authorized thereto; and thereupon it shall be the duty of the said State court to stay all further proceedings in such cause, and the said suit or prosecution, upon delivery of such process, or leaving the same as aforesaid, shall be deemed and taken to be moved to the said circuit court, and any further proceedings, trial, or judgment therein in the State court shall be wholly null and void. And if the de-
Defendant in actual custody. fendant in any such suit be in actual custody on mesne process therein, it shall be the duty of the marshal, by virtue of the writ of habeas corpus cum causa, to take the body of the defendant into his custody, to be dealt with in the said cause according to the rules of law and the order of the circuit court, or of any judge thereof in vacation. All
Attachments and bail. attachments made and all bail and other security given upon such suit or prosecution shall be and continue in like force and effect as if the same suit or prosecution had proceeded to final judgment and execution in the State court; and if, upon removal of any such suit or prosecution, it shall be made appear to the said circuit court that no copy of the record and proceedings therein in the State court can be obtained, it shall be lawful for said circuit court to allow and require the plaintiff to proceed de novo, and to file a declaration of his cause of action, and the parties may thereupon proceed as in action[s] originally brought in said circuit court; and, on failure of so proceeding, judgment of nolle prosequi may be rendered against the plaintiff, with costs for the defendant: *Provided*,
Construction of act of March 2, 1833. That an act entitled "An act further to provide for the collection of duties on imports," passed March second, eighteen hundred and thirty-three, shall not be so construed as to apply to cases arising under an act entitled "An act to provide internal revenue to support the Government, to pay interest on the public debt, and for other purposes," passed June thirtieth, eighteen hundred and sixty-four, or any act in addition thereto or in amendment thereof, nor to any case in which the validity or interpretation of said act or
Remedy for internal revenue officer, &c. acts shall be in issue: *Provided further*, That if any officer appointed under and by virtue of any act to provide internal revenue, or any person acting under or by authority of any such officer, shall receive any injury to his person or property, for or on account of any act by him done, under any law of the United States for the collection of taxes, he shall be entitled to maintain suit for damage therefor in the circuit court of the United States, in the district wherein the party doing the injury may reside or shall be found.

And all property taken or detained by any officer or other person under authority of any revenue law of the United States shall be irrepleviable, and shall be deemed to be in the custody of the law, and subject only to the orders and decrees of the courts of the United States having jurisdiction thereof. And if any person shall dispossess or rescue, or attempt to dispossess or rescue, any property so taken or detained as aforesaid, or shall aid or assist therein, such person shall be deemed guilty of a misdemeanor, and shall be liable to such punishment as is provided by the twenty-second section of the act for the punishment of certain crimes against the United States, approved the thirtieth day of April, anno Domini one thousand seven hundred and ninety, for the willful obstruction or resistance of officers in the service of process.

Property in custody to be irrepleviable.

Rescuing property.

July 13, 1866.

SEC. 68. *And be it further enacted*, That the fiftieth section of an act passed June thirtieth, eighteen hundred and sixty-four, entitled "An act to provide internal revenue to support the government, to pay interest on the public debt, and for other purposes," is hereby repealed: *Provided*, That any case which may have been removed from the courts of any State under said fiftieth section to the courts of the United States shall be remanded to the State court from which it was so removed, with all the records relating to such cases, unless the justice of the circuit court of the United States in which such suit or prosecution is pending shall be of opinion that said case would be removable from the court of the State to the circuit court under and by virtue of the sixty-seventh section of this act. And in all cases which may have been removed from any court of any State under and by virtue of said fiftieth section of said act of June thirtieth, eighteen hundred and sixty-four, all attachments made, and all bail or other security given upon such suit or prosecution, shall be and continue in full force and effect until final judgment and execution, whether such suit shall be prosecuted to final judgment in the circuit court of the United States, or remanded to the State court from which it was removed.

Repeal of § 50 of act of June 30, 1864.

Cases to be remanded to State court unless, &c.

Attachment, bail, &c., to remain in force.

MISCELLANEOUS PROVISIONS.

June 30, 1864.

SEC. 126. *And be it further enacted*, That for the purposes of this act the term "real estate" shall include all lands, tenements, and hereditaments, corporeal and incorporeal; that the term "succession" shall denote the devolution of title to any real estate; and that the term "person" shall be held to include persons, body corporate, company, or association.

Definition of terms in act of June 30, 1864.

June 30, 1864.

SEC. 182. *And be it further enacted*, That wherever the word State is used in this act, it shall be construed to include the Territories and the District of Columbia, where such construction is necessary to carry out the provisions of this act.

The word State in act June 30, 1864, to include Territories and District of Columbia.

July 20, 1868.

SEC. 104. *And be it further enacted*, That where not otherwise distinctly expressed or manifestly incompatible with the intent thereof, the word "person," as used in this act,

Definition of terms in act of July 20, 1868.

shall be construed to mean and include a firm, partnership, association, company, or corporation, as well as a natural person; and words of the masculine gender, as applied to persons, to mean and include the feminine gender; and the singular number to mean and include the plural number; and the word "State" to mean and include a Territory and District of Columbia; and the word "county," to mean and include parish, district, or other equivalent territorial subdivision of a State.

June 30, 1864.

Commissioner authorized to make regulations necessary by reason of alteration of laws.

SEC. 174. *And be it further enacted*, That the said Commissioner of Internal Revenue, under the direction of the Secretary of the Treasury, is authorized to make all such regulations, not otherwise provided for, as may become necessary by reason of the alteration of the laws in relation to internal revenue, by virtue of this act.

July 20, 1868.

Commissioner authorized to make regulations necessary by reason of change of law.

SEC. 103. *And be it further enacted*, That when any tax is imposed, and the mode or time of assessment or collection is not provided for, the same shall be established by regulation of the Commissioner of Internal Revenue; and the Commissioner is authorized to make all such regulations, not otherwise provided for, as may become necessary by reason of any change of law in relation to internal revenue made by this act.

June 6, 1872.

Act to take effect August 1, 1872, except where otherwise provided.

Commissioner authorized to make regulations necessary by reason of changes in laws.

SEC. 47. That this act shall take effect on the first day of August, eighteen hundred and seventy-two, except where otherwise provided. And the Commissioner of Internal Revenue is hereby authorized to make, with the approval of the Secretary of the Treasury, all such regulations not in conflict with any provision of law as may become necessary by reason of any changes in the internal-revenue laws made by this act.

June 30, 1864.

False swearing in any proceeding under this act to be deemed perjury, and so punished.

SEC. 42. *And be it further enacted*, That if any person, in any case, matter, hearing, or other proceeding in which an oath or affirmation shall be required to be taken or administered under and by virtue of this act, shall, upon the taking of such oath or affirmation, knowingly and wilfully swear or affirm falsely, every person so offending shall be deemed guilty of perjury, and shall, on conviction thereof, be subject to the like punishment and penalties now provided by the laws of the United States for the crime of perjury.

June 30, 1864.

Separate accounts to be kept of moneys receiv'd from the several States, districts, &c., and the several sources of revenue, with the compensation, &c., paid to officers.

SEC. 43. *And be it further enacted*, That separate accounts shall be kept at the Treasury of all moneys received from internal duties or taxes in each of the respective States, Territories, and collection-districts; and that separate accounts shall be kept of the amount of each species of duty or tax that shall accrue, so as to exhibit, as far as may be, the amount collected from each source of revenue, with the moneys paid as compensation and for allowances to the collectors and deputy collectors, assessors and assistant assessors, inspectors, and other officers employed in each of the respective States, Territories, and collection districts, an abstract in tabular form of which accounts it shall be the duty of the Secretary of the Treasury, annually, in the month of December, to lay before Congress.

Annual abstract to be laid before Congress.

SEC. 181. * * *Provided*, That, * * * [after] the thirtieth day of June, eighteen hundred and sixty-five,* the Secretary of the Treasury shall embrace in his annual estimates the amount which, in his opinion, will be required for the expenses of this branch of the public service.

June 30, 1864.

Secretary of the Treasury to embrace in his annual estimates expenses of internal revenue service.

SEC. 1. * * And hereafter the said Commissioner [of Internal Revenue] shall estimate in detail, by collection districts, the expense of assessing and the expense of the collection of internal revenue. (*Extract from An Act making appropriations for the Legislative, Executive, and Judicial expenses of the Government for the year ending the thirtieth of June, eighteen hundred and seventy.* Approved March 3, 1869. 15 *Stat., p.* 290.)

March 3, 1869.

Commissioner to estimate by collection districts expenses of assessing and collecting internal revenue.

SEC. 46. *And be it further enacted*, That if, for any cause, at any time after this act goes into operation, the laws of the United States cannot be executed in a State or Territory of the United States, or any part thereof, or within the District of Columbia, it shall be the duty of the President, and he is hereby authorized, to proceed to execute the provisions of this act within the limits of such State or Territory, or part thereof, or District of Columbia, so soon as the authority of the United States therein shall be re-established, and to collect the taxes, duties, and licenses, in such States and Territories, under the regulations prescribed in this act, so far as applicable; and where not applicable, the assessment and levy shall be made, and the time and manner of collection regulated, by the instructions and directions of the Commissioner of Internal Revenue, under the direction of the Secretary of the Treasury.

June 30, 1864.

Duty of the President in States and Territories where the laws cannot be executed.

SEC. 48. *And be it further enacted, That all goods, wares, merchandise, articles, or objects, on which taxes are imposed by the provisions of law, which shall be found in the possession, or custody, or within the control of any person or persons, for the purpose of being sold or removed by such person or persons in fraud of the internal revenue laws, or with design to avoid payment of said taxes, may be seized by the collector or deputy collector of the proper district, or by such other collector or deputy collector as may be specially authorized by the Commissioner of Internal Revenue for that purpose, and the same shall be forfeited to the United States; and also all raw materials found in the possession of any person or persons intending to manufacture the same into articles of a kind subject to tax for the purpose of fraudulent[ly] selling such manufactured articles, or with design to evade the payment of said tax; and also all tools, implements, instruments, and personal property whatsoever, in the place or building or within any yard or enclosure where such articles or such raw materials shall be found, may also be seized by any collector or deputy collector, as aforesaid, and the same shall be forfeited as aforesaid; and the proceedings to enforce said forfeiture shall be in the nature of a proceeding in rem in the circuit or district court of the United States for the district where such seizure is made, or in any other court of competent jurisdiction. And any person who shall have in his custody or possession any such goods, wares, merchandise, articles, or objects, subject to tax as aforesaid, for*

June 30, 1864.

July 13, 1866, § 9.

Taxable articles held by any person with intent to defraud the revenue may be seized by certain officers and forfeited.

But see §§ 36, 39, 69, 71, 89, 92, July 20, 1868.

Raw materials to be forfeited.

Tools, &c., found on premises to be forfeited.

Forfeiture to be enforced by proceedings *in rem*.

Penalty of $500, or not less than double the amount of taxes.

the purpose of selling the same with the design of avoiding payment of the taxes imposed thereon, shall be liable to a penalty of five hundred dollars, or not less than double the amount of taxes fraudulently attempted to be evaded, to be recovered in any court of competent jurisdiction; and the goods, wares, merchandise, articles, or objects, which shall be so seized by any collector or deputy collector, may, at the option of the collector, be delivered to the marshal of said district, and remain in the care and custody of said marshal, and under his control, until he shall obtain possession by process of law, and the cost of seizure made before process issues shall be taxable by the court: Provided, That *when the property so seized may be liable to perish or become greatly reduced in price or value by keeping, or when it cannot be kept without great expense, the owner thereof, the collector, or the marshal of the district, may apply to the assessor of the district to examine said property; and if, in the opinion of said assessor, it shall be necessary that the said property should be sold to prevent such waste or expense, he shall appraise the same; and the owner thereupon shall have said property returned to him, upon giving bond in such form as may be prescribed by the Commissioner of Internal Revenue, and in an amount equal to the appraised value, with such sureties as the said assessor shall deem good and sufficient, to abide the final order, decree, or judgment of the court having cognizance of the case, and to pay the amount of said appraised value to the collector, marshal, or otherwise, as he may be ordered and directed by the court, which bond shall be filed by said assessor with the United States district-attorney for the district in which said proceedings in rem may be commenced: Provided further, That in case said bond shall have been executed and the property returned before seizure thereof, by virtue of the process aforesaid, the marshal shall give notice of the pendency of proceedings in court to the parties executing said bond, by personal service or publication, and in manner and form as the court may direct, and the court shall thereupon have jurisdiction of said matter and parties in the same manner as if such property had been seized by virtue of the process aforesaid. But if said owner shall neglect or refuse to give said bond, the assessor shall issue to the collector or marshal aforesaid an order to sell the same; and the said collector or marshal shall thereupon advertise and sell the said property at public auction in the same manner as goods may be sold on final execution in said district; and the proceeds of the sale, after deducting the reasonable costs of the seizure and sale, shall be paid to the court aforesaid, to abide its final order, decree, or judgment.*

Custody of goods may be given to U. S. marshal.

Property perishable, &c., may be appraised and returned to owner, he giving bond for same.

If bond not given, property may be sold at auction.

June 30, 1864.

Provisions in act of June 30, 1864, for delivery of returns &c., imposition of fines, &c., apply to all persons, corporations, &c.

SEC. 49. *And be it further enacted*, That all the provisions hereinafter made for the delivery of returns, lists, statements, and valuations, and for additions to the duty in case of false or fraudulent lists or returns, or in case of undervaluation or understatement on lists or returns, or in case of refusal or neglect to deliver lists or returns, and for the imposition of fines, penalties, and forfeitures, shall be held and taken to apply to all persons, associations, corporations, or companies liable to pay duty or tax; and any additions to duties, fines, penalties, or forfeitures hereinafter imposed for failure to perform any duty required to be performed,

Fines, &c., imposed to be additional to those before

shall be held and taken to be additional to those herein-before [in act of June 30, 1864,] provided. provided in act June 30, 1864.

SEC. 97. *And be it further enacted*, That every person, firm, or corporation, who shall have made any contract prior to the passage of this act, [June 30, 1864,] and without other provisions therein for the payment of duties imposed by law enacted subsequent thereto, upon articles to be delivered under such contract, is hereby authorized and empowered to add to the price thereof so much money as will be equivalent to the duty so subsequently imposed on said articles, and not previously paid by the vendee, and shall be entitled by virtue hereof to be paid, and to sue for and recover, the same accordingly: *Provided*, That where the United States is the purchaser under such prior contract, the certificate of the proper officer of the department by which the contract was made, showing, acccording to regulations to be prescribed by the Secretary of the Treasury, the articles so purchased by the United States, and liable to such subsequent duty, shall be taken and received, so far as the same is applicable, in discharge of such subsequent duties on articles so contracted to be delivered to the United States and actually delivered according to such contract.

June 30, 1864.

Manufacturers delivering goods under contract made prior to this act are allowed to add to the price of such goods so much as will be equivalent to the duty subsequently imposed, &c.

Proviso, when the United States is the purchaser.

SEC. 115. *And be it further enacted*, That whenever by this act any license, duty, or tax of any description has been imposed on any person or corporate body, or property of any person, or incorporated or unincorporated company, having more than one place of business, it shall be lawful for the Commissioner of Internal Revenue to prescribe and determine in what district such tax shall be assessed and collected, and to what officer thereof the official notices required in that behalf shall be given, and of whom payment of such tax shall be demanded: *Provided*, That all taxes on manufactures, manufacturing companies, and manufacturing corporations shall be assessed, and the tax collected, in the district within which the place of manufacture is located, unless otherwise provided.

June 30, 1864.

Persons, &c., having more than one place of business.

Commissioner to determine the district of assessment and collection.

Proviso as to place of manufacture.

SEC. 180. *And be it further enacted*, That if any person liable and required to pay any tax upon any article, goods, wares, merchandise, or manufactures, as herein provided, shall sell, or cause or allow the same to be sold, before the tax to which such article, goods, wares, merchandise, or manufacture is legally liable, is paid, with intent to avoid such tax, or in fraud of the revenue herein provided, any debt contracted in the sale of such article, goods, wares, or merchandise, or manufactures, or any security given therefor, unless the same shall have been bona fide transferred to the hands of an innocent holder, shall be entirely void, and the collection thereof shall not be enforced in any court. And if any such article, goods, wares, merchandise, or manufacture has been paid for, in whole or in part, the sum so paid shall be deemed forfeited, and any person who will sue for the same in an action of debt shall recover of the seller the amount so paid, one-half to his own use, and the other half to the use of the United States.

June 30, 1864.

Debts contracted through the sale of articles, with intent to evade tax, to be void.

If paid, sum paid to be forfeited and may be sued for.

SEC. 17. *And be it further enacted*, That the privilege of purchasing supplies of goods imported from foreign coun-

March 3, 1865.

Goods may be

purchased by Government free of tax. tries for the use of the United States, duty free, which now does or hereafter shall exist by provision of law, shall be extended, under such regulations as the Secretary of the Treasury may prescribe, to all articles of domestic production which are subject to tax by the provisions of this act.

July 13, 1866.

Removal or concealment with intent to defraud the revenue, cause of forfeiture.

But see §§ 36, 39, 69, 71, 89, 92, act of July 20, 1868.

SEC. 14. *And be it further enacted*, That in case any goods or commodities for or in respect whereof any tax is or shall be imposed, or any materials, utensils, or vessels proper or intended to be made use of for or in the making of such goods or commodities shall be removed, or shall be deposited or concealed in any place, with intent to defraud the United States of such tax, or any part thereof, all such goods and commodities, and all such materials, utensils, and vessels, respectively shall be forfeited; and in every such case, and in every case where any goods or commodities shall be forfeited under this act, or any other act of Congress relating to the internal revenue, all and singular the casks, vessels, cases or other packages whatsoever, containing, or which shall have contained, such goods or commodities, respectively, and every vessel, boat, cart, carriage, or other conveyance whatsoever, and all horses or other animals, and all things used in the removal or for the deposit or concealment thereof, respectively, shall be forfeited; and every person who shall remove, deposit, or conceal, or be concerned in removing, depositing or concealing any goods or commodities for or in respect whereof any tax is or shall be imposed, with intent to defraud the United States of such tax or any part thereof, shall be liable to a fine or penalty of not exceeding five hundred dollars.

Casks, &c., boats, &c., horses, carts, &c., to be forfeited.

Fine or penalty.

July 13, 1866.

Search-warrant may be issued.

SEC. 15. *And be it further enacted*, That the judge of any circuit or district court of the United States, or any commissioner thereof, may issue a search warrant, authorizing any internal revenue officer to search any premises, if such officer shall make oath in writing that he has reason to believe, and does believe, that a fraud upon the revenue has been or is being committed upon or by the use of said premises.

July 13, 1866.

Misuse of revenue stamps, &c.

See §§ 43 and 72, July 20, 1868, as amended.

SEC. 16. *And be it further enacted*, That in case any person shall sell, give, or purchase or receive any box, barrel, bag, or any vessel, package, wrapper, cover, or envelope of any kind, stamped, branded or marked in any way so as to show that the contents or intended contents thereof have been duly inspected, or that the tax thereon has been paid, or that any provision of the internal revenue laws has been complied with, whether such stamping, branding, or marking may have been a duly authorized act or may be false and counterfeit, or otherwise without authority of law, said box, barrel, bag, vessel, package, wrapper, cover, or envelope being empty, or containing anything else than the contents which were therein when said articles had been so lawfully stamped, branded, or marked by an officer of the revenue, such person shall be liable to a penalty of not less than fifty nor more than five hundred dollars. And any person who shall make, manufacture, or produce any box, barrel, bag, vessel, package, wrapper, cover, or envelope, stamped, branded, or marked, as above described, or shall stamp, brand, or mark the same, as hereinbefore recited,

Penalties.

shall, upon conviction thereof, be liable to penalty as before provided in this section. And any person who shall violate the foregoing provisions of this section, with intent to defraud the revenue, or to defraud any person, shall, upon conviction thereof, be liable to a fine of not less than one thousand nor more than five thousand dollars, or imprisonment for not less than six months, nor more than five years, or both such fine and imprisonment, at the discretion of the court. And all articles sold, given, purchased, received, made, manufactured, produced, branded, stamped, or marked in violation of the provisions of this section, and all their contents, shall be forfeited to the United States.

In case of fraudulent intent.

Forfeiture.

July 13, 1866.

SEC. 17. *And be it further enacted*, That where any whiskey,* tobacco, or other articles of manufacture or produce, requiring brands, stamps, or marks of whatever kind to be placed thereon, shall be sold upon distraint, forfeiture, or other process provided by law, the same not having been branded, stamped, or marked as required by law, the officer selling the same shall, upon sale thereof, fix, or cause to be affixed the brands, stamps, or marks so required, and deduct the expense thereof from the proceeds of such sale.

Articles requiring brands, &c., sold on distraint, forfeiture, &c. shall be properly marked and stamped by the officer making sale.

See §§ 58 and 67, July 20, 1868, as amended.

July 13, 1866.

SEC. 62. *And be it further enacted*, That if any person or persons shall, directly or indirectly, promise, offer, or give, or cause or procure to be promised, offered, or given, any money, goods, right in action, bribe, present, or reward, or any promise, contract, undertaking, obligation, or security for the payment or delivery of any money, goods, right in action, bribe, present, or reward, or any other valuable thing whatever to any officer of the United States, or person holding any place of trust or profit, or discharging any official function under, or in connection with, any department of the Government of the United States, after the passage of this act, with intent to influence his decision or action on any question, matter, cause, or thing which may then be pending, or may by law be brought before him in his official capacity, or in his place of trust or profit, or with intent to influence any such officer or person to commit, or aid or abet in committing, any fraud on the revenue of the United States, or to connive at or collude in, or to allow or permit, or make opportunity for the commission of any such fraud, and shall be thereof convicted, such person or persons so offering, promising, or giving, or causing, or procuring to be promised, offered, or given any such money, goods, right in action, bribe, present, or reward, or any promise, contract, undertaking, obligation, or security for the payment or delivery of any money, goods, right in action, bribe, present, or reward, or other valuable thing whatever, and the officer or person who shall in anywise accept or receive the same, or any part [thereof,] respectively shall be liable to indictment in any court of the United States having jurisdiction, and shall, upon conviction thereof, be fined not exceeding three times the amount so offered, promised, given, accepted, or received, and imprisoned not exceeding three years; and the person convicted of so accepting or receiving the same, or any part thereof, if an officer or person holding any such place of trust or profit, shall forfeit his office or place; and any person so convicted

Bribing public officers.

Accepting bribes.

Penalty.

under this section shall forever be disqualified to hold any office of honor, trust or profit under the United States.

March 2, 1867.

Assessment of tax for articles sold without being properly stamped.

See § 60, act July 20, 1868, as amended, as to tobacco, snuff, and cigars.

SEC. 5. *And be it further enacted*, That if the manufacturer of any article upon which a tax is required to be paid by means of a stamp shall have sold or removed for sale any such articles without the use of the proper stamp, in addition to the penalties now imposed by law for such sale or removal, it shall be the duty of the proper assessor or assistant assessor, within a period of not more than two years after such removal or sale, upon such information as he can obtain, to estimate the amount of the tax which has been omitted to be paid, and to make an assessment therefor, and certify the same to the collector; and the subsequent proceedings for collection shall be in all respects like those for the collection of taxes upon manufactures and productions.

March 2, 1867.

Personation of revenue officer, &c.

SEC. 28. *And be it further enacted*, That if any person shall falsely represent himself to be a revenue officer of the United States, and shall in such assumed character demand or receive any money or other article of value from any person for any duty or tax due to the United States, or for any violation or pretended violation of any revenue law of the United States, such person shall be deemed guilty of a felony, and on conviction thereof shall be liable to a fine of five hundred dollars, and to imprisonment not less than six months and not exceeding two years, at the discretion of the court.

Penalty.

March 2, 1867.

Conspiring to commit an offence, or to defraud, &c.

SEC. 30. *And be it further enacted*, That if two or more persons conspire either to commit any offence against the laws of the United States, or to defraud the United States in any manner whatever, and one or more of said parties to said conspiracy shall do any act to effect the object thereof, the parties to said conspiracy shall be deemed guilty of a misdemeanor, and on conviction thereof shall be liable to a penalty of not less than one thousand dollars and not more than ten thousand dollars, and to imprisonment not exceeding two years. And when any offence shall be begun in one judicial district of the United States and completed in another, every such offence shall be deemed to have been committed in either of the said districts, and may be dealt with, inquired of, tried, determined and punished in either of the said districts, in the same manner as if it had been actually and wholly committed therein.

Penalty.

Offence begun in one district and completed in another, to be held to have been committed in either.

July 20, 1868.

April 10, 1869, § 1.

Penalty for knowingly or wilfully violating the law relative to distilled spirits, tobacco, snuff, and cigars, where there is no specific penalty imposed by any other section.

SEC. 96. *And be it further enacted*, That if any distiller, rectifier, wholesale liquor-dealer, * or manufacturer of tobacco or cigars, shall knowingly or willfully omit, neglect, or refuse to do or cause to be done any of the things required by law in the carrying on or conducting of his business, or shall do anything by this act prohibited, if there be no specific penalty or punishment imposed by any other section of this act for the neglecting, omitting, or refusing to do, or for the doing or causing to be done the thing required or prohibited, he shall pay a penalty of one thousand dollars; and if the person so offending be a distiller, rectifier, [or] wholesale liquor-dealer, * all distilled spirits or liquors owned by him, or in which he has any interest as owner, and if he be a manufacturer of tobacco

April 10, 1869, § 1.

Forfeiture.

or cigars, all tobacco or cigars found in his manufactory, shall be forfeited to the United States.

July 20, 1868.

Fraud relative to execution or signing of any document required by this act, &c.

SEC. 99. *And be it further enacted*, That any person who shall simulate or falsely or fraudulently execute or sign any bond, permit, entry, or other document required by the provisions of this act, or by any regulation made in pursuance thereof, or who shall procure the same to be falsely or fraudulently executed; or who shall advise, aid in, or connive at the execution thereof, shall, on conviction, be imprisoned for a term not less than one year nor more than five years; and the property to which such false or fraudulent instrument relates shall be forfeited.

July 20, 1868.

Secretary and Commissioner authorized to alter, renew, or change the form, &c., of stamps, marks, and labels.

SEC. 101. *And be it further enacted*, That the Secretary of the Treasury and Commissioner of Internal Revenue are authorized and empowered to alter, renew, or change the form, style, and device of any stamp, mark, or label used under any provision of the laws relating to distilled spirits, tobacco, snuff, and cigars, when in their judgment necessary for the collection of revenue tax, or the prevention or detection of frauds thereon; and to make and publish such regulations for the use of such mark, stamp, or label as they may find requisite. * * *

June 6, 1872, § 12.

July 20, 1868.

Internal-revenue laws imposing certain taxes to extend to articles produced within exterior boundaries of U. S.

SEC. 107. *And be it further enacted*, That the internal revenue laws imposing taxes on distilled spirits, fermented liquors, tobacco, snuff, and cigars, shall be held and construed to extend to such articles produced anywhere within the exterior boundaries of the United States, whether the same shall be within a collection district or not.

July 20, 1868.

Provisions of this act requiring use of stamps, when to take effect.

SEC. 108. *And be it further enacted*, That all provisions of this act which require the use of stamps shall take effect at the end of sixty days from the passage of this act: *Provided*, That if at any time prior to the expiration of the said sixty days it shall be shown to the satisfaction of the Secretary of the Treasury that a longer delay is necessary for the preparation and due delivery of any of such stamps, he shall be authorized to fix a day not later than the first day of December next[1] for putting said provisions, relative to the use of either of such stamps, into operation, and shall give public notice of the day so fixed and determined upon, which day shall then be held and taken to be the time when that portion of this act which requires the use of stamps shall have effect.

---

[1] TREASURY DEPARTMENT, *September* 17, 1868.

In pursuance of authority conferred on me by the 108th section of the act imposing taxes on distilled spirits and tobacco, approved July 20, 1868, notice is hereby given, that the provisions of the said act requiring the use of stamps for distilled spirits, are postponed so as to go into practical operation upon the second day of November next; and that the provisions of the said act requiring the use of stamps for tobacco, snuff, and cigars are postponed so as to go into practical operation upon the twenty-third day of November next.

H. McCULLOCH,
Secretary of the Treasury.

REPEALING AND SAVING SECTIONS.

June 30, 1864.

Provisions to remain in force for collecting taxes already accrued, &c.

SEC. 173. * * * * * * * * *Provided*, That all the provisions of said acts[1] shall be in force for levying and collecting all taxes, duties, and licenses properly assessed or liable to be assessed, or accruing under the provisions of former acts, or drawbacks, the right to which has already accrued, or which may hereafter accrue, under said acts, and for maintaining and continuing liens, fines, penalties, and forfeitures incurred under and by virtue thereof. And for carrying out and completing all proceedings which have been already commenced, or that may be commenced, to enforce such fines, penalties, and forfeitures, or criminal proceedings under said acts, and for the punishment of crimes of which any party shall be or has been found guilty: *And provided, further*, That no office created by the said acts, and continued by this act, shall be vacated by reason of any provisions herein contained, but the officers heretofore appointed shall continue to hold the said offices without re-appointment: *And provided, further*, That whenever the duty imposed by any existing law shall cease in consequence of any limitation therein contained before the respective provisions of this act shall take effect, the same duty shall be, and is hereby, continued until such provisions of this act shall take effect; and where any act is hereby repealed, no duty imposed thereby shall be held to cease, in consequence of such repeal, until the respective corresponding provisions of this act shall take effect: *And provided, further*, That all manufactures and productions on which a duty was imposed by either of the acts repealed by this act, which shall be in the possession of the manufacturer or producer, or of his agent or agents, on the day when this act takes effect, the duty imposed by any such former act not having been paid, shall be held and deemed to have been manufactured or produced after such date; and whenever by the terms of this act a duty is imposed upon any articles, goods, wares, or merchandise manufactured or produced, upon which no duty was imposed by either of said former acts, it shall apply to such as were manufactured or produced and not removed from the place of manufacture or production on the day when this act takes effect. * * * * * * * *

Offices not to be vacated by reason of this act.

Former duties to continue until corresponding provisions of this act take effect.

Articles manufactured before the passage of the several acts.

March 3, 1865.

Inconsistent provisions repealed.

Saving of taxes due or returnable, and of fines, &c., incurred.

SEC. 16. *And be it further enacted*, That all provisions of any former act inconsistent with the provisions of this act are hereby repealed: *Provided, however*, That no duty imposed by any previous act, which has become due or of which return has been or ought to be made, shall be remitted or released by this act, but the same shall be collected and paid, and all fines and penalties heretofore incurred shall be enforced and collected, and all offences heretofore committed shall be punished as if this act had not been passed; and the Commissioner of Internal Revenue, under the direction of the Secretary of the Treasury, is authorized

[1] Referring to acts and parts of acts repealed by previous provisions of this section.

to make all necessary regulations and to prescribe all necessary forms and proceedings for the collection of such taxes and the enforcement of such fines and penalties for the execution of the provisions of this act.

Commissioner to make necessary regulations, &c.

SEC. 70. *And be it further enacted*, That this act shall take effect, where not otherwise provided, on the first day of August, eighteen hundred and sixty-six, and all provisions of any former act inconsistent with the provisions of this act are hereby repealed: *Provided, however*, That all the provisions of said acts shall be in force for collecting all taxes, duties and licenses properly assessed or liable to be assessed, or accruing under the provisions of acts, the right to which has already accrued or which may hereafter accrue under said acts, and for maintaining and continuing liens, fines, penalties, and forfeitures incurred under and by virtue thereof, and for carrying out and completing all proceedings which have been already commenced, or that may be commenced, to enforce such fines, penalties, and forfeitures, or criminal proceedings under said acts, and for the punishment of crimes of which any party shall be or has been found guilty: *And provided further*, That whenever the duty imposed by any existing law shall cease in consequence of any limitation therein contained before the respective provisions of this act shall take effect, the same duty shall be, and is hereby, continued until such provisions of this act shall take effect; and where any act is hereby repealed, no duty imposed thereby shall be held to cease, in consequence of such repeal, until the respective corresponding provisions of this act shall take effect: *And provided further*, That all manufactures and productions on which a duty was imposed by either of the acts repealed by this act, which shall be in possession of the manufacturer or producer, or of his agent or agents, on the day when this act takes effect, the duty imposed by any such former act not having been paid, shall be held and deemed to have been manufactured or produced after such date; and whenever by the terms of this act a duty is imposed upon any articles, goods, wares, or merchandise, manufactured or produced, upon which no duty was imposed by either of said former acts, it shall apply to such as were manufactured or produced, and not removed from the place of manufacture or production, on the day when this act takes effect. And the Commissioner of Internal Revenue, under the direction of the Secretary of the Treasury, is authorized to make all necessary regulations and prescribe all necessary forms and proceedings for the collection of such taxes and the enforcement of such fines and penalties for the execution of the provisions of this act.

July 13, 1866.

When to take effect.

Inconsistent provisions repealed.

Provisions of former acts to be in force for certain purposes.

Former duties to continue until corresponding provisions of this act take effect.

As to manufactures in possession of manufacturer, &c.

Commissioner to make necessary regulations.

SEC. 34. *And be it further enacted*, That all acts or parts of acts inconsistent with this act, and all acts and parts of acts imposing any tax upon advertisements, or the gross receipts of toll-roads, are hereby repealed: *Provided*, That this act shall not be construed to affect any act done, right accrued, or penalty incurred, under former acts, but every such right is hereby saved; and all suits and prosecutions

March 2, 1867.

Inconsistent acts repealed; also tax on advertisements and gross receipts for acts already done in violation of any former act or acts of Congress relating to the subjects embraced in this act may be commenced or proceeded with in like manner as if this act had not been passed; and all penal clauses and provisions in existing laws relating to the subjects embraced in this act shall be deemed applicable thereto.

Saving clause.

March 31, 1868.

Saving of certain taxes.

See following amendment of this section.

SEC. 2. *And be it further enacted*, That nothing in this act contained shall be construed to repeal or interfere with any law, regulation, or provision for the assessment or collection of any tax which, under existing laws, may accrue before the first day of April, anno Domini eighteen hundred and sixty-eight. And nothing herein contained shall be construed as a repeal of any tax upon machinery or other articles which have been or may be delivered on contracts máde with the United States prior to the passage of this act.

Act of Mar. 3, 1869.

Amending § 2, March 31, 1868.

Be it enacted by the Senate and House of Representatives of the United States of America in Congress assembled, That the act to exempt certain manufacturers from internal tax, and for other purposes, approved March thirty-one, eighteen hundred and sixty-eight, be, and hereby is, amended in the second section thereof so as to remit all taxes upon naval machinery which had not accrued prior to the first day of April, eighteen hundred and sixty-eight.

July 20, 1868.

Inconsistent acts, &c., repealed.

Saving clauses.

SEC. 105. *And be it further enacted*, That all acts and parts of acts inconsistent with the provisions of this act are hereby repealed: *Provided*, That all the provisions of said acts shall be in force for levying and collecting all taxes properly assessed or liable to be assessed, or accruing under the provisions of former acts, the right to which has already accrued or which may hereafter accrue under said acts, and for maintaining, continuing and enforcing liens, fines, penalties, and forfeitures incurred under and by virtue thereof. And this act shall not be construed to affect any act done, right accrued, or penalty incurred, under former acts, but every such right is hereby saved; and all suits and prosecutions for acts already done in violation of any former act or acts of Congress, relating to the subjects embraced in this act, may be commenced or proceeded with in like manner as if this act had not been passed: *And provided further*, That no office created by the said acts and continued by this act shall be vacated by reason of any provisions herein contained, but the officers heretofore appointed shall continue to hold the said offices without re-appointment until their successors, or other officers to perform their duties, respectively, shall be appointed as provided in this act: *And provided further*, That whenever the duty imposed by any existing law shall cease in consequence of any limitation therein contained before the respective provisions of this act shall take effect, the same duty or tax shall be, and is hereby, continued until such provisions of this act shall take effect, and where any act is hereby repealed, no duty or tax imposed thereby shall be held to cease in consequence of such repeal, until the respective *correspective* corresponding provisions of this act shall take effect.

July 14, 1870.

Certain taxes under secs. 120, 121, 122 and 123 of act of June 30, 1864, as amended by acts of July 13, 1866, and March 2, 1867, to cease after August 1, 1870.

SEC. 17. *And be it further enacted*, That sections one hundred and twenty, one hundred and twenty-one, one hundred and twenty-two, and one hundred and twenty-three of the act of June thirty, eighteen hundred and sixty-four, entitled "An act to provide internal revenue to support the Government, to pay interest on the public debt, and for other purposes," as amended by the act of July thirteen, eighteen hundred and sixty-six, and the act of March two, eighteen hundred and sixty-seven, shall be construed to impose the taxes therein mentioned to the first day of August, eighteen hundred and seventy, but after that date no further taxes shall be levied or assessed under said sections; and all acts and parts of acts relating to the taxes herein repealed, and *that* all the provisions of said acts, shall continue in full force for levying and collecting all taxes properly assessed or liable to be assessed, or accruing under the provisions of former acts, or drawbacks, the right to which has already accrued or which may hereafter accrue under said acts, and for maintaining and continuing liens, fines, penalties, and forfeitures incurred under and by virtue thereof. And this act shall not be construed to affect any act done, right accrued, or penalty incurred under former acts, but every such right is hereby saved. And for carrying out and completing all proceedings which have been already commenced or that may be commenced to enforce such fines, penalties, and forfeitures, or criminal proceedings under said acts, and for the punishment of crimes of which any party shall be or has been found guilty.

All provisions of said acts continued in force for certain purposes.

June 6, 1872.

Inconsistent acts, &c., repealed.

SEC. 46. That all acts and parts of acts inconsistent with the provisions of this act are hereby repealed: *Provided*, That all the provisions of said act, shall be in force for levying and collecting all taxes properly assessed, or liable to be assessed, or accruing under the provisions of former acts, the right to which has *has* already accrued, or which may hereafter accrue, under said acts, and for maintaining, continuing, and enforcing liens, fines, penalties, and forfeitures incurred under and by virtue thereof. And this act shall not be construed to affect any act done, right accrued, or penalty incurred under former acts, but every such right is hereby saved; and all suits and prosecutions for acts already done in violation of any former act or acts of Congress relating to the subjects embraced in this act may be commenced or proceeded with in like manner as if this act had not been passed: *Provided*, That whenever the duty imposed by any existing law shall cease in consequence of any limitation therein contained before the respective provisions of this act shall take effect, the same duty or tax shall be, and is hereby, continued until such provisions of this act shall take effect; and where any act is hereby repealed, no duty or tax imposed thereby shall be held to cease in consequence of such repeal until the respective corresponding provisions of this act shall take effect.

Saving clauses.

Taxes imposed by existing law to continue until corresponding provisions of this act take effect.

APPENDIX.

AN ACT for the reduction of officers and expenses of the internal revenue, approved December 24, 1872.

Be it enacted by the Senate and House of Representatives of the United States of America in Congress assembled, That on the first day of July, eighteen hundred and seventy-three, or at such time prior thereto, in the districts respectively, as the Commissioner of Internal Revenue may find practicable, the offices of assessor and assistant assessor of internal revenue shall cease to exist; thereupon all duties imposed by law on assessors and assistant assessors, except as hereinafter otherwise provided, be, and the same are hereby, transferred to and imposed upon collectors of internal revenue, to be performed by them or their deputies; and that all returns and reports required by law to be made to the said assessors and assistant assessors shall be made to the said collectors, or to their deputies; and that each of said assessors shall, prior to the date aforesaid, and at the time set therefor by the Commissioner of Internal Revenue, transfer to such revenue officer as may be designated by the Commissioner of Internal Revenue for that purpose all books, papers, and other property belonging to the Government in his possession, or in that of any of his assistant assessors, and shall file with his final account an inventory thereof in detail, with the receipt of said revenue officer therefor; and from the time set for said transfer, his office and that of his assistants shall cease.

Abolishing the offices of assessor and assistant assessor. Collectors or deputies to perform the duties of the same.

Transfer of books, papers, and other property.

Assessor to file inventory and receipt with final account.

SEC. 2. That the Commissioner of Internal Revenue is hereby authorized and required thereafter to make the inquiries, determinations, and assessments of the following taxes, to wit:

Commissioner authorized to make assessments, &c., of the following taxes:

For deficiencies imposed by the provisions of section twenty of an act entitled "An act imposing taxes on distilled spirits and tobacco, and for other purposes," approved July twentieth, eighteen hundred and sixty-eight, as amended by subsequent acts.

Deficiency tax, under section 20 of act of July 20, 1868, as amended.

Semi-annually, upon the deposits, capital, and circulation of each person, bank, association, company, or corporation engaged in the business of banking, imposed by the provisions of section one hundred and ten of an act entitled "An act to provide internal revenue to support the Government and to pay interest on the public debt, and for other purposes," approved June thirtieth, eighteen hundred and sixty-four, as amended and supplemented by subsequent acts.

Tax on the deposits, capital, circulation of banks, &c., under section 110 of act of June 30, 1864, as amended.

Upon articles provided for in section five, and the first proviso of section fourteen, of an act entitled "An act to amend existing laws relating to internal revenue, and for other purposes," approved March second, eighteen hundred and sixty-seven.

Tax upon articles provided for in sections 5 and 14 of act of March 2, 1867.

Tax upon tobacco, snuff, and cigars provided for in section 60 of act of July 20, 1868, as amended by section 31 of act of June 6, 1872.

Upon tobacco, snuff, and cigars, provided for in section sixty of an act entitled "An act imposing taxes on distilled spirits and tobacco, and for other purposes," approved July twentieth, eighteen hundred and sixty-eight, as amended by section thirty-one of an act entitled "An act to reduce duties on imports and to reduce internal taxes, and for other purposes," approved June sixth, eighteen hundred and seventy-two.

Tax upon legacies and successions, and taxes liable to be assessed, &c., under former acts.

Upon legacies and successions, and of all other internal-revenue taxes liable to be assessed, or accruing under the provisions of former acts; and the said Commissioner shall certify such assessments, when made, to the proper collectors, respectively, who shall proceed to collect and account for taxes so certified in the same manner as assessments on lists are now collected and accounted for.

Special taxes to be paid by stamps.

SEC. 3. That all special taxes imposed by law, accruing after April thirty, eighteen hundred and seventy-three, including the tax on stills, or worms, shall be paid by stamps denoting the tax; and the Commissioner of Internal Revenue is hereby authorized and required to procure appropriate stamps for the payment of such taxes; and the provisions of sections twenty-six and one hundred and one of an act entitled "An act imposing taxes on distilled spirits and tobacco, and for other purposes," approved July twentieth, eighteen hundred and sixty-eight, and all other provisions of law relating to the preparation and issue of stamps for distilled spirits, fermented liquors, tobacco, and cigars, so far as applicable, are hereby extended, so as to include such stamps, and the Commissioner of Internal Revenue shall have authority to make all needful rules and regulations relative thereto. Every person engaged in any business, avocation, or employment, who is thereby made liable to a special tax, except tobacco peddlers, shall place and keep conspicuously in his establishment or place of business all stamps denoting the payment of said special tax; and any person who shall, through negligence, fail to so place and keep said stamp, shall, upon conviction, be sentenced to pay a penalty equal to the special tax for which his business rendered him liable, and the costs of prosecution; but in no case shall said penalty be less than ten dollars. And where the failure to comply with the foregoing provision of law shall be through willful neglect or refusal, then the penalty shall be double the amount above prescribed: *Provided*, That nothing contained in this section shall change, or in any way affect, the liability of any person for exercising or carrying on any trade, business, or profession, or doing any act for the exercising, carrying on, or doing of which a special tax is imposed by law, without the payment thereof.

Commissioner authorized to procure appropriate stamps for the payment of such taxes, and to make all needful regulations in relation thereto.

Special tax-stamps to be kept conspicuously in place of business.

Penalty.

Other liabilities of persons carrying on any business, for which special tax is required, not changed.

Collector to keep in his office, for inspection, an alphabetical list of persons paying special taxes.

SEC. 4. That each collector of internal revenue shall, under regulations of the Commissioner of Internal Revenue, place and keep conspicuously in his office, for public inspection, an alphabetical list of the names of all persons who shall have paid special taxes within his district, and shall state thereon the time, place, and business for which such special taxes have been paid.

SEC. 5. That section one hundred and ten of an act entitled "An act to provide internal revenue to support the Government, to pay interest on the public debt, and for other purposes," approved June thirtieth, eighteen hundred and sixty-four, as subsequently amended, be so amended that the returns therein required to be made shall be made and rendered semi-annually on the first day of December and the first day of June, in duplicate; one copy of which shall be transmitted to the collector of the proper district, and one copy to the Commissioner of Internal Revenue.

Amendment of section 110 of act of June 30, 1864.

SEC. 6. That the act entitled "An act imposing taxes on distilled spirits and tobacco, and for other purposes," approved July twentieth, eighteen hundred and sixty-eight, as amended by subsequent acts, be further amended as follows, to wit:

That section five be amended so that the duplicate statement therein required to be retained by the assistant assessor of the district shall, from and after the time when the office of said assistant assessor shall cease, be transmitted by the collector to the Commissioner of Internal Revenue.

Amending section 5 of act of July 20, 1868.

That section nineteen be amended so that one of the duplicate returns therein required to be sent to the assistant assessor of the district shall, from and after the time when the office of said assistant assessor shall cease, be transmitted by the collector to the Commissioner of Internal Revenue.

Amending section 19 of act of July 20, 1868.

That section twenty-eight be so amended that all of the additional commission of one-half of one per centum therein allowed shall be paid to the collector receiving the tax on all spirits produced after the office of the assessor shall cease under the provisions of this act: *Provided*, That the total net compensation of collectors, as now fixed by law, shall not be thereby increased.

Amending section 28 of act of July 20, 1868.

Total net compensation of collectors not to be increased by this amendment.

That section fifty-nine be so amended that in case any peddler refuses to exhibit a proper certificate from the collector of his or her district, and fails to show cause why the property seized shall not be forfeited, proceedings for its forfeiture shall be taken and had under the general provisions of the internal-revenue laws relating to forfeitures.

Amending section 59 of act of July 20, 1868.

That the provisions of section one hundred and three be extended and made applicable to the provisions of this act.

Provisions of sec. 103, act July 20, 1868, extended to this act.

SEC. 7. That section forty-three of an act entitled "An act to reduce duties on imports and to reduce internal taxes, and for other purposes," approved June sixth, eighteen hundred and seventy-two, be, and the same is hereby, repealed.

Repeal of section 43 of act of June 6, 1872.

SEC. 8. That the Commissioner of Internal Revenue shall, under the direction of the Secretary of the Treasury, require that each collector of internal revenue shall, before entering upon the duties prescribed by this act, give additional bond, conditioned that said collector shall faithfully perform the duties of his office according to the provisions of existing laws or of laws hereafter enacted.

Additional bond to be required of collector, under this act.

SEC. 9. That the Commissioner of Internal Revenue be, and hereby is, authorized to designate one of the heads of division as chief clerk of the bureau without additional compensation.

A head of division to be designated as Chief Clerk of Bureau.

[General nature—No. 37.]

AN ACT to remit the excise taxes upon alcohol used by universities and colleges for scientific purposes.

Alcohol may be withdrawn from bond for scientific purposes without payment of tax.

Be it enacted by the Senate and House of Representatives of the United States of America in Congress assembled, That the Secretary of the Treasury be, and he is hereby, authorized to grant permits to incorporated or chartered scientific institutions or colleges of learning to withdraw alcohol in specified quantities from bond without payment of the internal-revenue tax on the same, or on the spirits from which the alcohol has been distilled, for the sole and exclusive purpose of preserving specimens of anatomy, physiology, or of natural history belonging to such institutions, or for use in any chemical laboratory of such institutions: *Provided*, That application for permits shall be made by the presidents or curators of such institutions, who shall file a bond for double the amount of the tax on the alcohol to be withdrawn, with two good and sufficient sureties, to be approved by the Commissioner of Internal Revenue, and conditioned that the whole quantity of alcohol so withdrawn from bond shall be used for the purposes above specified, and for no other, and that the said presidents and curators shall comply with such other requirements and regulations as the Secretary of the Treasury may prescribe. And if any alcohol so obtained shall be used by any officer, as aforesaid, of such institutions for any purposes other than that above specified, then the said officers or sureties shall pay the tax on the whole amount of alcohol withdrawn from bond, together with a like amount as a penalty in addition thereto.

Bond to be filed.

Penalty.

Approved, February 21, 1873.

[General nature—No. 60.]

AN ACT to amend an act entitled "An act to reduce duties on imports and to reduce internal taxes, and for other purposes," approved June sixth, eighteen hundred and seventy-two, and for other purposes.

* * * * * * *

Section 5. That section fifty-five of the act of July twentieth, eighteen hundred and sixty-eight, as amended by the act of June sixth, eighteen hundred and seventy-two, be further amended by adding to the first paragraph of said section the words: "*Provided further*, That the bonds required to be given for the exportation of distilled spirits shall be cancelled upon the presentation of satisfactory proof and certificates that said distilled spirits have been landed at the port of destination named in the bill of lading, or upon satisfactory proof that after shipment the same were lost at sea without fault or neglect of the owner or shipper thereof."

Cancellation of bonds given for the exportation of distilled spirits.

Approved, March 3, 1873.

[GENERAL NATURE—No. 72.]

AN ACT to amend an act entitled "An act to prevent smuggling, and for other purposes," approved July eighteenth, eighteen hundred and sixty-six.

Be it enacted by the Senate and House of Representatives of the United States of America in Congress assembled, That the seventh section of the act entitled "An act to further prevent smuggling, and for other purposes," approved July eighteenth, eighteen hundred and sixty-six, is hereby amended so as to read as follows: That it shall be the duty of the several collectors of customs and of internal revenue to report within ten days to the district attorney of the district in which any fine, penalty, or forfeiture may be incurred for the violation of any law of the United States relating to the revenue, a statement of all the facts and circumstances of the case within their knowledge, together with the names of the witnesses, and which may come to their knowledge from time to time, stating the provisions of the law believed to be violated, and on which a reliance may be had for condemnation or conviction, and such district attorney shall cause the proper proceedings to be commenced and prosecuted without delay for the fines, penalties, and forfeitures by law in such case provided, unless, upon inquiry and examination, he shall decide that such proceedings cannot probably be sustained, or that the ends of public justice do not require that proceedings should be instituted, in which case he shall reports the facts in customs cases to the Sectary of the Treasury, and in internal-revenue cases to the Commissioner of Internal Revenue, for their direction; and for the expenses incurred and services rendered in all such cases the district attorney shall receive and be paid from the treasury such sum as the Secretary of the Treasury shall deem just and reasonable upon the certificate of the judge before whom such cases are tried or disposed of: *Provided, however*, That the annual compensation of such district attorney shall not exceed the maximum amount now prescribed by law; and if any collector shall in any case fail to report to the proper district attorney as prescribed in this section, such collector's right to any compensation, benefit, or allowance in such case shall be forfeited to the United States, and the same may, in the discretion of the Secretary of the Treasury, be awarded to such persons as may make complaint and prosecute the same to judgment or conviction.

Collectors to report to district attorney fines, &c., incurred.

Duty of district attorney in such cases.

Compensation of district attorney.

Approved, March 3, 1873.

[GENERAL NATURE—No. 82.]

AN ACT relating to the fractional parts of a barrel containing fermented liquors.

Be it enacted by the Senate and House of Representatives of the United States of America in Congress assembled, That section eighteen of the act entitled "An act to reduce duties on imports and to reduce internal taxes, and for other purposes," approved June sixth, eighteen hundred and seventy-two, be amended by striking out the proviso to said section, and inserting in lieu thereof the following: "In estimating and computing the internal tax on all beer, lager beer, ale, porter, and other fermented liquors, by whatever name such liquors may be called, the fractional parts of a barrel shall be halves, thirds, quarters, sixths, and eighths; and any fractional part of a barrel containing less than one-eighth shall be accounted one-eighth; more than one-eighth, and not more than one-sixth, shall be accounted one-sixth; more than one-sixth, and not more than one-fourth, shall be accounted one-fourth; more than one-fourth, and not more than one third, shall be accounted one-third; more than one-third, and not more than one-half, shall be accounted one-half; more than one-half, and not more than one barrel, shall be accounted one barrel; and more than one barrel, and not more than sixty-three gallons, shall be accounted two barrels, or a hogshead.

Fractional parts of a barrel containing fermented liquors, how accounted.

Approved, March 3, 1873.

[NOT OF GENERAL NATURE—No. 78.]

AN ACT to place at the disposal of the Commissioner of Internal Revenue certain copies of the new compilation of internal-revenue laws.

Be it enacted by the Senate and House of Representatives of the United States of America in Congress assembled, That of the seven thousand copies of the new compilation of internal-revenue laws ordered by section forty-five of the act of June sixth, eighteen hundred and seventy-two, to be printed for the use of Congress, eight hundred shall be for the use of the Senate, twelve hundred shall be for the use of the House of Representatives, and five thousand shall be for the use of the Commissioner of Internal Revenue.

Approved, March 3, 1873.

ERRATA.

The Attorney-General, in his opinion of April 9, 1873, holds that the following provision of the legislative, executive, and judicial appropriation act for the year ending June 30, 1871, remains in force, notwithstanding the 43d section of the act of June 6, 1872, that section having been repealed December 24, 1872, before it became practically operative. Accordingly that provision, as printed below, should be regarded as following section 7, act of June 30, 1864, on page 2 of this compilation.

SEC. 1. * * * * * *
And provided further, That the President may, at his discretion, divide the States and Territories respectively into convenient collection districts, or alter the same, or unite two or more districts or two or more States or Territories into one district, and may exercise said power from time to time as in his opinion the public interest may require. [*Extract from "An act making appropriations for the legislative, executive, and judicial expenses of the Government for the year ending the thirtieth of June, eighteen hundred and seventy-one," approved July* 12, 1870. 16 *Stat.*, *pp*. 230–239.]

On page 11, sec. 50, act July 20, 1868: The "agents" here referred to, instead of being paid under the act of March 2, 1867, are now paid from the general appropriation "for salaries and expenses of collectors, officers and agents," &c., &c. (See legislative, executive, and judicial appropriation act for the year ending June 30, 1874, approved March 3, 1873.)

On page 118, in foot note, "sec. 17," should be "sec. 170," the error occurring by displacement of the cipher in press-work.

INDEX.

A

D.

G.

H.

I.

S.

www.ingramcontent.com/pod-product-compliance
Lightning Source LLC
LaVergne TN
LVHW050529100826
845148LV00002B/497

* 9 7 8 1 4 2 5 5 1 9 1 6 2 *

EIRENE;

OR,

A WOMAN'S RIGHT.

BY

MARY CLEMMER AMES.

"Eirene—a name which signifies peace."
"The ornament she wore—a lowly heart."

NEW YORK:
G. P. PUTNAM & SONS,
ASSOCIATION BUILDING, TWENTY-THIRD STREET.
1871.